W9-BVJ-200

The
WILL *of* GOD
— as a —
WAY *of* LIFE

ALSO BY GERALD SITTSER

A Grace Disguised

The
WILL of GOD
as a
WAY of LIFE

Finding and Following the Will of God

GERALD L. SITTSER

Author of A Grace Disguised

ZondervanPublishingHouse
Grand Rapids, Michigan

A Division of HarperCollins*Publishers*

We want to hear from you. Please send your comments about this
book to us in care of the address below. Thank you.

ZondervanPublishingHouse
Grand Rapids, Michigan 49530
http://www.zondervan.com

The Will of God as a Way of Life
Copyright © 2000 by Gerald L. Sittser

Requests for information should be addressed to:

ZondervanPublishingHouse
Grand Rapids, Michigan 49530

Library of Congress Cataloging-in-Publication Data

Sittser, Gerald Lawson, 1950-
    The will of God as a way of life : finding and following the will of God /
Gerald L. Sittser.
      p. cm.
    Includes bibliographical references.
    ISBN 0-310-22656-2 (alk. paper)
    1. God—Will. 2. Christian life—Presbyterian authors. I. Title.
BV4509.5.S58 2000
248.4—dc21
                                              00–043281
                                            CIP

This edition printed on acid-free paper.

All Scripture quotations, unless otherwise indicated, are taken from the New Revised
Standard Version of the Bible. Copyright © 1989 by the Division of Christian
Education of the National Council of the Churches of Christ in the United States of
America. Used by permission. All rights reserved.

Interior design by Todd Sprague

Printed in the United States of America

00 01 02 03 04 05 06 /❖ DC/ 10 9 8 7 6 5 4 3 2 1

To my children:
Catherine, David, and John,
who are so clearly the will of God for me.

CONTENTS

ACKNOWLEDGMENTS

I will tell the story of how I came to be writing about the will of God in chapter 1. Still, a little explanation here will help. I have been thinking about this topic since I was in college. This book, therefore, is the culmination of years of reflection, conversation, and struggle. My principal aim in writing this book is to provide perspective, not to outline five easy steps to discovering the will of God. If, after reading this book, readers take stock of their lives and discern how they can live for God right where they are, then I will consider it a success.

I first tested these ideas on students many years ago. Their questions and insights only reinforced what I have always known—students are the real teachers. I worked out these ideas with people who had a vested interest, for students are intensely interested in discovering God's will for their lives. They helped me to develop the ideas presented here. I thank them for their eagerness to learn, which made them such good teachers for me.

Books are the by-products of community, although usually only one name appears on the jacket cover. I wish to thank some of the many people who contributed to this project along the way. Jim Edwards and Karen Peterson Finch provided useful criticism of early proposals. Laura Bloxham urged me to read novels, which gave me insights into the human struggle to find God's will. Marcia Everett sent me useful material to read, some of which made its way into the book, and in addition, she offered a thorough critique of the rough draft. My sister and brother-in-law, Diane and Jack Veltkamp, gave me wonderful support. Bill Robinson, Forrest Baird, Andrea Palpant, Tad Wisenor, Katie Wisenor, Bob Mitchell, Janelle Thayer, Todd and Monica Holdridge, and Kelly Walsh read a rough draft and provided helpful criticism. I take sole responsibility for what I have written. I give these friends the credit for challenging me to write it as well as I could.

I was fortunate to publish an earlier book with Zondervan, entitled *A Grace Disguised: How the Soul Grows Through Loss.* The staff there accomplished a rare feat. They helped me to do my best as an author, and they also treated me well as a person. I am deeply grateful to them for their support.

This support has been evident in the publication of this book as well. John Topliff, head of marketing, has worked hard to get both books into the hands of readers. Ann Spangler, the editor of my first book, helped start this book as well. Her instincts for ideas and words have been superb. Sandra Vander Zicht, Senior Acquisitions Editor, read the rough draft and urged me to do better. So I tore apart what I had written and started over; I am grateful to her for setting high standards. Verlyn D. Verbrugge, Senior Editor, tidied up the prose when I lost all capacity to spot misspelled words, poor grammar, redundancies, and awkwardness of phrasing. These three editors, professionals of the highest caliber, helped to make this project a pleasure from beginning to end. I am almost sad it is done.

I owe the greatest debt, however, to my three children: Catherine, David, and John. They gave me the time I needed to finish the book, and they even showed interest along the way. But their real contribution to this book has been more subtle and significant. They have taught me more about the will of God than they will ever know simply because they *are* the will of God for my life. I dedicate this book to them with love, affection, gratitude, and loyalty.

PART I

KNOWING GOD'S WILL

1

WE NEVER KNOW HOW
THINGS WILL TURN OUT

I spent the first twenty years of my life feeling certain I knew the will of God for my life. I was going to practice medicine. I was as sure about the future as I was about the difficulty of getting there. While still in high school, I talked seriously with a plastic surgeon about joining his practice when I completed my education, and he invited me to his summer home to show me slides of his work. By the time I entered college, I was eager to enroll in science and math courses to prepare for medical school. I had one goal in mind. Everything else was a distraction and inconvenience to me, like having to do chores on a hot summer day.

But I made a fatal mistake in selecting a college. Hope College, located in Holland, Michigan, was a *liberal arts* institution, not a college of science. It did not even offer a Bachelor of Science degree. It required students to take a broad range of general studies courses. If I ever wanted to earn a degree from Hope, therefore, I would have to read Dostoyevsky, listen to Beethoven, study the causes of the Crimean War, and write a persuasive essay.

I was about as eager to study the liberal arts as I was to read a dictionary for weekend pleasure. But I had no choice. In my first semester I signed up for a freshman writing class. For years I had read literature only under duress and had avoided writing altogether, except when my teachers forced me to put pen to paper. Fortunately, my writing professor, Dr. Nancy Miller, knew my type. Savvy and sociable, she was adept at handling people like me. When I griped one day about the writing requirement, she ignored me as if I had just made a bland comment about the

Detroit Lions. When I told her that I simply did not need the
course because I was not planning to write for a career, she
replied, "You never know, Jerry, what you'll end up doing."

She was right, of course. I ended up doing something far different from what I had assumed was God's will for my life. I did
not attend medical school; I enrolled in seminary. I did not
become a medical doctor; I became a minister instead. Later I
returned to graduate school to earn an advanced degree. Now I
serve as a college professor, and I write in my spare time. Words
are therefore central to what I do. The writing course I took my
freshman year of college became very useful to me, and my writing teacher proved to be a prophet. As it turns out, both course
and teacher helped to prepare me for a vocation I never imagined
at the time I would be doing.

INABILITY TO PREDICT THE FUTURE

From this experience, I learned a valuable lesson I will never
forget: *We never know how things will turn out.* What appears in
our minds to be the pathway we should take might change as suddenly as weather in the Midwest. So we would be wise to be attentive and responsive to God along the way, even in matters that
appear to have little significance, such as crafting good papers in
a freshman writing class. Perhaps our attention to these little
things *is* the will of God, and our preoccupation with the future
a foolish distraction.

As I look back on my forty-nine years, I see a pattern emerge.
At various points along the way I thought I knew the pathway I
was supposed to take, but I ended up doing something quite different. This different "something" turned out to be the will of
God. At twenty, I was sure that God wanted me to pursue a career
in medicine; I became a minister instead. At thirty, I was planning
to stay the course in pastoral ministry; now I am a college professor. At forty, I didn't aspire to be an avid writer; now I am fin-
ishing this, my fifth book. At every step along the way I thought
I knew God's will for my life. I thought I had it all figured out.
But it did not turn out as I had planned.

It occurred to me a few years ago that either I had developed
the bad habit of missing the will of God for my life, or I had a

mistaken notion of what this will was and is. The first alternative terrified me, for I had lived far too long and had made too many irreversible decisions—like getting married and having children—to wish I could start over in a vain attempt to get back on track. Besides, I have had too much evidence at my disposal—such as contentment of life and joy in my work—to assume that I had missed the will of God. It struck me as odd that I could wander that far off course without intending to, and yet not know it.

So I concluded that I had misunderstood what God's will really is. Like a detective who had followed leads to one dead end after another, I decided to pursue another course altogether. I began to explore a different way of approaching the will of God. It proved to be one of the most exciting decisions I ever made.

SUFFERING LOSS

The inability to predict the future was the first clue that set me searching in a different direction. But it was not the only clue I had. A second clue came from suffering loss. I married my wife, Lynda, when I was twenty-one. I was confident that I had found the right woman. It never occurred to me then that there could have been others, all equally pleasing to God. Lynda and I did have occasional fights along the way, as most couples do. But I never once doubted that Lynda was the perfect match for me. I assumed that I would grow old with her, as if marrying the "right" person guaranteed such an outcome.

We struggled for years with infertility. But Lynda finally conceived and over the course of six years gave birth to four children, two boys and two girls. She had just turned forty when she gave birth to John, our youngest. Our friends said that God had given us the "two-million-dollar" family. Both she and I felt like we were living on top of the world. We were experiencing the bliss of knowing and doing the will of God.

This bliss came to a sudden end in the fall of 1991. A drunken driver, driving eighty-five miles an hour on a lonely stretch of highway in rural Idaho, jumped his lane and collided with our minivan as we were returning from a powwow at a nearby Indian reservation. Lynda, my four-year-old daughter, Diana Jane, and my mother, Grace, who had been visiting us for the weekend, were all killed in the accident. John, then only two, was seriously injured. Catherine (then eight), David (seven), and I were injured, though not badly enough to require hospitalization.

This experience thrust me into a permanent state of dizziness, and I had trouble regaining my balance for a long time. I had assumed that my marriage to Lynda was the will of God, that our family of six was the will of God, that the happy, stable, prosperous life we enjoyed together was the will of God. We were, as so many said, "the ideal family." How could God allow such a tragedy to happen?

I could not believe that God had suddenly changed his mind about what he willed for us—a good marriage and a healthy family. How, then, could my life as a single father of three traumatized children also be the will of God? The accident forced me to reconsider my assumptions about God's will. Did God plan only "the good life" for me? If so, I wondered how I could integrate suffering into my understanding of God's will? Or did God plan something very different for me, something still good, but also hard and painful at the same time? If so, I had to face the prospect that my approach to the will of God was entirely mistaken.

This second clue—a horrible truth to learn—sent my mind reeling. I spent hours every day in silence, unable and probably unwilling to make any sense of it. At first I could not think about it in rational terms. I felt groggy with pain, like someone just coming out of surgery. But over time I attempted to reflect on my experience and ponder what it all meant.

I also started to read the Bible with fresh eyes. The Bible provided the third and final clue. As I will explain in the next chapter, I discovered that the Bible says very little about the will of God as a future pathway that we must discover and then follow. Instead, the Bible warns us about anxiety and presumption concerning the future, assures us that God is in control, and commands us to do the will of God we already know in the present. Over time I scrutinized my assumptions and reconsidered the "conventional" approach to the will of God I had followed up to that point.

THE CONVENTIONAL APPROACH

I am not sure how or where I first learned the conventional approach to the will of God. I think I simply accepted it from the very beginning as gospel truth without much scrutiny, much as I accept the way letters are arranged in the alphabet.

Conventional understanding of God's will defines it as a specific pathway we should follow into the future. God knows what this pathway is, and he has laid it out for us to follow. Our responsibility is to discover this pathway—God's plan for our lives. We must discover which of the many pathways we *could* follow is the one we *should* follow, the one God has planned for us. If and when we make the right choice, we will receive his favor, fulfill our divine destiny, and succeed in life.

In this model, then, when a decision has to be made, life suddenly becomes like a maze. There is only one way out. All the other ways are dead ends, every one of them a bad choice. God, of course, knows the right way. He has, after all, willed it for us, and we must discover that will. The consequences of our choices are therefore weighty. If we choose rightly, we will experience his blessing and achieve success and happiness. If we choose wrongly, we may lose our way, miss God's will for our lives, and remain lost forever in an incomprehensible maze.

As a result, we pray for guidance, we look for signs, we seek advice, we read the Bible for insight, and we search our hearts. We wait in the hope that God will give us a clear signal. We think that a clear voice from heaven would be nice. The moment finally arrives, however, when we must choose. We must enter one job-training program among the many we could enter. We must select one college among the many to which we have applied. We must accept or decline a job offer. We must marry or get out of the relationship. We must buy the new home or stay put. We must take one pathway, turning away from all the others.

Meanwhile, a nagging question hovers in the back of our minds. Doubt plagues us like the memory of a bad dream that refuses to go away. What if we make the wrong decision? What if we miss the will of God for our lives? What if our choice sends us down a dead-end street? What if we are stuck forever having to live with the consequences of a bad decision?

WHAT'S REALLY IMPORTANT, ANYWAY?

For many years I followed this conventional approach to analyzing and discovering the will of God for my life. Not that I did it consciously or critically. If I had been more critical, I would have certainly raised questions about it. I simply assumed it as true and then pursued it with considerable anxiety. I wanted to get it right the first time around.

But over time I discovered problems with this conventional approach. For one, it focuses our attention on supposedly important decisions concerning the future, not on little, seemingly unimportant decisions we make every day. For example, we think long and hard when we choose a college, a job or career, or a spouse. This makes good sense, considering how consequential these choices are. But we give little thought to how much TV we watch or how often we talk on the phone or how seldom we praise our children. Yet the little choices we make every day often have a cumulative effect far exceeding the significance of the big choices we occasionally make about the future.

As I look back now on the ordeal of making the decision during my college days between medicine and ministry, I am both amused and embarrassed. I was preoccupied with that decision for months. I prayed, sought advice, and thought long and hard about the benefits and defects of both options. I wanted to know which one was God's will for my life. But regardless of how fervently I searched, I could not make a decision with the assurance that I would know, beyond a shadow of a doubt, that the one I chose was his will. Like a traveler on a long journey who comes to a major crossroad with no signposts marking the way, I had to choose without the sure knowledge that I was going to end up on the right path. I felt confused and miserable.

Meanwhile, I did not realize how much the ordeal of choosing between the two had affected me. I had become as self-absorbed as a child standing in front of a mirror and as unpleasant to be around as a nervous cat. My wife, Lynda, finally jolted me out of my self-absorption. "Who really cares what you decide?" she asked. "I just want my husband back!" Ironically, I was worrying so much about my decision that I had ignored what was staring me right in the face. I was neglecting Lynda, losing interest in my studies, and overlooking mundane responsibilities. I thought almost exclusively about myself.

As it turns out, Lynda asked the right question. It broke the spell of obsession. I began to ponder the choice itself. "Does it really matter which option I choose?" I asked myself. I was familiar with physicians and pastors who were rogues. So I knew that neither profession guaranteed that I would become a good person or serve a noble cause. Few professions, I discovered in the process, are inherently good or bad, including medicine and ministry. On the one hand, I could become the next Albert Schweitzer or the next Billy Graham. On the other hand, I could also become the next Nazi physician or the next evangelistic huckster. How I functioned in either field of service would depend on the quality of my character, the depth of my convictions, and the degree of my competence.

I finally concluded that the choice of medicine or ministry was beside the point, for if I was not attentive to the little choices I made every day—to be a diligent student, a kind husband, a disciplined Christian—then whatever path I chose would never lead to the kind of fruitfulness I really desired for my life.

We do not, therefore, need to fret when we have to make big decisions about the future, worrying about the terrifying possibility that we might miss God's will for our lives. We simply need to do what we already know in the present. God has been clear where clarity is most needed. The choices we make every day—to love a spouse after an argument, to treat an unkind coworker with respect, to serve food at a soup kitchen, to pray for God's help when we do not feel much need for it—determine whether or not we are doing the will of God. If we have a problem, it is not lack of knowledge; rather, it is our unwillingness to respond to the knowledge we have.

As we will see, of course, we still have to make difficult choices regarding the future, as I did when I had to choose between medicine and ministry. We have to make many such choices, and they are rarely easy to make. But these choices are secondary all the same. Who we choose to become and how we choose to live every day creates a trajectory for everything else. Perhaps that is why the Bible says so little about God's will for tomorrow and so much about what we should do to fulfill his will today.

IS GOD HIDING SOMETHING?

The conventional approach to discovering the will of God has a second problem. It betrays a false and negative view of God. It implies that God has for some reason "hidden" his will and thus forces us to look for it, as if God were playing the celestial equivalent of "hide-and-seek" with us. According to this way of thinking, God hides his will, and we must go searching for it. In the process, he appears to delight in making things difficult for us. He prefers hiding over being found, frustrating us over making us joyful.

Raising my own children, however, has changed my understanding of both God and the game. When my children were little, we used to play hide-and-seek, usually indoors during the winter or on rainy days. Sometimes I would hide, and sometimes my kids would hide. I was better at hiding than my kids were. But I always gave them hints, like little squeaks or hoots, to help them find me. When they discovered my whereabouts, they would squeal with delight because they loved to find me.

The joy of the game came in being found, not in hiding. The hiding only increased the joy of being found. Hugs and laughter always followed. What mattered most in the game was the relationship between my kids and me, and the game nurtured this relationship. I never once wanted to hide so well that they would never find me.

Playing that simple game with my little children helped clarify my understanding of the will of God. Is his will something we must discover, or is it something we already know? Is it something God has hidden and we have to figure out, or is it something we must simply do? I assume, rightly or wrongly, that God is always clear when he needs to be. He does not play a celestial game to frustrate us. He cares about us much more than we care about our children. He delights in us. He wants us to do his will because he knows this will bring us true happiness. God has enough trouble persuading us to do that will. Why would he make it more difficult on him and on us by hiding it? Has God made his will that obscure and inaccessible?

What if we do make a wrong choice? Does a wrong choice imply that we have forever missed the will of God for our lives? We choose to become, say, a chef when God wants us to be a teacher. We choose to marry Ellen when God wills us to marry Sarah. Is God so mean that he would cut us off from the good plans he has for us just because we make one "wrong" decision? Perhaps we would have been a better teacher than chef; we can still serve God as a chef. Perhaps we would have been better matched with Sarah than with Ellen; we can still build a good life with Ellen.

Too many of us conclude in the face of difficulty and suffering that we must have made a choice outside the will of God. Then we spend the rest of our lives wishing that we had chosen differently. Ironically, we waste the opportunity we do have, however severe our circumstances, to do God's will right where we are and to build our relationship with him. The conventional approach to the will of God leads to second-guessing and wishful thinking, which contradicts God's gracious provision for us in Christ.

My own suffering put me on to this insight. Was my experience of loss outside the will of God? If so, then was I doomed to live for the rest of my life with God's second best, or even worse than that? At first I rejected the idea that God had caused our car accident or even allowed the accident. But I also recoiled from the idea that God was utterly powerless in the face of it, as if it were as much of a surprise to him as it was to me.

One question kept haunting me: Did God will my suffering? If I answered yes to that question, then God appeared mean, like a sadistic bully. I knew it would be hard for me to trust such a mean God. Yet if I answered no to the question, then God appeared impotent, like a general without artillery and army. I knew that it would be just as hard for me to trust such a weak God. Who, I wondered, would ever want to follow a God who is either a sadist or a weakling? Given the choice, the thought even raced through my mind that it might be better to abandon faith altogether and go it alone. In other words, I felt utterly bewildered as I contemplated the role that God played in the accident.

Eventually, however, I began to ask another question. I had thought so much about God's role in the ordeal that I had neglected to think about my own. How, I wondered, does God want me to *respond* to the tragedy? I reasoned that God had his business, which I could not for the life of me understand, and I had my business, which I did understand. I figured that, however God was involved, I had work to do. I could spend the rest of my life blaming God, and even feel justified for doing so. But what good would that do if I let that tragedy ruin the rest of my life—and not only mine, but also the lives of my children and my grandchildren and who knows how many more? I wanted to stop the bleeding, heal the wound, and get on with life. I knew that such a response was God's will.

Several months after the accident, I read the book of Job. One insight kept haunting me. Job experienced nothing but isolation and alienation when he suffered, as if he were a single atom floating alone in the universe. What Job did not realize is that the almighty God was watching him and that the host of heaven was waiting breathlessly to see if God's confidence in Job was secure. God's very reputation depended on Job's response. Thus, though Job felt alone, he was in fact *not* alone. Job believed that God had abandoned him, but God had done nothing of the sort. If anything, God had risked believing in Job, an action that represents a strange reversal of what we would consider a normal relationship with God.

God was not playing a game with Job. He was present and active in ways that Job did not and could not understand. In the meantime, Job had work to do. God's will for him was to endure in faith, which Job did—though not without great agony.[1]

THE FUTURE'S NOT OURS TO SEE

There is one final problem with the conventional approach to discovering the will of God. Our preoccupation with what lies ahead betrays a desire to control a future that simply cannot be controlled. We want the security of knowing what the future will bring rather than risk trusting God as the unknown future gradually unfolds before us. We keep hoping that light will shine to illumine the entire journey ahead so that we will know everything ahead of time. This way we will be spared from the difficulty of having to trust God as we discover and do his will. We will know so much about the future that a relationship with God will become largely irrelevant, as irrelevant as a teacher is to someone who thinks that she can learn everything from a textbook.

This longing to know the future has obsessed the human race since the dawn of time. People have consulted soothsayers, prophets, shamans, witches, priests, and diviners of every kind to discern what the future holds and what they will therefore do in the future. Seers have read the entrails of slain animals, cracks in shells, the flight path of the eagle, and the placement of the stars to predict what the gods are up to and what the future will bring. The Mesopotamians observed the stars and created the twelve signs of the zodiac. Gypsies study tea leaves, tarot cards, and crystals.

Celestial signs provide information necessary for horoscopes, which many people still read in the morning newspaper. Astrology supposedly allows one to predict everything from wars to weather. The late medieval prophet Nostradamus wrote voluminously about events in the future that some people, especially those who write for publications like the *National Enquirer*, take seriously. Though she has faded from the public eye since her death, Jeanne Dixon still receives some attention for her predictions about the future, however often she is wrong (which is most of the time). These various methods of prediction and control reveal the depths of our longing to know what God—or fate—has planned for us in the future. Who does not want to know the future? Who does not strive to discover the will of God for their lives?[2]

Well, then, what does the future hold for me? What does the future hold for any of us? We simply do not know, we cannot know, and *we should not know*. If we did know the future, we would be too overcome with utter surprise or terror (or both) to respond wisely and make the most of it. Before life is done, we will undoubtedly be shocked by what happens to us. At the age of thirty, I did not think I would ever be the father of four children, yet I had four children by the time I turned forty. At the age of forty, I did not seriously consider what would happen if I lost Lynda and had to raise children alone, yet as I approach fifty I am widowed and caring for my three children without the help of a spouse.

Do I dare even hazard a guess about the future? Do I really *want to know* what the future will be? How would such knowledge really help me? How would it help any of us? On the one hand, if we foresaw that our future was going to be hard and painful, full of suffering, we would recoil, fretfully awaiting its awful reality and wishing we could change it. But at the same time we would miss the wisdom and character that suffering engenders. And if, on the other hand, we learned that our future was going to be easy and pleasant, we would become dull and complacent, which would only diminish our capacity to enjoy the pleasant future that was going to be ours.

This book is my attempt to clarify how we can understand and discover the will of God for our lives. Its central idea is neither an abstract notion nor a curious piece of information one might find in an old newspaper. What I have learned through experience and reflection and have now put to writing has brought me freedom, security, and confidence. It can do the same for you.

As is obvious from the foregoing, three experiences have dramatically altered my thinking on the will of God. First, I ended up taking a different pathway from the one I had assumed God wanted for my life. This change of direction challenged my inordinate preoccupation with the future. Second, I faced catastrophic suffering, which undermined my quest for control and security. Finally, I turned to the Bible for fresh insight. The Bible has challenged me to reconsider my entire approach to discovering the future will of God, as we will see in more detail in the next chapter.

2

OUR ASTONISHING FREEDOM

When I began to search the Scriptures for insight concerning God's will for the future, I took note immediately of what the Bible does *not* say on this topic. James warns us to exercise restraint and avoid presumption when we make decisions about the future because we can never be sure what the future holds.

> Come now, you who say, "Today or tomorrow we will go to such and such a town and spend a year there, doing business and making money." Yet you do not even know what tomorrow will bring. What is your life? For you are a mist that appears for a little while and then vanishes. Instead you ought to say, "If the Lord wishes, we will live and do this or that." As it is, you boast and brag. All such boasting is evil. Anyone, then, who knows the good he ought to do and doesn't do it, sins.[1]

James is clearly concerned about believers who were confident that they knew God's will concerning the future, which gave them a false sense of security. They thought they knew what tomorrow would bring—prosperity, in their case. James calls it pure presumption. None of us, he writes, can have certainty about tomorrow, except the certainty that we will face limitations, hardships, and even death. All knowledge of the future is conditional. "If the Lord wishes" should be attached to every plan we make. But we do know what we should do in the present. In James's mind, what we know about God's will in the present is more important than what we think we know about God's will concerning the future. Instead of being presumptuous about the future, we should be attentive to God's will in the present.

Søren Kierkegaard, a nineteenth-century existential philosopher, tells the story of a man who was invited to a friend's house for dinner but was killed on the way by a falling roof tile. The man had accepted the invitation, but he failed to show up, although the reason for his failure to appear was obviously beyond his control. Kierkegaard wonders how his host would have responded had his friend accepted the invitation but qualified himself by saying, "I will come, definitely, believe me, except in case a roof tile falls down and kills me, because then I cannot come." Would his host have viewed this elaborate acceptance as a jest? Or would he have taken the comment in earnest? Perhaps both, Kierkegaard writes, are appropriate responses, for the condition attached to his acceptance is serious as well as silly. However peculiar, the comment is appropriate considering how perilous life is in this world. We can make our plans, but we can never be certain how they will turn out. Something as absurd as a falling roof tile can change our plans as quickly as a tornado destroys a house.[2]

In the Sermon on the Mount, Jesus exhorts us not to be anxious about tomorrow but to concentrate on what we must do today. We ought to trust that the God who clothes the lilies of the field and cares for the birds of the air will also meet our needs. This God will take care of tomorrow; thus, we must concentrate our energies on today. "So do not worry about tomorrow, for tomorrow will bring worries of its own. Today's trouble is enough for today."[3]

Jesus' teaching on God's will is deceptively simple here. He instructs us not to worry, as unbelievers do, about present circumstances or future problems. Instead, he commands, "Strive first for the kingdom of God and his righteousness, and all these things will be given to you as well."[4] This verse says nothing about how to discern God's will for our lives, as the conventional approach described in chapter 1 defines it. Jesus demands instead that we establish right priorities and put first things first.

We may have ten important decisions to make and a hundred possible pathways we could follow. We may wish that God would tell us exactly what to do, where to go, and how to choose. Yet Jesus only requires that we make sure our heart is good, our motives are pure, and our basic direction is right, pointing toward the "true north" of the kingdom of God. We can, in good conscience, choose from among any number of reasonable alternatives and continue to do the will of God. In the end what matters most is that we seek first God's kingdom and righteousness.

Jesus wants us to devote our time and energy to all the little tasks we must do every day, not just to the big decisions we occasionally have to make. The little responsibilities we do prepare us for big responsibilities later on, little actions set the stage for big ones, and faithfulness in things that appear to have only modest importance enables us to respond wisely to duties that seem— and perhaps are—very important.

> Whoever is faithful in a very little is faithful also in much; and whoever is dishonest in a very little is dishonest also in much. If then you have not been faithful with the dishonest wealth, who will entrust to you the true riches? And if you have not been faithful with what belongs to another, who will give you what is your own?[5]

The apostle Paul argues in a similar vein. His letter to the Romans explores the great questions of human sin and divine salvation. Paul probes the problem of exploiting grace by indulging in sin and of wanting to do right and still doing wrong. He describes the role of the Holy Spirit in the Christian life and the place of the Jews in God's redemptive plan. His letter is heady stuff, complex, nuanced, and demanding. Yet when Paul wishes to drive home the single most important lesson for believers— what God wills for us in response to how he has acted on our behalf—the apostle becomes as simple and direct as Jesus. The will of God involves serving and honoring God in the present and has little to do with big plans for the future:

> I appeal to you therefore, brothers and sisters, by the mercies of God, to present your bodies as a living sacrifice, holy and acceptable to God, which is your spiritual worship. Do not be conformed to this world, but be transformed by the renewing of your minds, so that you may discern what is the will of God—what is good and acceptable and perfect.[6]

Likewise, when Paul warns believers in Ephesus to avoid sinful behavior and to live holy lives, he writes, "Be careful then how you live, not as unwise people but as wise, making the most of the time, because the days are evil. So do not be foolish, but understand what the will of the Lord is."[7] And what is that will? Is it some specific, secret plan God has for us and wants us to spend days, weeks, even years, discovering? Not at all. Rather, it consists of a sober life, living in the power of the Holy Spirit, and offering praise and gratitude to God for his goodness. Paul's main concern is about how believers conduct themselves in ordinary life.

No, biblical authors do not ignore the future. They simply have a different view of it than we do. They believe that God worked through Christ to redeem the past and that God will work out all things for good in the future.[8] God had the first word; he will also have the last. As biblical writers state time and again, Christ will eventually return and establish God's kingdom on earth. God controls the future because he is sovereign. Human beings are powerless to determine the future because we are finite. Thus, the biblical authors emphasize how believers should live in the present, which is the only moment we have to know God and to do his will.

Paul underscores the importance of the present moment when he wrote to the Corinthians, "See, now is the acceptable time; see, now is the day of salvation!"[9] Paul's confidence that God controls the future enabled him to obey God in the present, even under conditions that were far less than ideal. He lived in integrity, righteousness, and faith. He was faithful to God, even in his suffering, because he believed that God would make all things right.

> As servants of God we have commended ourselves in every way: through great endurance, in afflictions, hardships, calamities, beatings, imprisonments, riots, labors, sleepless nights, hunger; by purity, knowledge, patience, kindness, holiness of spirit, genuine love, truthful speech, and the power of God.[10]

Of course, Jesus' followers still had to make decisions about the future, just as we do. Paul, for example, had to decide when to start his missionary journeys, where to go, and how to work. He and his assistants prayed, fasted, and waited on God.[11] But Paul trusted in the Holy Spirit, and he changed plans when he learned that God wanted him to move in a different direction.[12] Nevertheless, the New Testament offers no hint that Paul agonized about the will of God as it pertained to the future. He gave himself to the present because he was eager to use what little time he had to do what he already knew God wanted him to do.

If we sense any agony in the heroes of Scripture, it is not in discovering the will of God but in doing it. Jesus knew his mission—that it would culminate in his crucifixion. He asked his Father in heaven to "remove the cup" so he could be delivered from the agony of execution and separation from his Father, yet he submitted to his Father's will and embraced his destiny of suffering and death: "Yet, not my will but yours be done."[13]

Likewise, the apostle Paul did not seem to wrestle much with the problem of discerning the will of God for his life. It was *doing* the will of God that created both zeal and fear in him. He spoke with great foreboding about disobeying God's will for his life: "Woe to me if I do not proclaim the gospel!"[14]

I am not suggesting that this view of what God wants us to do will spare us from the difficulty of having to make choices about the future. Nothing can do that for us. We are not like creatures of instinct that hunt prey or fly south or build nests because it is in our nature to do so. We are human beings, and we must choose. Whatever our choices, we must always make God's kingdom and righteousness our greatest passion in life.

A STARTLING CONCLUSION

As I struggled with the issue of discovering God's will in light of my own personal uncertainty, intense suffering, and in-depth biblical study, I came to a startling conclusion. The will of God concerns the present more than the future. It deals with our motives as well as our actions. It focuses on the little decisions we make every day even more than the big decisions we make about the future. The only time we really have to know and do God's will is the *present moment*. We are to love God with heart, soul, mind, and strength, and we are to love our neighbors as we love ourselves. These are the basic responsibilities Jesus challenges us to pay attention to, just as a basketball coach emphasizes the fundamentals of dribbling, passing, and shooting.

Jesus' teaching about the simple will of God is therefore always relevant in every situation imaginable, whether we are doctors or ministers, single or married, young or old, healthy or sick. It is the daily choices we make to honor and serve God—in the manner of our conduct at home or at work, in our use of time and talent, in our willingness to do mundane tasks, in our devotion to service, in our commitment to live sacrificially—that determine whether we are doing the will of God. We already know the will of God for our daily lives, however cloudy the future appears to be. That we do not know what God wants us to do tomorrow does not excuse us from doing his will today.

This perspective on the will of God gives us astonishing freedom. If we seek first God's kingdom and righteousness, which *is* the will of God for our lives, then *whatever choices we make concerning the future become the will of God for our lives*. There are many pathways we *could* follow, many options we *could* pursue. As long as we are seeking God, all of them can be God's will for our lives, although only one—the path we choose—actually becomes his will.

In other words, God does not have one will for our lives but many wills. God does not, for example, have one person selected for you to marry whom you must "find." Instead, there are many people you could marry, if you choose to marry at all. Nor does God have one career mapped out for you that you must figure out. Instead, there are many careers you could do and perhaps will do. Of course we must still make choices, and some will be difficult to make. Yet we can be confident that what we choose becomes God's will for our lives.

God is thus surprisingly flexible about the future because he is supremely inflexible in the present. You are free to marry Bill or Edward, just as you are free to become a computer scientist or a day-care provider. But you are *not* free to put anything before or above God. God must be first and foremost in our lives. Once we seek first God's kingdom and righteousness and entrust our lives wholly to him, the world suddenly becomes full of possibilities. As Paul claims with utter boldness, "For all things are yours, whether Paul or Apollos or Cephas or the world or life or death or the present or the future—all belong to you, and you belong to Christ, and Christ belongs to God."[15] All things are ours in Christ. God works all things to our ultimate and eternal advantage, including the future. The only significant condition is that we surrender our lives to Jesus Christ and follow him as Lord.

Thomas Merton, a Trappist monk and author of many books on spirituality, believed that the present moment is pregnant with incredible possibilities. "Every moment and every event of every man's life on earth plants something in his soul. For just as the wind carries thousands of winged seeds, so each moment brings with it germs of spiritual vitality that come to rest imperceptibly in the minds and wills of men." But we must be sensitive to these moments. We must be attentive to God as he works in our lives day by day. "Most of these unnumbered seeds perish and are lost, because men are not prepared to receive them: for such seeds as these cannot spring up anywhere except in the good soil of freedom, spontaneity and love." We become good soil, Merton concluded, by seeking God in the present moment—the only moment we have.[16]

What does this principle mean in practical terms? God wills that *we do the obvious* every day, that is, to honor God. As Ignatius of Loyola, founder of the Jesuits, wrote in his *Spiritual Exercises*, "In every good choice, in so far as it depends upon us, the direction of our intention should be simple. I must look only to the end for which I am created, that is, for the praise of God our Lord and for the salvation of my soul. Therefore, whatever I choose must have as its purpose to help me to this end."[17]

Thus we should seek God, repent of our sins, and practice spiritual discipline. We should love our family and our friends and our neighbors. We should get involved in a Christian community. We should cultivate character, serve the needy, and do our calling in life. Above all, we should trust God and surrender our lives to him.

Thomas à Kempis, author of the fifteenth-century spiritual classic *The Imitation of Christ*, writes, "Vanity of vanities, and all is vanity, except to love God and to serve only him. This is the highest wisdom: to see the world as it truly is, fallen and fleeting; to love the world not for its own sake, but for God's; and to direct all your effort toward achieving the kingdom of heaven."[18]

WHY THE AMBIGUITY?

Do I like to live with the ambiguity of this theology? Not at all! When I think about it, it seems that all my choices are left almost entirely up to me, as if God doesn't care about them.

Nevertheless, there may actually be good reasons for the ambiguity. For one, it keeps us from dividing life into sacred and secular. As C. S. Lewis has argued, God does not want just a few religious things from us—say, a tithe or a few hours of voluntary service or weekly attendance at a Bible study. As our Creator and Redeemer, he lays claim on every moment of our lives and has rightful jurisdiction over us. In the Christian faith, all of life is religious and falls under God's authority. He gives all things to us; he demands all things from us. God doesn't want something from us; he simply wants us.[19]

Religious activities are no more inherently valuable than any other activities. Of course, they do serve a useful purpose. Weekly worship enables us to focus our attention on God's goodness and inestimable glory. Prayer and Bible reading help us to receive God's wisdom and grace, as if we were thirsty hikers drinking water from a fresh mountain stream. Such activities illumine and inspire us. But they are no more important to God than a child's bedtime story is to a mother who sees motherhood as far grander than a few moments with a child at the end of the day. God wants us to surrender everything to him—both those things that have the appearance of religion and those that do not. Thus, the ambiguity of seeking God's kingdom first has a positive purpose to it. It keeps us from confining our religious life to a certain day of the week or to a certain set of activities.

Francis de Sales, known during his lifetime in the seventeenth century as a wise counselor and master of the spiritual life, believed that the effects of true devotion, which he defined as living one's whole life for God, would naturally spill over into the rest of one's life and erase any distinction between what is religious and what is secular. Such devotion would influence and transform every area of one's life as varnish adds a beautiful sheen to everything it covers.

> True devotion does even better. Not only does it not spoil any sort of life situation or occupation, but on the contrary enriches it and makes it attractive. Devotion makes the care of the family peaceful, the love of husband and wife more sincere, the service of the ruler more loyal, and every sort of occupation more pleasant and more loveable.[20]

There is a second reason for the ambiguity of Jesus' words in seeking God's will. They prevent us from putting God off. When Jesus taught "Seek first God's kingdom" and "Let the day's own trouble be sufficient for the day," he was insisting that we treat the present moment as the proper time—the only time, really—to follow and serve God. It is not enough to refrain from worrying about a future beyond our control; rather, we should be fully present to what is immediately at hand, like a child playing her favorite game on a beautiful summer day. If we associate God's will with some great future work we hope to do for God, it is so easy to overlook the little works we can and should be doing every day. It is far too easy to use our future aspirations (e.g., "What a wonderful contribution I will make as a surgeon") as an excuse for ignoring God in the present.

College students are notorious for claiming the right to sow "wild oats" during their college years because they assume they will take a more serious turn when, as adults, they enter the "real" world and begin careers, marry, and raise children. But such a decision to put off doing the will of God can form bad habits. We put it off until we get our first job. Then we decide to wait until we get married and have children. Then we excuse ourselves until we settle comfortably into middle age. In other words, we continue to postpone doing God's will until there is no time left. It is never now; it is always later.

But the time to do the will of God is *now*—always now and never later. As I tell my children, "You will never find it easy to love your siblings, at least not at first. It will only get easy with practice. So you might as well start now."

If anything, the sooner we get started, the better it will be—for us, not for God. God does not command us to do his will for his sake, as if he were some puny dictator needing to have his ego flattered by groveling subjects. God commands us to seek him because our deepest longing in life is for him. We are incomplete without him. If we put off doing his will, we sacrifice our own happiness and fulfillment. We have been created for God, and nothing less than complete surrender is going to satisfy us. As Augustine, who served as a bishop in North Africa in the early fifth century, wrote so eloquently in his *Confessions*:

And so we humans, who are a due part of your creation, long to praise you—we who carry our immortality about with us, carry the evidence of our sin and with it the proof that you thwart the proud. Yet these humans, due part of your creation as they are, still do long to praise you. You arouse us so that praising you may bring us joy, because you have made us and drawn us to yourself, and our heart is unquiet until it rests in you.[21]

Finally, the ambiguity of seeking God's kingdom first gives us freedom, confidence, and security to make decisions. If we truly seek God above all, then we will *always be doing the will of God*, no matter where our particular choices lead us, because seeking God's kingdom first *is* God's will. When we come to a crossroads with no signposts to guide our way, we then have the *freedom* to choose what we want, we can be *confident* that God will go with us whatever we decide, and we will enjoy the *security* of knowing that our decisions become his will. In other words, we simply cannot lose. We cannot make a decision that is "outside" the will of God because we are already "inside" that will. As it turns out, the weightiest choice we make is never between two future options—say, taking a job in California or staying in Iowa—but between two ways of life, one for God, the other against God.

But is it *that* easy? Yes, if we choose the "easy" life of complete devotion to God. Jesus taught, "My yoke is easy, and my burden is light,"[22] although the initial step of submission to his yoke may strike us at the time of decision as anything but easy. Yet whether or not it is easy is beside the point. Many things start out difficult but become easy over time, such as learning a new sport or playing a new musical instrument or studying a new subject. Following God works the same way. It contradicts our selfish nature, yet it is true to our nature as well. God made us for himself; our deepest longings are for him. The life we ought to lead—the life we really *want* to lead—is a life lived every day for God.

As we will see, God does have a plan for our lives. We will discover that plan, however, as we simply do the will of God we already know in the present moment. Life will then gradually unfold for us. We will discover at just the right time what we need to know and do. We will walk through a door into one room and then, over time, recognize which door we should take next—or, if clear guidance is lacking, simply choose another door and walk through it. That process will continue as we move from one room to the next and progress from one phase of life to the next. We will discern God's will as naturally as we learned how to walk—one step at a time. We will never have to look back, never have to fret over decisions, never have to worry that God has abandoned us.

Over time we will begin to see a pattern emerge—that the course our lives took was exactly what God intended. We will observe this pattern, however, *only by looking back* on what has already happened, only by viewing our life story in retrospect. In the meantime, let's concentrate our energy on the present moment. God, we can be sure, will be clear when he needs to be. And he has been supremely clear about one thing—*that we must seek him first.*

3

OBSTACLES THAT GET IN THE WAY

I am not sure that Christians in the Third World share the relatively modern and distinctively Western preoccupation with discovering the will of God. Our confusion is partly the result of living in the postmodern world. Contemporary culture presents us with an inordinate number of choices, pressures us to live busy, fragmented lives, and isolates us from community. These characteristics of life in our world—choice, busyness, and isolation—seem to make it all but impossible for us to discern God's will.

We have so many choices that the sheer number overwhelms us, as if we were shopping at a giant mall. We are so much on the run that we find it difficult to make choices that keep the whole of life in mind. We live such isolated lives that few people know us well enough to give us wise counsel when we have to make choices. As we will see in this chapter, God's will for us is to learn to choose quality of life over quantity of options, to slow down and integrate our lives as best we can, and to build friendships with people who know the whole of us, not just isolated parts of us. His will challenges us to resist and even to reverse some of the trends of contemporary culture itself.

TRADITION!

A pastor recently told me about a conversation he had had with a friend about courtship and marriage. He asked his friend, who had been raised in India, "When did you first fall in love with your wife?"

"Oh, I suppose about three years after we were married," he replied.

The pastor was incredulous. "How can that be?" he asked.

"Our marriage was arranged. We didn't meet until a week before the wedding. We didn't have time to fall in love before we were married. The love came later on."

Obviously this Indian did not have to discover God's will for a life partner. His parents did that for him. Instead, he had to learn how to love the woman who had been chosen for him. He learned to love her over time and through the course of ordinary life. That was the will of God for his life.

This man was describing a different world from the one we know in modern Western culture. It is the world of traditional society. The musical *Fiddler on the Roof* tells a story of a Jewish family who lives in just that kind of society. Pointing to a fiddler perched precariously on a steep roof and trying to scratch out a tune without breaking his neck, Tevye, the father of the family, asks, "How do we keep our balance?" And he himself answers, "That I can tell you, in one word—TRADITION!"

It was tradition that enabled his little village to maintain its existence in an unstable and hostile world. It was tradition that showed each of its residents how to eat, work, and dress. It was tradition that reminded them of their Jewish identity. Tradition required the papa to provide for the family and find husbands for his daughters, and it mandated the mama to keep a peaceful, quiet, kosher home. Tradition created order and stability in the community. As Tevye concludes, it was because of tradition that "every one of us knows who he is and what God expects him to do." Consequently, the Jews in that village did not have the freedom—and did not face the pressure—to choose spouses, occupations, or anything else. Tradition chose for them.

Tradition also helped to create community in Tevye's little village. "We all get along together perfectly well," Tevye said with mischief in his eyes, obviously exaggerating the harmony that existed among the villagers. Still, the people of Anatevka worked together, worshiped together, danced together, studied the Torah together, and drank together. They married their sons and daughters to the children of their dearest friends. They served one

another and defended one another. If there were conflicts, as there
inevitably are in any community of people, they worked them out
because the community of Anatevka was a whole. They *had* to
work them out because there was nowhere else to go. Anatevka
provided stability for the lives of these Jews and enabled them to
make decisions in light of what was best for the community, not
simply what was best for the individual.

Our modern and postmodern world has jettisoned the rule of
tradition. We strive to multiply the number of choices we have.
We value freedom and opportunity, and we cherish independence.
It is unthinkable for us to limit freedom and eliminate the wide
variety of choices we have or to sacrifice our independence for
the sake of community. Occasionally I ask my students, "Do you
trust my judgment?" They usually reply that they do. Then I ask
them, "How many of you would be willing to allow me or someone else you trust to choose a life partner for you." Thus far no
one has accepted my offer. Their freedom to choose is too important to them. Their independence is so valuable that they would
rather go it alone, even though they will probably make many
poor choices along the way.

SO MANY CHOICES

The freedom to choose can become a burden, as we all know
from personal experience. Having choice is one thing; having *too
many* choices is quite another. Like visiting a huge Super Wal-Mart
or scanning a five-page menu at a restaurant, we are often overwhelmed and immobilized by the number of choices we have to
make. Where do we even begin? How do we sort out the options
and establish priorities? Thus, what used to be decided by tradition
in India or in the world of *Fiddler on the Roof* has been relegated
to personal choice today. We can choose whatever we wish. As a
friend of mine said to me recently, "I have never seen a happy child
at Toys R Us. There are simply too many toys there and too many
choices that they have to make. It overwhelms kids."

My two teenage children will soon have to choose a college,
and they will be courted by dozens of colleges before they make
their decision. Twenty-five years ago colleges did not deploy an
army of recruiters as they have been doing more recently. Today

admission staffs pound the pavement to recruit high school students to their colleges. They rely on sophisticated strategies, advanced computer technology, slick publications, and weekend experiences to persuade high school students to choose their school over others. Considering the staggering number of good options my children will have, which college will they choose? How will they decide? How will they discover what God's will is? It would be far easier if I decided for them. That day, however, is long gone. My children will have to choose for themselves. They feel overwhelmed already. So do I—and we have just begun.

The Internet has become a metaphor for contemporary life. I am no fan of the Internet, but I have surfed it enough to know that it contains about as much information as the ocean contains drops of water. We have access to anything we want; we can buy almost any clothes we want; we can learn about virtually any topic we want. The Internet provides an overwhelming number of options, but those options give us more choices than we could ever hope—or want—to make.

Why do we want so many choices? C. Leslie Charles, author of *Why Is Everyone So Cranky?* argues that modern society has raised our expectations for what life can and should deliver. The advertisement industry alone feeds our hunger for more, better, faster, and newer, making us feel entitled to whatever it is we want. We see what is available and assume we have a right to it—to be happy, rich, beautiful, and powerful. So we live by an unstated set of selfish rules: I am entitled to what I want when I want it. I am entitled to special privileges because I am who I am. I not only have a right to pursue happiness, I deserve to be happy, and I'll do whatever it takes to achieve it. I deserve the newest, the biggest, the best, and the most. It's my right.[1]

We assume, therefore, that we have a right to choose whatever our heart desires and to expand the number of our choices. The more choices we have, the better life will be. Little do we realize, however, that number of choices can be deceiving because quantity does not imply quality. If we were given the choice of ten different ways to die, would having such a wide variety of options make us happy?

BUSY BEYOND BELIEF

It is bad enough that we have to make so many choices. It is even worse that life has become so busy. Busyness clouds our judgment, too, especially our ability to discern and make wise choices. We have so much to do, and our packed schedules often deprive us of the time needed to reflect deeply over the choices we have to make.

My circumstances as a widower with three active children might set me apart from most of my married friends, but my hectic schedule is not unusual for middle-class people. If anything, I have one advantage. I have a ready excuse for saying "no" because everyone seems to understand. "Oh," they say, "we know how busy you are, raising those three kids all by yourself." My married friends cannot use that excuse. Still, they seem no less frazzled than I am. When I take a few moments on a Sunday evening to plan the calendar and menu for the week, I am always amazed by the sheer number of tasks I must do, the number of places I must go, and the number of people I will meet over the course of one short week. As syndicated columnist Ellen Goodman once commented, we used to say "Fine!" when people asked "How are you doing?" Now we say "Busy!"

Even now as I sit down to plan my schedule for the week, I feel almost proud that my calendar is full of appointments, activities, and duties, as if my busyness is a kind of status symbol establishing my worth as a human being. I will teach at the college, spending time with students both inside and outside the classroom. I will prepare lectures, make up exams, and grade papers. I will attend several meetings with colleagues and administrators. I will receive and respond to many e-mail messages each day. I will talk shop on the telephone with scholars and friends.

I will also drive my children to early-morning practices, to afternoon music lessons, and to evening youth-group meetings. I will attend their weekend athletic events or recitals. I will make lunches and cook dinner, do laundry, clean house, and pick up messes (all with the help of my children, of course). I will chat with neighbors, talk on the telephone with friends, read and sort mail, and take care of literally hundreds of other details that come up. Then, if there is time, I will try to exercise or to sit down for a few minutes to read a novel or magazine. Such is the nature of my busy life.

My children are less busy than I am, to be sure, but they are busy, too. Like many middle-class children growing up in America, they play sports, take music lessons, and attend a church youth group. I grew up in the 1950s and 1960s, and I can't remember being as busy then as my children are today, nor can I recall my mother being as busy then as I am now.

Something has happened to change the way we live. I, for one, welcome the opportunities, but I deplore the busyness. I have not heeded Mahatma Gandhi's famous words, "There is more to life than increasing its speed." Nor have I listened to the warnings of Francis de Sales, "Nothing done impulsively and in a hurry is ever well done.... We always do fast enough when we do well.... Drones make more noise and are more in a hurry than the bees but they make no honey. Thus those who rush around with tormenting anxiety and noisy solicitude do neither much nor well."[2]

As if our present busyness is not enough, we are often under constant pressure to accept new responsibilities, and we fear that we will miss out on something important or let someone down if we decline. Yet rarely do we consider the implications of the choices we make. Each new responsibility puts us deeper into the hole of distraction, stress, and overcommitment.

When I am asked, for example, to speak at a weekend retreat in another city or state, I force myself to consider the hidden *costs*. Not only does the time away from my routines demand something from me, but also the time I need to prepare, the energy I must find to speak well, the interest in people I want to show while I am at the retreat, the housework I will have to do when I return home, and the loss of a weekend I would have otherwise had with my kids. Strangely, I often feel guilty when I decline an invitation. I wonder sometimes what drives me to take on so many responsibilities, what makes me prone to be so busy, what deludes me into thinking I can do it all and have it all. I am like a man who is on a mission to everywhere.

Thomas Merton lamented this idolatry of busyness, which in his mind destroys our capacity for living contented and contemplative lives. Ironically, our very productivity keeps us from hearing the voice of God and doing the will of God.

How many there are who are in a worse state still: they never
even get as far as contemplation because they are attached to
activities and enterprises that seem to be important. Blinded by
their desire for ceaseless motion, for a constant sense of achievement, famished with a crude hunger for results, for visible and
tangible success, they work themselves into a state in which
they cannot believe that they are pleasing God unless they are
busy with a dozen jobs at the same time.[3]

A huge industry marketing time-management techniques has
emerged in the last twenty-five years to help us handle the complexity, stress, and pressure of life today. We learn to squeeze
thirty more minutes of productivity out of each day, to get more
done in less time, and to marshal our energy with the intensity
and focus of a magnifying glass. Years ago I read a book on time
management that promised me *total success* if I followed the
author's proven strategy. I could do "anything I wanted," the
author claimed, and I could gain "complete control over my life."
I did find his ideas helpful, and I did learn how to manage my time
better. But his book, however helpful, ignored the bigger problem of busyness and fragmentation. Is productivity in itself a
virtue? Is my commitment to success always a good thing? Is it
worth it to become master of the world at the expense of the soul?

The problem is exacerbated because we have made work itself
an idol. Max Weber, a leading social theorist writing in the early
twentieth century, argued in *The Protestant Ethic and the Spirit of
Capitalism* that what to the Puritans in seventeenth-century
America was an expression of discipline, obedience, and even joy
has become for us an obligation. The Puritans strove to honor
God by working hard. Then it was a matter of religious conviction, which for the most part they freely chose. Now it is a matter of survival, and it has been turned into a virtual pathology.

We earn high grades to get into graduate schools in order to
secure jobs with the best companies, hoping to rise to the top of
our profession and earn a six-figure income. We work all the time.
We *have* to work all the time to stay competitive. "The Puritan
wanted to work in a calling; we are forced to do so. . . . In [the
Puritan] view the care for external goods should only lie on the
shoulders of the 'saint like a light cloak, which can be thrown

aside at any moment.' But fate decreed that the cloak should become an iron cage."[4]

As a result, we develop techniques to manage time, resources, and people. We learn to compete and strain to win. We break the speed limit to get to meetings on time, use a cell phone and e-mail in order to master the art of "multi-tasking," and drive ourselves until we reach the point of exhaustion, just to stay competitive. We do not think much about changing the system because we are too intent on succeeding in it.

Jesus taught, "For those who want to save their life will lose it, and those who lose their life for my sake will find it. For what will it profit them if they gain the whole world but forfeit their life? Or what will they give in return for their life?"[5] Sadly, in society today each of us faces the terrifying possibility that should we fail to manage our time and resources properly, to get involved in everything we can, or to push our children to extraordinary heights of achievement, we will be left behind, passed over for promotion, forced to live on a modest income, and consigned to the dreaded status of being ordinary.

Does God will that we live so insanely? Can we discover God's will, whatever we mean by that phrase, as long as we live such busy, frenzied lives? Does it really matter that we realize our ambitions if, in the end, we lose our very souls? Surely such a price is too high.

LOSS OF COMMUNITY

We also live fragmented lives. We often feel forced to move in different directions simultaneously, to relate to a wide variety of people, and to jump from one world to another. Many of us live in four, five, even six separate universes—neighborhood, church, work, club, team, committee, and so forth—each having little connection with the other. The only thing that gets us from one universe to the next is the wormhole of our automobiles. If there is any continuity among those universes, it is the solitary self.

Let's face it, each of us finds it difficult to maintain integrity, consistency, and even sanity as we rush from one universe to the next, from one responsibility to the next. Does anyone—even spouse or best friend!—know how we really live? Does anyone know who we really are? Is there anyone who holds us account-able? Most of us could invent a different identity, value system, and personality for each of our many worlds, and no one would ever know. Many of us already do, at least to some degree. A man uses profanity at work, tells off-color jokes at the club, ignores his neighbors, and yet demonstrates sincere piety at church—with little awareness of these discrepancies in his life.

In *The Pilot's Wife*, novelist Anita Shreve tells the story of Kathryn Lyons, who learns the devastating news that her hus-band, a pilot flying international routes, has been killed in a plane crash during a transatlantic crossing. What appears at first to be a tragedy turns into a nightmare when she discovers that her hus-band, Jack, had another life that she knew nothing about. She knew him as her husband, friend, and lover, as a father to their daughter, and as a professional pilot. But she learns over time that he had another wife and another child and that he had been work-ing for the Irish Republican Army as well. These discoveries com-pletely contradict what she knew about him while he was alive. As the sordid plot unfolds, she has to face facts that tell a very dif-ferent story about his life. "How do you ever know that you really know a person?" she asks wistfully toward the end of the novel.[6]

The need for community is universal. But community means one thing in traditional societies and another thing in our society. We interact with many communities, but rarely does one group of people—family or best friends or church members—see the entirety of our lives and know us well. Instead, people relate to us as a coworker, not as a person who is married to Jane or Sally. They know us as a partner on the basketball court at the local YMCA, not as a member of a local church. They know us as a summer sailor, not as a neighbor living next door. How we expe-rience community, therefore, is as fragmented as our personal lives. We know so little about other people, and they know so lit-tle about us, even though we see them every day.

It would amaze us if we counted up the number of people we meet in any given week. A few are good friends, some are acquaintances, but most are strangers. I have shopped at a local Safeway for over eight years now. I have walked into that store well over five hundred times. I know a few employees by name, but I know little else about them, and I know nothing about the vast number of people who grow the food I eat and who process, package, ship, and shelve it. Likewise, I fly on airplanes piloted by people I have never met. I live in a safe and secure community policed by people I will never know. My life, in other words, rests in the hands of thousands of complete strangers. I depend on them, yet I know nothing about them.

Add to that list the thousands of people I do know and see at the college, in church, on the soccer fields, or in the grandstands. I bump into hundreds of people every week, yet I really know only a few of them. Sometimes I feel isolated and lonely, a man with no friends. I live like a stranger in the very world I call my own. Is my experience so different from anyone else's?

The Internet can also isolate. It feeds paranoia because it cuts us off from intimate relationships. The Internet has allowed "urban legends" to spread quickly. Urban legends are stories popularly believed to be true, but which usually have no basis in fact. As one story goes, a woman died at an ATM machine after licking an envelope laced with cyanide. In another story, a woman contracted AIDS after accidentally sitting on an infected needle in a movie theater. These stories, both untrue, have gone from one friend to another through e-mail, and by now have been read by millions of people, persuading them to become ever more suspicious and fearful of others around them.

In an age of fax machines and e-mail, we do not relate to people face-to-face. If anything, we feel wary and critical of everyone but our closest friends. "In a culture where interaction with others is increasingly optional," writes commentator Chuck Colson, "is it any surprise that mistrust and suspicion are also increasing? How can we trust our neighbors if we don't even know them? No wonder so many people fall for bogus e-mail warnings that warn of hidden dangers lurking in the most innocent settings."[7]

How can we discover God's will for our lives without guidance and support from a community? Huge corporations move employees around with little consideration given to friendships, family, neighborhood, and church. Young adults fall in love and marry with little parental involvement. Sometimes parents do not even meet their future son- or daughter-in-law until the decision to marry has already been made. People choose a vocation without receiving advice from friends and family who know them best. We become like a goose trying to fly south without a flock to fly along with. No wonder we lose our way so often.

Friends who teach at seminaries tell me many students receive a personal "call" to ministry—surely a matter of considerable relevance to the will of God!—without the confirmation a home church can provide. These students have little experience in ministry, even less understanding of what professional ministry requires, and no intimate relationships with older mentors. In many Third World churches, by contrast, mature members of a local church are drafted into leadership by the church itself. They are then sent somewhere for training. The church in America does not follow that same pattern, probably to its peril.

Our struggle to discern God's will for our lives reflects the fragmentation and isolation we experience. We make decisions in a vacuum because we lack consistent contact with people who know us well and can give us sound advice about our strengths and weaknesses. Participation in a real community can turn what might appear to be difficult choices into easy ones, complex choices into simple ones. Community informs, clarifies, and illumines, but only if we *belong* to such a community.

Participation in a community can change everything. It certainly did for Anne Lamott, a novelist and essayist who lives in San Francisco. Her journey to faith was about as difficult as crossing the Himalayas barefoot. She was an alcoholic and drug addict, and she lived on the edge for years. She found her way to faith through the influence of a little church comprised mostly of poor and marginal people. She wanted her son to grow up in the loving environment of this church, too. So, like many parents do with their children, she made him go. The reason for her action was simple, and it says a great deal about the sense of community that most people seem to miss.

The main reason is that I want to give him what I found in the world, which is to say a path and a little light to see by. Most of the people I know who have what I want—which is to say, purpose, heart, balance, gratitude, joy—are people with a deep sense of spirituality. They are people in community, who pray, or practice their faith.... They follow a brighter light than the glimmer of their own candle; they are part of something beautiful.[8]

Lamott became a member of that "beautiful" little community. She also discovered there what it meant to do the simple will of God. "Our funky little church is filled with people who are working for peace and freedom, who are out there on the streets and inside praying, and they are home writing letters, and they are at the shelters with giant platters of food."[9]

Not that traditional society is an ideal we should seek to recover. The town of Anatevka in *Fiddler on the Roof* was no "Garden of Eden," as the matchmaker in the musical lamented. Traditional societies have their own problems. They are often narrow and oppressive, and they force people to assume roles that do not fit their desires and interests. I for one prefer the freedom of living today. Still, that freedom comes with a price.

We have too many choices to make. We are too busy. Though we meet hundreds of people every week, we live in relative isolation and loneliness. Under these conditions, how is it possible for us to discover the will of God? Life seems too complex, frenzied, and lonely to allow us to discover anything about God at all. We will turn in the next chapter to examine how we can begin to establish order in our lives—to choose quality over quantity, to set a pace that is good for our souls, and to live in a healthy community. In short, we will explore simple obedience as the way of doing God's will.

4

SIMPLE OBEDIENCE
AS A WAY OF LIFE

My children want the freedom to make choices. When I take them to the local mall for a shopping expedition, they always notice with glee the new stores that have opened since the last time they were there. The latest is American Eagle, a store my daughter likes to browse. New stores mean more choices, and more choices, they assume, are a good thing.

My children are not unusual. Most middle-class adolescents in our culture angle to get as much freedom of choice as they can—to spend unlimited time and money at the mall, to surf the net hour after hour, to view whatever new movie appears on the marquee of the local multiplex, to attend every dance, party, and game they can. But is this quest for freedom altogether healthy? Like the serpent in the Garden of Eden, it can beguile us into overlooking the dangers involved in the face of so many choices.

Two hundred years ago the Founding Fathers of the United States of America decided to gamble on freedom. At the time, however, the American people had few opportunities to express that freedom because they lived in a simple society offering limited choices and requiring hard work to survive. We live in a different world today. The market economy and the technological revolution have changed all that. We now have freedom to make almost unlimited choices.

I see the impact on my teenagers in particular. The number and range of choices they have overwhelm and confuse them. They wander through life as if in a constant state of vertigo because of so many options. It is not, however, a problem unique to teenagers. All of us feel immobilized at times by the choices we have to make. Freedom appears as much an enemy as it is a friend. However much we cherish it, we feel cursed by it, too. What good are all those choices if we fail to choose what is good and right and true?

TWO KINDS OF FREEDOM

Perhaps we misunderstand what true freedom is. Popular American culture defines freedom as the absence of external restraint and the protection—as well as the expansion—of personal rights. These rights are outlined in the Constitution, which grants us the freedom to believe, speak, and in large measure behave the way we want.

We can believe in many gods, one God, or no God. We can speak and write whatever enters our minds, even if it is false, sordid, or inflammatory. We can pursue any interest we want, as long as other people are not harmed by it. We can read bestsellers, collect guns, keep snakes as pets, surf the net for pornography, or paint our living room black. We can make gobs of money and give it all away or spend it on foolish and vain pleasures. We have the right to pursue what is noble or vain, wise or foolish, visionary or selfish. No one in the United States has to be a Presbyterian; no one has to vote Democrat; no one has to believe that evolution is true or atoms contain energy or Abraham Lincoln was a great president.

Freedom is literally marketed to us. I read an advertisement recently that was trying to persuade me to buy a new cologne. The cologne is appropriately named "Freedom." The ad copy read: "Go where you want to go. Do what you want to do. Live how you want to live. That's what Freedom is all about. . . . Freedom. A New Sound in Fragrance." Of course the ad mentioned nothing about *where* we should go, *what* we should do, or *how* we should live. This appears entirely irrelevant. It is not what we do with our freedom that matters (except, of course, to buy this new product!). It is that we have freedom.

This quest for freedom has even wormed its way into Christianity. While pollsters keep reporting that Americans are still overwhelmingly religious, they are discovering that many are also drifting away from traditional Christian belief. Americans want to experiment with new religious ideas (like Taoism or Hinduism), reject such orthodox doctrines as the exclusivity of Jesus as the only way to God, or undermine traditional moral standards (like faithfulness to marriage vows). In "Spirit Search," an article about new tastes in American religious belief, *Boston Globe* reporter Scot Lehigh suggests Americans want the freedom to design their own religion. "God may have had the first word, but he sure isn't having the last one. As we enter the 21st century, Americans have shrugged loose the strictures of Scripture and are busy remaking the religious rules—and even the nature of faith itself—to their own liking."[1]

Lehigh admits that not all "traditionalists" are pleased with this trend. Some theologians wonder what good Christianity is if it is always "evolving with the times." If popular standards prevail, then Christianity does nothing more than reflect what people already believe, how they feel about life, and what they want from God. It puts people, not God, in charge of religion. Such religion upholds human freedom, to be sure, though sometimes at the expense of truth.

By contrast, the Bible defines freedom in different terms. True freedom comes when we become enslaved to Christ. "If any want to become my followers, let them deny themselves and take up their cross daily and follow me. For those who want to save their life will lose it, and those who lose their life for my sake will save it. What does it profit them if they gain the whole world, but lose or forfeit themselves?"[2]

Jesus taught that if we wish to find true life, we must die to our sinful and selfish selves. If we hope to win in a way that counts for eternity, we must lose in the ways that matter only in the temporal world. If we want to be first in the kingdom, we must be last in the world. We must take up our cross and follow Jesus. As Dietrich Bonhoeffer, a German Christian theologian martyred during World War II, argued in *The Cost of Discipleship*, "Because Jesus is the Christ, he has the authority to call and to demand obedience to his word. Jesus summons men to follow him not as a teacher or a pattern of the good life, but as the Christ, the Son of God."[3]

In other words, true freedom is found by surrendering ourselves to God and dedicating our wills to a life of obedience. This is what Evelyn Underhill, a novelist, teacher, and mystical writer who lived in the early twentieth century, called the act of consecration of the self. Though having many choices seems attractive to us, only *one* choice is sufficient and right—the choice of obedience. "Surely the very essential of a dedicated life is our free acquiescence in this: that simple act of acceptance which combines rightful action with perfect obedience, unquestioning acceptance of a job or of a mission, and the effort to accomplish our assignment."[4]

Alexis de Tocqueville, a French nobleman who visited America in the 1830s, understood this difference between the popular American definition of freedom and a Christian definition. He believed that the reason America could be so generous in providing the civil freedoms as outlined in the Bill of Rights was because Christianity functioned to restrain the American people from abusing those freedoms and disciplined them to use their freedom wisely and rightly. Christianity shaped American values—its "habits of the heart"—and enabled the American people to stop short of using freedom as an excuse to practice vice. De Tocqueville concluded:

> Despotism may be able to do without faith, but freedom cannot. Religion is much more needed in the republic they advocate than in the monarchy they attack, and in democratic republics most of all. How could society escape destruction if, when political ties are relaxed, moral ties are not tightened? And what can be done with a people master of itself if it is not subject to God?[5]

What does this discussion of biblical freedom have to do with our quest to discover God's will? As it turns out, our lust for freedom as American culture defines it has influenced the way we search for the will of God. The hidden assumption behind the conventional approach to the will of God is that having many options is a good thing, but only one option is God's will for us. The burden then falls on us to figure out which is the right and true one.

God's will is like the one present under the Christmas tree intended for us, though there are many other presents there, all of which *could* be ours. We must somehow discern which is ours, in spite of the fact that none of the packages has a tag with a name. We are therefore absolutely confounded in our search for which one is God's will for us.

But what if there were only one package under the tree? Then having no tag on it would be no problem. What if choice itself is beside the point, as much a distraction as a benefit? What if the freedom we value so much—the freedom to have anything we want—keeps us from experiencing the freedom we really need—to choose what God wants us to choose?

The will of God has to do with what we already know, not what we must figure out. It is contained in Jesus' command that we seek first God's kingdom and righteousness. The will of God, then, consists of one clear mandate—that we make God the absolute center of our lives. Ironically, it is exactly in making this choice that we find true freedom. It is the freedom of obedience. That is the will of God for all of us.

THE BIBLE ON FREEDOM

Both the Old Testament and the New Testament teach this truth—that freedom comes in obedience. The children of Israel were slaves in Egypt for four hundred years. Then God sent Moses to set them free. He confronted the pharaoh, who refused to release the Hebrew slaves. But ten plagues forced him to yield to God and to grant the Hebrews their freedom. Thus, the Hebrews departed from Egypt and traveled into the desert. There, in the desert, they found negative freedom—freedom *from* oppression. They were free to live on their own. But they had not yet discovered positive freedom—the freedom of living *for* God.

This positive kind of freedom they learned at Mount Sinai, where Moses received the Ten Commandments. These commandments were not intended to oppress the people of Israel again, as if they had been delivered from a human despot only to be subjugated to a divine despot. The Ten Commandments promised them *true* freedom, the freedom that comes from functioning according to God's design and fulfilling a divine purpose in their lives.

What instructions are to a new computer, the Ten Commandments are to people. They show us how to run properly.

They are the divine instructions to the human machine, helping us to live well, productively, and happily. Sadly, the people of Israel spurned these commandments time and again. They preferred to live in anarchy, and they paid dearly for their foolishness.[6]

The apostle Paul was dogged in his ministry by the same problem Moses dealt with. He had supporters who embraced his theology of grace because they felt it gave them license to do as they pleased. They took advantage of grace, using it as justification for willful disobedience. They even boasted about their sin because it demonstrated just how free they really were. They accepted no restraints, no demands, no limitations, like orphans left to shift for themselves.

A group of believers in the church of Corinth were especially adept at exploiting the freedom they had in Christ. They claimed the right to do anything they wanted. They even applauded a man for living adulterously with his stepmother, and they filed lawsuits against each other if someone violated their rights.[7] As part of his rebuttal Paul actually quotes their favorite slogan—"All things are lawful for me"—in his reply: "'All things are lawful for me,' but not all things are beneficial. 'All things are lawful for me,' but I will not be dominated by anything."[8] Paul goes on to counter this Corinthian definition of freedom with a Christian definition: "Do you not know that your body is a temple of the Holy Spirit within you, which you have from God, and that you are not your own? For you were bought with a price; therefore glorify God in your body."[9]

Jesus too announced that if we want true freedom, we must surrender our lives to God. Freedom is found not in doing whatever we want but in doing what God commands. We find freedom when we obey God. Once again, such obedience *is* the will of God for our lives.

The obedience to which Jesus and the Scriptures call us, however, is anything but oppressive. It is far different from the legalism that the Pharisees, Jesus' main opponents, imposed on their followers. They took the Old Testament law seriously, but their seriousness led them into legalism and self-righteousness. They forced people to submit to a yoke of bondage and required external observance, not inward change. For example, they followed detailed customs concerning the Sabbath. They would not light fires, carry wood, or prepare food on the Sabbath. But they missed the whole point of the Sabbath. As Jesus charged, the Pharisees strained at a gnat and swallowed a camel. They reduced obedience to petty rules and neglected to pursue justice, righteousness, and mercy.[10]

Jesus did not confront their oppressive legalism, however, by advocating license. He taught and practiced the true meaning of obedience—an obedience that plunged to the heart of the matter, affirming God's real intent. For example, while the Pharisees followed elaborate rituals when they washed their hands, Jesus demanded purity of heart. "Now you Pharisees clean the outside of the cup and of the dish, but inside you are full of greed and wickedness. You fools! Did not the one who made the outside make the inside also? So give for alms those things that are within; and see, everything will be clean for you."[11]

Dietrich Bonhoeffer understood Jesus' distinction between legalism and true obedience. Referring to Jesus' radical commands, he wrote:

> Again, it is no universal law. Rather is it the exact opposite of all legality. It is nothing else than bondage to Jesus Christ alone, complete breaking through every programme, every ideal, every set of laws. No other significance is possible, since Jesus is the only significance. Beside Jesus nothing has any significance. He alone matters.[12]

Jesus was not distant and detached when he taught his own set of rules for the human community (e.g., the Sermon on the Mount). His rules were not arbitrary, petty, and irrelevant. Jesus lived by his own rules, tested them in real life, and proved that they were good and livable. His rules are life-giving and life-changing. He thus embraced the commands of the Old Testament, which were extensions of God's promises, and obeyed them perfectly. He wants his followers similarly to embrace what the apostle Paul calls "the obedience of faith."[13]

If obeyed in faith, God's commands will turn our lives upside down and inside out. They will make us wonderfully new, holy, and mature, like a tall and stately tree. As C. S. Lewis observed, "You must realise from the outset that the goal towards which He is beginning to guide you is absolute perfection; and no power in the whole universe, except you yourself, can prevent Him from taking you to that goal. That is what you are in for."[14]

God lays claim to us and promises to transform us until we become the creatures he always intended us to be. If Christ represents the perfect picture of what God wants us to become, then the commands of Scripture are like the directions that will get us there. There is nothing trivial and superficial about God's plan. His commands are radical because his plans are complete. He wants to make us new in every way. Such transformation will also set us free.

Jesus called this the "narrow gate."[15] It is not narrow as we often understand narrowness, as if Jesus were calling us to become hyper-conservatives. His way is narrow because it squeezes all selfishness out of us. It deprives us of the right to live for ourselves. Jesus demands everything from us, not because he wants to make life miserable for us but because he wants to give us purpose and joy. He knows that real life is gained by giving our lives up to God.

Token obedience betrays an errant theology. We think that real life is gained by what we keep to ourselves, not by what we give to God. So we do the minimum in terms of obedience—just enough to get by—so that we have plenty of choices left over for ourselves. In our way of thinking, God's commands are like emptying the garbage or doing taxes. They are part of the deal of being a Christian, but hardly a welcomed part. So we fulfill our obligation to God and, once that is finished, start to enjoy life again.

But Jesus will have none of that. He rejects all token obedience. He keeps demanding more because he knows his followers will find true life only by obeying God, not by living for themselves. Thus, while the Mosaic law forbids murder, Jesus forbids hate. While the Mosaic law condemns adultery, Jesus condemns lust. The narrow way Jesus taught is the way of complete obedience, an obedience that leads to freedom from self and freedom to live for God.[16]

ARTISTS AND ATHLETES HAVE IT RIGHT!

To summarize our discussion thus far, freedom as our culture defines it allows us to do anything we want. Freedom as the New Testament defines it, however, allows us to become what God, our Creator and Redeemer, wants. In rejecting the "freedom" of license and embracing biblical freedom, we experience the true freedom of being children of God. Both artists and athletes understand the nature of true freedom. They give up their freedom to do whatever they want, subject themselves to strict discipline, and in the end gain the freedom to perform at the highest levels of artistic and athletic achievement. Loss of freedom actually leads to freedom. It is the freedom of obedience, gained by following a strict regimen of practice.

The famous Suzuki method, used to teach students how to play musical instruments, is founded on this principle. John, my youngest child, began taking piano lessons two years ago. Before he started, he would occasionally sit down at the piano and pound on the keys. He enjoyed complete freedom, but what he produced was a cacophony of sound, not music. To learn to make music, he has been placed under severe restraint—not always to his liking, as he is quick to tell me about once a week (or more). His arms must be held just so, his wrists must bounce just right, his fingers must plunk the keys according to strict rhythm. It is slow, arduous work. Before it is all over I estimate that he will play variations on "Twinkle, Twinkle, Little Star" (the national anthem of the Suzuki method) thousands of times until both he and I are ready to go insane.

But over time such discipline will enable him to play beautiful music—if, that is, we make it that far. I am confident of that outcome because my daughter was required to follow the same method. Catherine resisted, just as John does. On many occasions I grew weary of making her practice, and the monotony of playing "Twinkle" was enough to turn the most dedicated parent away from music forever. Our home, I am ashamed to say, was not always the picture of harmony during those early years of lessons. But we persisted, in spite of procrastination, protest, pressure, and conflict.

Now Catherine's days of "Twinkle" are long past. She has learned to discipline herself, and she plays Mozart, Debussy, Chopin, and Beethoven with precision and feeling. She makes beautiful music, and I relish listening to it. As a musician, she has experienced the benefits of obedience and has found true freedom in playing with excellence. She has become accomplished.

Athletes learn the same lesson. To become competitive in a sport, they must learn to follow a regimen. They must give up the freedom to do whatever they want in order to gain a deeper kind of freedom to perform well as an athlete. My older son, David, has played soccer for years. We used to spend hours practicing in the front yard, and I coached his team for five years. At first I pretended to play hard when we squared off against each other, but I would usually let him win. Had I tried my hardest, I would have beaten him every time.

During those early years he often missed the ball entirely when he tried to kick it hard. His dribbling made him look as if he had two left feet. But he kept at it. Now he can juggle the ball with his feet as effortlessly as I can catch a ball with my hands. His passes and shots on goal are crisp and accurate. In the great reversal that every mom or dad expects and longs for, David must now play far below his ability when we scrimmage each other in the front yard so that I have a chance to score a goal or two. I wish he was as merciful to me as I used to be to him. He has become a competitive soccer player. He makes the game look natural and easy. It was not natural and easy at first, but it became that way through obedience to a regimen of discipline.

The performance of artists and athletes seems effortless and seamless, fluid and natural, because they have developed complete self-mastery over their bodies. Great runners skim over the track as if they were phantoms, virtuoso pianists play as if they were pouring water over the keys, polished writers use words as if the words chose themselves. But runners, pianists, and writers perform at the highest level only because they have at one time followed a routine of practice, developed self-discipline, and learned obedience. They found freedom by giving it up.

God calls us to follow that same pattern of obedience in ordinary life so that we can experience that same freedom. Rigor of obedience determines outcome in life, no matter what we do. The quality of our friendships, for example, will affect our decisions about courtship and marriage. If we fail to honor and cherish friends, we will be less likely to find a good marriage partner for ourselves, to say nothing about becoming a good marriage partner for someone else. Diligence of study will ensure success in whatever profession we choose to pursue. If we fail to study, we will never achieve what we have dreamed of accomplishing. Integrity of character, basic skills in reading and writing, affection and loyalty in friendships, and godliness of life are universally relevant, no matter where we live and what we do. Obedience is God's will for our lives, and obedience leads to freedom.

TWO LESSONS FROM VIETNAM

Last night I attended a performance of *Miss Saigon* with Catherine, David, and six other friends. The musical tells the story of Chris, a Marine officer stationed in Saigon during the Vietnam War, and Kim, a young prostitute. Chris meets Kim at a popular bar on the night she begins to practice her new profession. The scene is a madhouse. Dozens of Marines and prostitutes are drinking, dancing, and cavorting together while wild music plays in the background. Their obsession with sex, money, and pleasure drives them into a wild frenzy, as if they were starving animals feeding on a fresh kill.

Chris and Kim immediately fall in love and begin to live together. They long for genuine love, not cheap sex. They are desperate to find something real in a world that seems to have gone mad, though the world they create for themselves is anything but real. Two weeks later Chris is forced to escape Saigon because the Vietcong are about to invade the city. He has to leave Kim behind. He tries later on to locate her but eventually gives up. He falls in love with an American woman, marries, and settles down. But three years later he learns that Kim and he had a son together. He flies to Bangkok, accompanied by his new wife, to meet Kim and their child. Kim is devastated when she learns that Chris is married. The story ends tragically when Kim commits suicide so that her son will be free to return with Chris to America.

Chris's experience and the behavior of the Marines in the opening scene of the musical were true to life. Many American soldiers embraced their freedom with a vengeance, feeling little pressure to restrain their appetites without the watchful eye of friends, family, church, and community. If anything, the temptation to drown their fears in sex, alcohol, and drugs was too much for them. So during off-duty hours they slept around, drank themselves into a stupor, and experimented with drugs. The results were often devastating: children born out of wedlock, drug addiction, and violence. Many of these soldiers had enormous difficulty readjusting to life in America after the war, and their problems persisted for years.

But there is another side to the story. It is a personal one. My brother-in-law, Jack, spent a year as an officer in the Air Force. He was stationed on a base near Bangkok during the Vietnam War. He was married to my sister, Diane, and she was already pregnant with their first child when he was shipped out. Tammelyn was born a month after he began his tour of duty.

Jack did not see Tammelyn or Diane for an entire year. He, too, faced the temptation of having absolute moral freedom while he was overseas. But he decided to remain faithful to my sister. He gave up his freedom, in other words, for something more valuable to him. My sister helped, too. Every day she sent him a long letter; every day she sent him photos of his baby daughter; every day she sent him a cassette tape capturing the ordinary sounds of their household. Jack plastered the walls of his bedroom with those photos, as if to remind himself of the reality of a world that seemed so far away.

I was there at the airport when Jack returned after his year away. I witnessed their glorious reunion, as if I was eavesdropping on a miracle. That moment will remain forever imprinted on my memory. Jack stepped off that plane, embraced my sister, and cradled his baby daughter for the first time. They were delirious with joy. Diane and Jack went on to build a good life together. They have now been married for thirty-four years. They have raised five children and have two grandchildren. Jack has set up a successful dentistry practice, and he and Diane have served their church and community well.

I still think about Jack's year in Southeast Asia. I reflect on what it must have been like for him to say "no" to temptation, to give up the extraordinary freedom he had there, and to remain true to his wife and baby daughter. The choice he made is like a metaphor of the theme of this chapter. He had one kind of freedom, the freedom to live an unrestrained life, to "go where you want to go, do what you want to do, live how you want to live," as the advertisement for "Freedom" reads.

But he gave up that freedom. He chose another kind of freedom, the freedom of obedience. I have observed with respect and appreciation what that freedom has produced in their lives, in their family, and in their community. That is the kind of freedom I wish for my life and my family. It is the freedom of living a life for God, of following God's will. The *one* pathway we must follow may limit freedom as culture defines it, but it gives us freedom as the Bible defines it. When we seek first God's kingdom and righteousness, we will do the will of God *and* experience true freedom.

PART II

DISCERNING OUR CALLING IN LIFE

DISTINGUISHING BETWEEN CALLING AND CAREER

Career and calling. Two words we have probably all used. Though I am not always comfortable with them, I am going to use them in this chapter since they are the best ones we have to convey the ideas I want to explore.

Career is a secular word. We use it often, though without giving much thought to it. I define *career* as a particular line of work a person does that earns an income, requires education or training, and keeps society running. A career usually provides power and status of some kind and helps us to feel as if we fit into society as contributing members.

Calling is a theological word, perhaps less familiar to us, and its meaning is more ambiguous. I define *calling* as a God-given purpose to use one's time, energy, and abilities to serve God in the world.

There is obviously overlap between the two words. Many people fulfill their calling in life through a job or career. Nevertheless, a calling is different from a career in at least four ways. We will explore these differences in more detail in the next three chapters, so I will only mention them briefly here at the outset.

First, a calling transcends a career in the same way an athlete transcends the sport he or she plays. One simply *is* an athlete, by nature and ability; one *plays* a sport. The primary calling of every Christian is to follow God, regardless of ability, position, opportunity, or background. Whether young or old, ordinary or extraordinary, poverty-stricken or pampered, everyone is called by God to trust, serve, and obey him. As we have observed in Part

I, this is God's will for human life—our primary calling. As Os Guinness, a contemporary Christian author and social critic, argues: "Calling is the truth that God calls us to himself so decisively that everything we are, everything we do, and everything we have is invested with a special devotion, dynamism, and direction lived out as a response to his summons and service."[1]

Second, a calling often uses a career, though it should never be reduced to a career. I have a friend who teaches pathology in a local medical residency program. He is a career doctor, but his calling is bigger than his career. He uses his position in medicine to accomplish goals that most secular doctors overlook. My former nanny, Monica, works as a first grade teacher in a public school. What she does with students in the classroom and how she relates to parents outside the classroom, to say nothing about the way she prays for her school, sets her apart from most teachers I know.

Third, a calling involves work that can send us in directions where traditional careers do not go. Recently I met a woman who has twenty children, six biological and fourteen adopted. Far from looking harried and harassed by the bedlam in her home, she communicates a spirit of calm, joy, and energy, as if she were a dancer gliding across the stage. How she functions as a mother of twenty children seems well matched for who she is as a person. She is fulfilling her calling, though she does not have a traditional career.

Finally, a calling for most Christians is not singular but plural, which is why using the word is somewhat misleading. A Christian's calling in life is rarely to a single duty, unless that duty involves something like serving as a monk. Most of us have multiple callings. We must learn how to do them all, keeping in mind the importance of simplicity, balance, and flexibility (the subject of chapter 7).

As I reflect on my own life and experiences in the context of my daily professional work, I see that although I have pursued three careers in succession, not to mention the dozens of jobs I held when I was much younger, I have had one calling. But I also observe that I have had multiple roles to play in the pursuit of my calling, all of which are included in God's will, embody his calling in my life, and serve a greater purpose.

In spite of its messiness and complexity, I intend to use the term *calling* because it forces us to recognize how messy and complex life in the world can be. There is nothing neat and tidy about how we discover our calling—or callings, as the case may be— nor about how we fulfill them in ordinary life. Rarely does our journey through life follow a straight and clear path from beginning to end.

THREE CAREERS, ONE CALLING

As I mentioned in chapter 1, I decided to attend seminary because I sensed a "calling" to ministry, although I had little idea what that calling really implied. I thought that ministry had something to do with being at church a lot, preaching sermons, running meetings, visiting people, and helping the needy. Ministry was a job. To get to the point where I could do that job, I had to attend seminary first—which, I assumed, would prepare me.

So I attended Fuller Seminary in Pasadena, California. The education I received there was superb. I learned to study the Bible, to think theologically, and to hone my skills. But I received another education that was equally valuable. During my first year at Fuller I joined a youth ministry team at a large local church, Lake Avenue Congregational Church. The youth director, Chuck Miller, challenged me to think about a biblical vision for ministry, not simply the job of ministry. He introduced me to the idea— then revolutionary to me—that ministry consisted of investing in people's lives to help them become mature Christians. He taught me to establish three "priorities" in ministry—commitment to God, to church, and to world—and to organize a ministry so that I would do the "work of God without sacrificing the people of God." Under his tutelage I changed my view of ministry. It became less a job and more a genuine calling to help people grow in Christ.

When I graduated from Fuller, I became an associate pastor of a Reformed church in Paramount, California. My job description was outrageously demanding, though I had no idea at the time because I was too excited about it. I was supposed to develop a youth ministry program for junior high, senior high, and college students, to oversee the Christian education program of the church, to develop a practical plan for evangelism, and to provide pastoral care for the young married couples at the church.

The senior pastor, Harold Korver, was a masterful pastor and leader. He was also a superb mentor for me. I arrived shortly after the church had lost its third youth pastor in four years. Suspicion was high and expectations were low among church members. I added to the problem because I was young, brash, and immature. The church was wary of starting all over again with still another youth pastor. Thus Harold gave me some direct advice. "Sittser," he said sharply, "cut the mustard or get out. You have a job to do. So do it."

Because I was responsible to develop a program that did not yet exist, I could not hide behind a ministry that someone else had started. If anything was going to get done, I was the one who would have to do it. I worked hard during the four years I served there, which put tremendous strain on my marriage, an area of life that I did not, at least at that time, define as a real "calling." Using what I had learned during my years in seminary, I started to invest in people, especially the youth, many of whom became committed Christians. I look back on those years with deep appreciation for what I learned and for how the church supported me.

When I had been there about three years, my wife, Lynda, spontaneously mentioned that I would do well serving as a college chaplain, a position I had never considered before. She had obviously thought about it and was quick to identify the benefits: I could work with people at a formative stage of their life, I could be as intense and demanding as I wanted to be, and I could study during the summer months. She also suggested it might be good for our relationship.

Six months later I received a call from the president of Northwestern College, a small Christian liberal arts college in Orange City, Iowa, who invited me to apply for an opening in the chaplain's office. I applied for the position and was offered it. So I changed institutions, job descriptions, and locations and went to work as a college chaplain. I stayed there for six years. I discovered that the college setting suited me well. I loved working with students, and I developed deep friendships with faculty as well.

Again, it was Lynda who first encouraged me to think about enrolling in a graduate program. She thought that being a college professor would allow me to express my deepest interests and convictions—exploring the "big questions," reading great books, teaching, and mentoring students. So I started a course of study at the University of Chicago and earned my Ph.D. in the history of Christianity. During my final year there I applied for a position at Whitworth College in Spokane, Washington. I have been working at Whitworth for over ten years now.

When I view this journey in retrospect, I see a pattern emerge. It has little to do with how I made the decision to take one job over another, but it has much to do with how I actually functioned in each job once I started it. Without always knowing it, I was operating according to an intuitive sense of calling. I realize now that, though I have had three careers—pastor, chaplain, and professor—I have had one basic calling. I have always functioned as a bridge between two different worlds—the world of the academy, where ideas rule, and the world of the church, where practical concerns dominate. My calling is to make the academic study of theology accessible to ordinary people and to help prepare a generation of students for leadership in the church and in the world.

That I ended up serving in an academic setting is not particularly important. There may be a hierarchy of prestige and power in the way the secular world evaluates a person's work, but there is no such hierarchy in the way Christians should evaluate a calling. All have equal value in the eyes of God and all are equally useful for his kingdom work in the world, regardless of income earned or education required or notice received from cultural elites. Evelyn Underhill makes this point well. All vocations, she wrote, have value. "Some will be fulfilled in prayer, some in action, and some in both. Some are called to redemptive suffering, some to an intellectual life, some to very practical and homely labor. It doesn't matter which as long as ... we sanctify it by giving it supernatural intent."[2]

We do the will of God when we fulfill our calling in life, a calling that is uniquely ours, like a set of fingerprints. A calling grows out of our temperament, our talents, and our experiences in life, though these are not the only factors that affect a calling, as we will see. Ultimately a calling comes from God. It is part of who we are, of what God has put in us, and of how God wants us to serve his kingdom. Though we have to discover our calling, we should also recognize that it is already in us, very much a part of our identity, waiting to be discovered and expressed, like perennial seeds that, once planted, produce flowers that come up year after year.

The process of discovering our calling is as subtle as sign language, where every movement and gesture counts for something. If anything, a calling probably discovers us as much as we discover it. In his sermon "The Calling of Voices," Frederick Buechner, a contemporary novelist and preacher, explores the divine nature of our calling. A calling itself lays claim to us as we discover it. Buechner defines a calling as "the work that [a person] is called to in this world, the thing that he is summoned to spend his life doing." He believes that a calling is like a mandate. It places demands on us. "We can speak of a man's choosing his vocation, but perhaps it is at least as accurate to speak of a vocation's choosing the man, of a call's being given and a man's hearing it, or not hearing it."[3]

This idea of a calling was especially important to the leaders of the Reformation in the sixteenth century. John Calvin, for example, believed that God has assigned to each Christian a specific calling in life, which provides a person with a meaningful job to do, a way to serve the world, and a sense of divine purpose. He affirmed that every person is given a calling, and that every calling is unique. "Every individual's sphere of life, therefore, is a post assigned him by the Lord that he may not wander about in uncertainty all the days of his life. . . . Our present life, therefore, will be best regulated if we always keep our calling in mind."

Since God is the one who calls us into specific forms of service, every calling has dignity and purpose to it, regardless of what the powerful and famous may think.

> And everyone in his respective sphere of life will show more patience, and will overcome the difficulties, cares, miseries and anxieties in his path, when he will be convinced that every individual has his task laid upon his shoulders by God. If we follow our calling we shall receive this unique consolation that there is no work so mean and so sordid that does not look truly respectable and highly important in the sight of God![4]

THE PROBLEM WITH CAREERS

As we have already noted, a calling is not the same thing as a career, though the two are related. A career involves some kind of socially useful work. It usually requires specific education or training, promises advancement, provides compensation, and produces something considered valuable to society.

A career serves the needs, welfare, and interests of the larger society. Thus, engineers design cars, which assembly-line workers assemble, executives advertise, car dealers sell, insurance agents insure, commuters drive, and mechanics fix, until the cars end up in the junk-yard. Then junk dealers sell them for used parts until there is nothing left but rusted metal, which owners of foundries buy and use for scrap metal to make steel for another round of automobiles. Careers, in other words, function symbiotically, creating a circular system that keeps perpetuating itself as if it were a kind of economic ecosystem.

There are three possible problems with careers. First, not everyone's calling fits into a specific career. Sometimes people work at jobs because they need the income, though the labor they provide has little to do with their deepest interests and motivations. In my younger years I piled lumber, shoveled coal, flipped burgers, built apartments, and sold shoes because I needed the money. All were productive jobs and now provide me with hilarious stories to tell my kids or use as sermon illustrations, but none embodied my sense of calling. Some people spend their entire lives doing work that offers little satisfaction and little sense of calling because they have families to support and bills to pay. We even have a phrase for that: "dead-end jobs."

Second, sometimes a career can actually prevent a person from discovering or pursuing a calling. A career has incredible power to socialize people within its own area. When a professional basketball player justifies a strike by arguing that he simply wants to make enough income to "provide for his family"—never mind that many professional athletes make more *in one year* than most people do over a lifetime—we see the results of socialization. A career can cause a person to embrace values that advance his or her own interests or those of a social group, not the needs of society.

I think of a young student who aspires to be a medical missionary in the Third World. Years later, however, he finds himself settled in a comfortable suburban practice that supports his lavish lifestyle. "I had to think about my own professional security and advancement," he insists. Or a woman is inspired during her college years to pursue a career in law so that she can provide legal services in the inner city. But she ends up handling messy though profitable divorce cases. She excuses her change of direction by saying, "There is no money in justice."

I have witnessed this tragedy firsthand in college teaching. A bright student wants to become a college professor and scholar as a way to reach Generation Z, "the lost generation." But graduate school has a deleterious effect on him, and what graduate school starts, his first teaching post finishes. His scholarly interests become increasingly obscure, his writing abstruse and inaccessible. He cares less and less about the ordinary, tedious work of classroom teaching and more and more about research. He spends as little time as possible with students, whom he sees as a distraction. Instead, he attends as many scholarly conferences as he can, where he prances around like a rooster trying to impress and intimidate. His idealism and vision gradually disappear. He has forsaken the calling that once motivated him—not a bad thing in itself for people do, after all, change their minds—but he does not replace that calling with another that reflects his Christian convictions.

Third, some callings never translate into formal careers. Sometimes those for whom this is true feel "left out in the cold." Our modern obsession with careers, especially with the power, status, and income they provide, has marginalized people who have chosen not to pursue one. Some homemaker fathers and mothers see their parental role as central to their sense of calling and have been deprived of cultural validation because they have no formal careers. Many people, especially retirees, have cut themselves loose from a career in order to devote more time and energy to volunteer service, but they are put on the shelf by a culture that evaluates the worth of people according to a career, not according to their devotion to service. Little do we realize what would happen to our society—what in fact *is* happening to our society—without the contributions to the common good that homemakers, retirees, and volunteers make.

I am not suggesting that living in suburbs, handling divorce cases, or becoming scholars is wrong. But what should concern us is the subtle and insidious ways that a career can undermine our commitment to serve God. Most careers have enormous infrastructures—graduate schools, professional guilds, bureaucratic institutions (like unions), methods of evaluation, standards of success—that impose values not always compatible with Christian convictions. Careers far too often emphasize competition over cooperation, wealth over generosity, power over service, and ideology over truth. They can become self-serving. Having a career, therefore, runs the risk of subverting our commitment to God.

WHAT IT MEANS TO HAVE A CALLING

I have been negligent thus far in addressing the critical issue of whether the concept of a "calling" applies only to Christians. I have used (and I will continue to use) examples drawn from the secular world that have nothing to do with Christianity or Christian service—fields such as athletics, sales and service, medicine, law, and other fields that serve the common good. Does every person have a calling? If so, then what is distinctively Christian about a calling?

As you will recall, God wills above all that we seek him through his Son, Jesus Christ. God gives us grace not only when we seek him, but even before we seek him. He is the one whom we seek; he is also the one who does the seeking. God gives us the grace of salvation. He wants to make us right with him.

But God gives another kind of grace, too. The Reformed tradition calls it "common grace" because it refers to the grace that God gives to all people. It is the grace of creation, not of redemption. Many people, non-Christian as well as Christian, serve God *indirectly* by using their gifts for a worthy cause. People with little or no interest in Christianity can contribute to God's work in the world, even though they do not realize what they are doing and whom they are serving. As we learn from the book of Isaiah, even the pagan king Cyrus served God's greater plan by allowing the Jews to return to their homeland.[5]

Non-Christians, therefore, can and do contribute to the common good, whatever their convictions and motivations happen to be. Doctors of all types can heal sick people, lawyers can advocate justice, entrepreneurs can start helpful businesses, and teachers can educate students. God uses all kinds of people to accomplish his purposes.

A calling applies to our earthly life. It honors God, however unintentionally, by contributing something positive to the world that God has made, works now to redeem, and plans one day to restore when Jesus returns to establish his earthly kingdom. People in distinctively religious professions, therefore, are not the only ones who have a calling. So do construction workers, architects, seamstresses, artists, government representatives, army officers, and accountants, though their work is not at all directed toward specifically religious activities. This principle applies to everyone, Christian and non-Christian alike, who serve God when they advance the cause of justice, truth, beauty, and goodness.

After God had provided detailed designs for the construction of Israel's tabernacle, including the ark of the covenant, he called two men, Bezalel and Oholiab, to do the work. They were called as craftsmen because they were good at using their hands to build things. "Bezalel and Oholiab and every skillful one to whom the LORD has given skill and understanding to know how to do any work in the construction of the sanctuary shall work in accordance with all that the LORD has commanded."[6] God loves the world—not just people in the world but the world itself. He expresses that love by calling people to do something useful in and for the world. He uses their work to advance his divine purposes of creating beauty, caring for the needy, providing meaningful work, restoring relationships, and repairing a broken world.

A calling contributes uniquely to God's work in the world. People with a calling have a sense of higher purpose and see the bigger picture. For example:

• Selling insurance is a career, the success of which is determined by the size of policies sold, whether people need the insurance or not; helping people to become good stewards of their resources is a calling.

- Managing a sporting goods store is a career; challenging people to use their leisure time to find refreshment and renewal is a calling.
- Teaching social studies at a junior high is a career; providing instruction, support, and guidance to adolescents going through a difficult passage in life is a calling.
- Functioning as a secretary is a career; organizing an office so that details are handled efficiently, but never at the expense of people, is a calling.

A career causes people to think of income, power, position, and prestige. A calling inspires people to consider human need, moral standards, and a larger perspective.

A career does not define a person, nor does it determine a calling. If anything, the opposite occurs. God defines the person and gives that person a calling. Then he or she is free to use a career for God's kingdom purpose. As Os Guiness puts it, "A sense of calling should precede a choice of job and career, and the main way to discover calling is along the line of what we are each created and gifted to be. Instead of, 'You are what you do,' calling says: 'Do what you are.'"[7]

My two boys had the same first grade teacher. They have had many good teachers since then, but they still refer to her as their favorite teacher. I have often wondered what makes her so effective. She certainly teaches the basic subject matter well, as evidenced by the skills students develop. She manages the class exceptionally well, too. She maintains order but never dominates the students. She encourages conversation and creativity, but she never permits chaos. There is goodness and kindness in her as well. She loves her students, and they know it and feel it. Teaching is more than a job to her; it is a calling. It is an extension of who she is, how she sees the world, what drives her.

A calling is a way of seeing the world with the eyes of the heart. No two people see the world in exactly the same way. Imagine ten people arriving at the scene of a terrible accident. Though they witness the same event, they all see something different and respond in different ways. One man sees confused motorists unsure of what to do, so he begins to direct traffic. A woman sees the details of the accident, immediately calls 911 on her cell phone, and describes the scene with astonishing accuracy. A retired teacher sees two traumatized children whose mother is lying lifeless on the side of the road; she wraps her arms around them to comfort them. A nurse sees catastrophic injury and immediately checks vital signs. A pastor sees a witness to the accident sobbing uncontrollably and tries to calm her down. A young woman, still in her teens, sees a spiritual battle unfolding and prays. Other people see chaos, so they get blankets, flares, and emergency supplies out of their cars and put them to good use. Everyone responds differently to the accident because they see differently. What they see is determined by something deep within them.

How we see the world around us points the way to our calling. Some people see poor organization wherever they go. They join an institution and make it run more efficiently. Other people see poor health, whether in body, mind, or spirit, and develop careers to bring physical, psychological, or spiritual healing to people. Still others see poor housing, and they work at nonprofit organizations like Habitat for Humanity to alleviate the problem.

I know in my head that there is much that is wrong in the world, yet I do not see it with the eyes of my heart. I do not concern myself much with inept government, although I read about it in the newspaper almost every day. It probably ought to bother me more than it does, since it is such a big problem. I do not respond with alarm to national health-care problems, although I am aware of such social crises as teenage smoking and the AIDS epidemic. I do not lie awake at night tossing and turning about global warming and the pollution of our oceans, about illiteracy in our inner cities, or about refugees in eastern Europe, although I am aware of these problems and occasionally contribute money to remedy them.

But there are things I do see with the eyes of my heart. I see Christians who have at their disposal a legacy of two thousand years of faith but live as if they were spiritual orphans. I see churches filled with immature Christians who do not know how to connect Christian faith to life experience. I see college students who have four or five precious years to make important decisions about what they want to become and to accomplish in life and who need guidance as they lay a foundation for future success.

How do we discover our calling? Or better, how, as Buechner asked, does our calling discover us? We discover it by embarking on a journey. The journey to get there is a necessary part of the calling itself. Many of us will not know at an early age what our calling is. That does not mean we have no calling. It is already in us, like a bulb lying dormant in the frozen ground, waiting for spring to arrive, so that it can burst through the ground. Our deep sense of calling should send us on a journey of discovery. We have to travel to get where God wants us to go. It is not an easy path we must follow.

6

Discovering What We're Supposed to Do

Idid not intend to become a writer. I did not even want to be writer. The very idea made me feel as insecure as a stage actor with a bad memory. How I fell into writing—and it was about as accidental as a fall—says something important about how we discover our calling, or perhaps how our calling discovers us.

I served as a college chaplain in my late twenties. Soon after arriving on the campus of Northwestern College, I initiated a discipleship seminar for Christian students. That seminar was important to me, for it was the one time during the week when I could teach students about the Christian faith in depth. It was important to students, too, for many were eager to take a fresh look at Christianity after having been raised in traditional churches.

The students who attended the weekly seminar became leaders of small discipleship groups on campus. To prepare them to lead the groups, I decided to write weekly study guides for their small groups. I provided a resource, therefore, that had an immediate and practical purpose. I did not consider what I wrote each week as real "writing" because I did not intend it for formal publication. I was like a weekend gardener trying to raise enough food to provide for the family. The suggestion that I was a farmer would have been ridiculous to me.

The college occasionally invited speakers to visit the campus for a few days to address students, faculty, and members of the community. One of those speakers was Leighton Ford, an evangelist with the Billy Graham Evangelistic Association. He conducted several evangelistic rallies at the college and in the community. One morning, while sitting in my office, he picked up a few copies of the study guides I had written and perused them. He liked what he read and suggested I try to get them published. He even recommended a publisher he thought would be appropriate.

"That sounds wonderful," I said politely, "But who am I to them?"

He smiled, "It doesn't matter who you are. It matters who I am." Then, on his initiative and without my knowledge, he wrote friends at the publishing house and told them about me. One of the editors contacted me and asked me to send my study guides to him. They became the foundation for my first book, *The Adventure: Putting Energy into Your Walk with God.*

Leighton Ford took the initiative—it was an act of pure generosity on his part. But I had laid the groundwork for years by writing material that had no other purpose than to train students. I was fulfilling my calling as a writer long before I published anything or even thought of myself as a writer (which I still have trouble doing). I eventually became a *published* writer by writing before there was any thought or possibility of publication.

Discovering our calling can be like going on a journey. The experiences we have along the road have a cumulative effect, preparing us for future service. In other words, knowing God's will requires more than mere information about what we might be doing in the future, as if we were soldiers being given orders for our next tour of duty. We come to know the will of God as a life calling through experience itself. We discover what our calling is in the same way an artist paints on a canvas or a person falls in love. We learn by trying, by experimenting, by doing. Our calling is inseparable from the journey. In one sense, it *is* the journey.

Experience teaches us, prepares us, and seasons us for what lies ahead. If we are attentive to God in this present moment—which, as we have already learned, *is* the primary will of God for our lives—we will begin the glorious process of that discovery. We will learn as we go and become ready for what lies ahead. We will grow in character and conviction, gain necessary skills, and become mature. In due time our sense of calling will emerge, unfolding like a glorious landscape that we see on a road trip across America.

If I had tried to divine the future as I imagined it would be or thought it should be—or as I thought God had "willed" it for me—I would not have been able to see with any degree of clarity what I have ended up doing. Where I have arrived is a far different place from where I had planned to be. As I now look back, however, I see a pattern that makes sense to me. What I did at one stage anticipated what came later on, even though I could not see it at the time.

NOT WHAT WE EXPECT

Imagine standing in a room with an open door. As you look through that door, you see another room with an open door, which opens up to still another room with an open door, and so on. You can see through open doors to at least ten successive rooms. Let's say that you are convinced that your calling is in that tenth room, which you can see clearly from where you are standing. You want to get there as quickly and directly as you can, traveling through those ten open doors like an arrow flying fast and straight to its target. But what you do not realize is that once you walk through just one open door and enter another room, you will see other open doors in that room that you could not have seen before entering it. Going through one of those doors may lead you in an entirely different direction.

We cannot predict the future. We will go places, do things, meet people, face challenges, accomplish goals, and pursue careers that fall outside our present field of vision. We can see only a little ways ahead of us. But as we proceed, there will be strange twists and turns along the way. There will be surprises that we did not and could not anticipate.

I am not suggesting that it is impossible to know our calling at a young age. I know people who discerned their calling when they were still in elementary school. They knew beyond a shadow of a doubt that God was calling them to be a doctor or a teacher or a scientist. Still, how they fulfilled that calling did not always line up with their expectations. They ended up doing what they wanted to do, but not necessarily in the way they expected to do it. They planned to practice medicine, but perhaps not in an inner city clinic. Or they planned to teach elementary school, only in the United States, not in Cairo, where they eventually landed.

SHACKLETON'S HISTORIC FEAT

Take Earnest Shackleton as an example. He wanted to be a great explorer during "the heroic age" of exploration in the late nineteenth and early twentieth centuries. He aimed to be the first to reach the South Pole, but bad weather and short supplies turned him back. So he tried instead to be the first to cross the entire Antarctic continent by dogsled. He had a special ship built that would get him to his point of departure, and he carefully selected twenty-eight men and fifty-five dogs to accompany him on the perilous journey. The ship got within eighty miles of where his party planned to begin the expedition. Then pack ice moved in and encircled the ship, preventing further progress. When the ice began to move, the ship with its crew and cargo drifted north for hundreds of miles until all hope of starting the expedition was lost.

Shackleton found himself in dire circumstances. His ship had broken apart and sunk. His crew was stranded on a frozen sea. They had supplies to last, and they had three lifeboats, but they were hundreds of miles from the open ocean and hundreds more from land. So they waited. Finally, spring arrived and the ice broke up. They launched their small lifeboats and headed for land. They landed on Elephant Island, a small, uninhabited wasteland of an island that had nothing on it but rock, glaciers, penguins, and seals.

They built a shelter, hunted for food, and passed the time. Shackleton knew, however, that someone would have to make a run to an island with a human settlement, or they would all perish on Elephant Island. So he launched one of the lifeboats and, accompanied by five men, sailed for some twenty days through wild seas and in horrible weather until they reached South Georgia Island. Unfortunately, they landed on the wrong side of the island. So Shackleton and two of his men took thirty-six hours to cross an uncharted island covered with huge glaciers and mountains rising as high as ten thousand feet. Finally, they reached a whaling station. It took them four more months before they could reach the rest of the crew stranded on Elephant Island. Not one man, however, was lost, though they had been cut off from all contact with civilization for twenty-two months.

Shackleton did accomplish his lifelong ambition, though not in the way he had expected or planned. He never crossed the Antarctic, but he did cross a massive ice pack, a stretch of treacherous ocean, and an uncharted island. Amazingly, he survived it all. He faced obstacles and odds that few other explorers ever dreamed of facing, to say nothing of conquering.

Shackleton knew that he had accomplished something extraordinary. He realized after it was all over that his ambition in life had been fulfilled, however strangely and circuitously. He had achieved greatness as an explorer, only a different greatness from what he had expected. "In memories we were rich," he wrote in his journal after they had reached South Georgia Island. "We had pierced the veneer of outside things. We had 'suffered, starved, and triumphed, groveled down yet grasped at glory, grown bigger in the bigness of the whole.' We had seen God in His splendors, heard the text that Nature renders. We had reached the naked soul of man."[1]

AN UNFOLDING DISCOVERY

We discover our calling, then, not by trying to plan our life out ten years in advance but by being attentive to what God is doing through immediate circumstances and in the present moment. Over time our sense of calling unfolds simply and naturally, as scenery unfolds to backpackers hiking their way through the mountains. Rarely will we be able to see the whole pathway stretched out before us at any one time. Sometimes we will only be able to see far enough ahead to keep going.

In *Traveling Mercies*, an autobiography telling the story of her conversion, writer Anne Lamott recalls a sermon she heard that underscored the importance of paying attention to what is immediately at hand, not what is in the distant future, and to what God is doing now, not what God might do someday.

Pastor Veronica said that when she prays for direction, one spot of illumination always appears just beyond her feet, a circle of light into which she can step. She moved away from the pulpit to demonstrate, stepping forward shyly ... and then, after standing there looking puzzled, she moved another step forward to where the light had gone, two feet ahead of where she had been standing, and then again, "We in our faith work," she said, "stumble along toward where we think we're supposed to go, bumbling along, and here is what's so amazing—we end up getting exactly where we're supposed to be."[2]

Lamott's pastor is right. The pathway will continue to appear, no matter how confusing the route might be. We will be given just enough light to know where our next step should be. It is all a journey, as Shackleton discovered. The journey itself is a glorious thing. Failure will serve us as well as success, hard times will show us the way as readily as easy times. According to Elisabeth Elliot, God calls us within our own frame of reference and in ways that are appropriate, given our journey through life. "God leads me, I believe, within my own frame of reference. What I am, where I am, and how I got there, all have a great deal to do with what my frame of reference is. God can be counted on to choose the right avenue of approach."[3]

Take, for example, Renee, a woman who works in a large corporation. She strives to succeed at work by fitting in and exceeding expectations. At the same time, she is a single mother of three young boys—a role she takes seriously, especially since her husband died. Raising her boys is a job she must do alone, without the benefit of a husband's help and income. So she has two full-time jobs (businesswoman and homemaker), and she wants to do them well. She knows other women at work who face similar circumstances.

Renee observes that much of what her coworkers do in the office could be done at home. She suggests that the corporate hierarchy allow these women to work at home for a month to see if they would be able to work as productively there as they do in their offices. The corporate hierarchy dismisses her idea out of hand. "It just wouldn't work," they insist. She notices—it is hard not to notice!—that the top executives are all male. They evaluate her suggestion from a male perspective, reflecting the concerns that males typically have. But she is convinced that their concerns, though valid, can be addressed.

Two years later the corporation merges with another, and she loses her job in the shuffle. She works two part-time jobs for a few months to make ends meet. But she continues to carry a burden for single working mothers. Finally she borrows money from a Christian friend and starts her own company, HomeWorks. She employs women, supplies them with computers and software, and contracts with corporations to do special projects that women (as well as men!) can do at home. They are paid according to their productivity. Her company is wildly successful in making money and in meeting the needs of single mothers.

Renee has discovered her calling—helping women make good income while working at home—through the frustrations and failures of her own life experience. She was attentive to the will of God she already knew and responded to the needs around her. She did not compromise her commitment to raising her sons. Her calling emerged out of the struggle itself.

Discovering our calling is as much an art as it is a science. It is an intuitive process that defies simple steps and easy formulas. We need to be attentive to the signs, which provide hints and impressions and give us a sense of direction. We will undoubtedly face subtlety, ambiguity, and confusion along the way. But we must keep going and keep seeking as we keep doing.

OUR DEEPEST MOTIVATION

There are six signs to look for in this process. First, we should look within ourselves to see what motivates us. We must come to know ourselves—what captures our interest, what gives us energy. For whatever reason, some people seem to have an inner compulsion or drive that propels them toward a calling. Something deep within motivates them to start a new business or to compose a symphony or to teach in an inner city school, as if they *have* to do it, not only because they have the talent for it, which every calling requires, but also because they have the interest, energy, and passion for it. It is simply *in* them.

Mozart, for example, had music in him from the moment he was born. He was so precocious that he achieved fame as a performer and composer while he was still a young boy. Picasso painted brilliantly as a teenager. Francis of Assisi had a magnetic personality that attracted a following even before he became a Christian. That quality served him well when he founded the most influential religious order of the Middle Ages, the Friars Minor (better known as the Franciscans). Thomas Edison did not choose to become an inventor. He simply *was* an inventor. His basic orientation in life was imaginative and inventive. These people could no more *not* do their callings than cows could not chew their cud or geese could not fly south.

I am not sure if it is even possible to understand the mystery of human motivation. Evelyn Underhill, whose writings I have just begun to read, was born in England and educated at King's College, Oxford. In 1921 she became lecturer in philosophy of religion at Manchester College, Oxford. For many years she wrote novels and poetry, but she received lasting fame and exercised significant influence as a spiritual writer. The mystical voice within her *had* to find expression in words, especially as it applied to everyday life. She called it "practical mysticism." She wanted to help people discover how accessible and livable true spiritual devotion was. "The spiritual life is not a special career, involving abstraction from the world of things. It is a part of every man's life; and until he has realised it he is not a complete human being, he has not entered into possession of all his powers."[4]

Jonathan Edwards (1703–1758), a Puritan pastor and the leader of the First Great Awakening in America, is considered America's greatest theologian. He had a mind for theology that was as central to his nature as the beating of his heart. He kept a journal most of his life, recording his observations of the world around him and within him. Even during his teenage years he wrote with a level of precision and insight few people ever achieve. What drove Edwards to probe and ponder the mysteries of life with such obvious passion? It was simply in him to do it.

Eric Liddell is known to most of us through the film *Chariots of Fire*, which won the Academy Award for Best Motion Picture in 1981. Known as "the flying Scotsman," Liddell won a gold medal in the 1924 Olympics in a race he was not even supposed to run. He became a hero in his native Scotland and around the world. He could have cashed in on the fame, but he left for China a year after the Olympics to serve as a missionary. He lived the rest of his life in relative obscurity.

What made Liddell leave behind fame and fortune to do mission work in China? His biographer asked the same question and discovered it was a simple and easy decision for him. "Here again in Eric's life," she writes, "there was none of the obvious heart-searching that the story-teller is always hunting for. There seems to have been no soliloquy on the lure of stardom and how difficult it was to tear himself away; no dark night of the soul. . . . Eric just always seems to have known that this was what he would do."[5] Liddell had no choice. He *had* to go, to surrender himself to his calling from God.

TALENT

A second critical element in discovering our calling is talent. Proper talent is obviously necessary. Good intentions are not enough; we must have the gifts to get the job done. Still, the intersection between inner motivation and talent is complex, as we will see.

As portrayed in the film *Amadeus*, Salieri, a music composer of modest ability, spent his later years burning with jealousy over the work of a younger and better composer, Mozart. After hearing Mozart's music, Salieri discovered how pedestrian his own music was. He prayed (what is probably a fictional prayer), "O Lord, if you had to give me the calling, why could you not have given me the gift to go with it?" That prayer sends shivers into my soul because it reminds me of my own insecurity whenever I speak, teach, or write. I want to know that I am doing what God gifted me to do, not simply what I fancy myself doing.

At least Salieri understood his limits. Not everyone does. My wife, Lynda, was a professional musician, a soloist, and a choir director. She usually had someone in one of her choirs convinced that he (or she) was called by God to be a soloist, though without having the voice for it. "If God calls someone," Lynda often said to me, "one would think that God would have given that person the ability to do it." It is painful to learn that what we want to do might not be what we can do because we lack the talent. If we fail to learn this lesson, we will try to do things that would have been better left undone. We will try to preach sermons that would have been better filed away, to lead organizations that would have been better led by someone else, or to teach students who would have been better taught by someone with a higher aptitude for teaching.

Of course, talent alone is not enough. It provides a clue, but it falls short of being the sine qua non of a calling. On the one hand, some people will never be able to use all the talent they have. Eric Liddell could have been a professional runner, Jonathan Edwards a famous scientist. Some athletes could play more than one sport professionally, though the demands of competition force them to stick to only one. Some students could master any subject they care to study, but time does not allow it. So how can talented people decide what to use of their sizable reservoir? A sense of calling will help them sort it out.

On the other hand, some people excel in lines of work for which they appear to have only modest ability. Steve Largent was for many years the Seattle Seahawks' most successful receiver. He never claimed to have great ability, and opponents agreed. But Largent had drive and savvy and love for the sport, which compensated for his average talent and turned him into an accomplished professional football player. The same is true of John Stockton, point guard for the Utah Jazz. He is barely six feet tall, a virtual midget for a professional basketball player. He is not particularly fast or strong. Yet he has set the NBA record for assists and steals, and he has helped to lead the Jazz into the NBA playoffs almost every year he has played. His mastery of the sport surpasses what his modest abilities would seem to allow.

We note the same phenomenon in the Scriptures. Paul admitted that his ability as an orator was inadequate for the task, that his presence as a speaker was anything but impressive.[6] If we were to reduce Paul's abilities to a resume, we would not have considered him for the job. But Paul was dogged and determined. He worked harder than all the other apostles and endured suffering of every kind.[7] He refused to give up. How do we explain someone like the apostle Paul? Abilities and background alone do not tell the whole story. His motivation came from another source. It came from God.

LIFE EXPERIENCE

Third, life experiences can have a similar effect. Sometimes what happens *to* us pushes us toward a calling. A young widow whose husband dies of cancer goes to work for a hospice. A college student who hated junior high becomes a popular and effective counselor in a junior high school. A woman who endured years of abuse opens a clinic for battered women. A man who grew up in a lukewarm church becomes a successful evangelist. In each case, life experience awakened them to their life calling.

Sometimes the propelling event can be an insignificant experience that happens at just the right time. One event, which appears at the time to be very ordinary, can have extraordinary consequences. *Masterpiece Theater*, a PBS program, recently ran a dramatic presentation of the true story of British actress Coral Atkins. While attending a charity event for a children's home, Atkins met a little girl whose painful past and obvious need for love awakened terrible memories of Atkins' childhood. She was so moved by the experience that she gave up her glamorous career as an actress to start a home for disturbed children, a venture that turned out to be both wonderful and harrowing. The course her life took turned on that one ordinary experience of attending a charity event.

The experience of suffering can have a similar effect, as Anthony Storr, lecturer in clinical psychiatry at Oxford, argues in *Solitude: A Return to the Self*. He recounts stories of people whose suffering in prison set them on a course of writing or gave them insight that they would not otherwise have had. Their confinement isolated them, stirred their creativity, and enlarged their perspective on life. It inspired them to write on the human condition.

John Bunyan, for example, wrote his autobiography, *Grace Abounding* (1666), and began his classic work, *The Pilgrim's Progress*, during the twelve years he spent in the Bedford county jail for his Nonconformist beliefs. His works convey profound insight into temptation and suffering. His experience in jail helped him perceive the depths of human sin and to explore the wonder of God's plan of salvation. Dostoyevsky developed his philosophy of life and laid out plots for several of his stories and novels during the years he spent in a Siberian prison camp. His suffering became like a voice, calling him to ask and answer the most profound questions in life. Dostoyevsky would have been a writer whether or not he spent time in prison. He would not have written, however, with the same insight and power.[8]

OPEN AND CLOSED DOORS

A fourth factor in discovering our calling is opportunity. They constitute what Elisabeth Elliot categorizes as "circumstances." She believes that God can and does use circumstances to lead us. "Circumstances are without question a part of God's will. . . . It is a normal assumption of faith that he will use circumstances to nudge me in the right direction."[9]

Opportunities represent the proverbial "open door" that comes along every so often. The apostle Paul uses this expression to refer to opportunities he was given—or opportunities he prayed for—to preach the gospel in regions previously closed to him.[10] He had doors opened to continue his apostolic calling even in such odd and odious places as a prison, where he inspired fearful believers and witnessed to pagan prison guards.[11]

But Paul also had doors opened to him for the first time. There is a period after Paul's conversion—the so-called silent years—when Paul disappeared from public eye. While in Cilicia he received an invitation from Barnabas to join the ministry in Antioch in Syria, a church that had become largely Gentile. Paul traveled to Antioch and became active as a leader in that church. It was there that he and Barnabas eventually received their call to plant churches for Gentiles as well as Jews.[12]

Experiences during one's college years provide opportunities that sometimes engender a sense of calling. Some Whitworth students who have worked as counselors at summer camps later become directors of youth programs. Other students who have spent a semester in Latin America return to do economic development work. Still other students who have enrolled in semester-long internships in nonprofit organizations go to work for the same organization after graduation. Colleges like Whitworth excel in providing such opportunities for students to test their gifts and discover their calling.

Opportunities can also result from a benefactor's generosity. I did not ask Leighton Ford to write a letter on my behalf. It never even occurred to me that I might have publishable material until he mentioned it. He took the initiative to open the door for me, as he has done for many others. He considers it a part of his own calling to use his vast network of contacts to give young Christian leaders a chance to get started. He communicates with these leaders by phone and through e-mail, suggests their names when churches and organizations are looking for fresh leadership, and offers them advice when they need it.

Some opportunities appear to be a matter of pure chance. John Calvin, a lawyer by training, was converted to Christ and embraced the Reformation faith sometime in the early 1530s. He had already published a commentary on the philosopher Seneca, so he was already known for his brilliance.

While traveling to Strasbourg in 1536, he was forced by unforeseen circumstances to take a detour through Geneva. At that time Geneva was facing tremendous upheaval, for the city council had just voted to make Geneva a Reformation city, though they had little idea what it meant. When William Farel, one of the leaders of the fledgling movement, heard that Calvin was passing through, he paid him a visit at the hotel and asked him to stay in Geneva to help organize the new church. By nature a reserved man, Calvin wanted nothing to do with such leadership. He felt committed to pursuing a life of solitude and scholarship, so he refused Farel's request.

But Farel would not be put off so easily. In words now famous, Farel told Calvin that if he did not remain in Geneva and help lead the movement, "God will condemn you." It was hardly a welcomed opportunity, but Calvin knew that he was supposed to stay. "I felt as if God from heaven had laid his mighty hand upon me to stop me in my course ... and I was so terror-stricken that I did not continue my journey."

As a result, Calvin stayed in Geneva until he died, except for a brief three years when opponents on the city council ordered him to leave. During his twenty-five years in that city, Calvin preached thousands of sermons, provided pastoral care for a large congregation, published his *Institutes of the Christian Religion*, and wrote commentaries on almost every book of the Bible. He helped to organize a church that became a model for other Reformation leaders in Europe. He participated in important meetings with church leaders from all over Europe. Yet his entire career as a pastor and church leader in Geneva resulted from a chance detour and a brief encounter with William Farel.[13]

Open doors, then, can give us a clue about our calling, but so do closed doors. Parker Palmer, an educator, speaker, and author, argues that a calling implies *limits*. In choosing to pursue one calling, we eliminate other possible callings. We have to make choices, bypassing options that may look good to us. We must therefore discern what we are *not* supposed to do. As Palmer writes, "The truth is that I cannot be anything I want to be or do anything I want to do."

Thus, we must discern what is in us, recognize our limits, and allow doors to close as well as open. "The God who created us does not ask us to conform to some abstract norm for the ideal self. The God who created us asks us to honor the nature that is our birthright from God, which means both our potentials and our limits. When we fail to do so, reality happens—God happens—and the way closes behind us."[14]

A friend of mine left the parish ministry in the mid-1980s to pursue a doctorate in New Testament. He felt that God was calling him to teach in a Christian college or seminary. In order to help support his growing family during this time, he began to work part-time in a major Christian publishing house. As the completion of his program approached, he sent out numerous applications to Christian colleges and seminaries. But every door he reached out to open remained locked, whereas a full-time position opened up in that publishing company, where he could use his skills and expertise. That is where he is working to this day.

THE VOICE OF PEOPLE

The fifth factor that can assist us in discovering our calling is participation in a community. Rarely does a person discover a calling in isolation from a community. Only friends know us well enough to size up our gifts, to listen to our dreams, to challenge our thinking, and to encourage or discourage our plans. They help us recognize our strengths and weaknesses and discover who we are and what we ought to do with our lives. Though God is Lord of the universe, he does not work in a vacuum. He uses people as well as circumstances to help us discern our calling.

Elisabeth Elliot suggests that advice from the community of faith embodies one of the "natural means" God uses to guide us and to help us discover our calling. "The times when we find ourselves entirely alone in the making of a decision are rare," she writes. Friends can give us particularly good advice, though we must be sure to discern their motivation and perspective.

> A person who loves God and has had some experience in finding his will is the kind we should look for. I have been ... blessed in having several friends of my own age who have helped me often. But I have been especially blessed through the advice of men and women much older than I. They see things I don't see. They've been over roads I've never traveled. They have perspective I couldn't possibly have.[15]

Many Whitworth students majoring in religion have found such a community in our religion department. I am surprised by how honest they are with each other. "I just can't see you doing youth ministry," one student will say to another. "I think you have all the gifts to be a senior pastor." "I think you would make an excellent teacher or college professor." Not that these students exercise absolute authority. They do not speak for God, and they have on occasion been wrong. But they can and do provide perspective. They are "signs" that point the way.

Mentors often fulfill a similar purpose. The apostle Paul challenged several of his proteges to pursue a calling. Timothy, for example, grew up in a believing home. Both his mother and grandmother nurtured him in the faith. While still a young man he met the apostle Paul, who became his mentor. When Timothy began to struggle in his pastoral work, Paul charged him to carry out his duties with courage and conviction, in spite of his youthfulness, inexperience, and timidity:

> Let no one despise your youth, but set the believers an example in speech and conduct, in love, in faith, in purity. Until I

arrive, give attention to the public reading of scripture, to exhorting, to teaching. Do not neglect the gift that is in you, which was given to you through prophecy with the laying on of hands by the council of elders. Put these things into practice, devote yourself to them, so that all may see your progress.[16]

JOYFUL SERVICE

There is one final sign—the sign of joy. Some people believe mistakenly that we discover our calling by identifying the one thing we would least like to do, as if misery was *the* infallible sign of a calling. I disagree with that perspective. God wants us to live joyfully. He calls us to serve him with gladness of heart. We will know our calling not only if we feel driven to it but also if we find joy in it. God loves a cheerful giver, wrote Paul. He also loves a cheerful servant.

Once again, Elisabeth Elliot offers sound advice. She admits that she used to think God's calling would require her to do the thing she least wanted to do. But then she reconsidered that negative perspective. "A better understanding of Scripture has shown me that even I, chief of miserable offenders that I know myself to be, may now and then actually want what God wants. This is likely to be the case more and more as I practice obedience, but it can also be a very simple and natural thing."[17]

We should not confuse happiness and joy. We will never experience complete happiness on earth. The world is a tormented place. Farmers must deal with tenacious weeds, entrepreneurs with fickle consumers, teachers with unruly students, ministers with lukewarm church members. However much we take pleasure in our calling, we will grow weary with the work, feel irritation with colleagues and coworkers, endure periods of boredom, and fight structures that make our work unnecessarily complicated. We live in a fallen world.

I have been a college professor for ten years. I have graded upward of 15,000 papers. Some of them were a pleasure to read. Some were not. But I learned early on that if I wanted to be a good college professor, I would have to assign and grade lots of papers, because students learn best by writing. Grading papers is by no means the most fulfilling part of college teaching. Duty drives me to do it, however tedious and boring and hard.

Hard is one thing; miserable is another. We might not always be happy doing our work, but we can nevertheless be joyful, taking "pleasure in our toil," as the book of Ecclesiastes charges us to do. Such joy will come from knowing that we are doing something that is suitable to our nature and fruitful for God's kingdom work. Frederick Buechner argues that amidst all the voices that are trying to get our attention and to give us direction in discerning God's call, the voice we should listen to most attentively "is the voice that we might think we should listen to least, and that is the voice of our own gladness." This voice of gladness, which reminds us of the joy we find in the work we do, may turn out to be the most reliable sign of all.[18]

LEARNING TO LISTEN

These, then, are six signs we should look for; they are not easy steps we can take or formulas we can follow. The discovery of a calling is not a simple process, nor should it be. It is rare that a person hears a voice from heaven. The apostle Paul did, but Timothy did not, nor did most of Paul's companions in the faith. I have not yet met a person who has heard God speak to him or her as one person speaks to another. For most of us our calling will emerge over time and through experience. We will discover it by simply living and learning, failing as well as succeeding, experimenting, and, above all, listening. What we should listen for is not so much a voice *from* God but the voice *of* God as he speaks to us through reflection, talents, experience, opportunity, community, and the gladness of our own hearts.

Listening itself is an art, as we will discover in chapter 16. Mother Teresa recognized that assuming a posture of silence is the proper way to begin praying, for silence helps us to listen to God. "I always begin my prayer in silence, for it is in the silence of the heart that God speaks. God is the friend of silence—we need to listen to God because it's not what we say but what He says to us and through us that matters."[19]

Thomas Kelly, a Quaker philosopher who died in the 1940s, also suggested that we learn to listen to God by practicing silence. Such listening in silence will enable us to hear God's voice and discern our calling. "Deep within us all there is an amazing inner sanctuary of the soul, a holy place, a Divine Center, a speaking Voice, to which we may continuously return. Eternity is at our hearts, pressing upon our time-torn lives, warming us with intimations of an astounding destiny, calling us home unto Itself."[20]

God assures us that we will discover our calling. He is the one who calls; he will enable us to hear, understand, and accomplish our calling. We will succeed, though we might not succeed as the world defines success. Earlier in the chapter I mentioned a number of well-known people—Mozart, Dostoyevsky, Bunyan, Edwards—to illustrate how we may discover our calling. Few of us will succeed as they did. Unlike them, most of us will not be remembered long after we die. If anything, our calling may lead us into obscurity rather than fame. We may receive little acclaim for what we do. But why should we even want that? Laying up "treasures in heaven," as Jesus called it, does not leave much capital left over for investments on earth. Though our calling may have earthly value, it may not receive much earthly applause.

Heaven judges success differently from earth. If we fulfill our callings with integrity, faithfulness, and love, we will bear fruit for God's kingdom. God will honor us in heaven, whether or not people recognize our service here on earth. In *The Great Divorce* C. S. Lewis describes a procession in heaven to honor a great saint who has just died. The narrator of the story wonders if it is someone he would have heard of on earth. By the sight of the magnificent procession, that would appear to be likely. But the narrator's guide responds, "It's someone ye'll never have heard of. Her name on earth was Sarah Smith and she lived on Golders Green."

The narrator comments, "She seems to be . . . well, a person of particular importance?"

His guide responds, "Aye. She is one of the great ones. Ye have heard that fame in this country and fame on Earth are two quite different things."[21]

Sarah Smith was great in the eyes of heaven because she fulfilled her calling without regard to earthly honors. She did the will of God for God's sake and for the world's good. Though the world forgot, God did not. He honored her for it.

MANAGING OUR
MANY CALLINGS

Now for a wrinkle in the argument. I am going to appear to contradict myself.

As I mentioned in chapter 5, I feel uncomfortable using the term *career*. Instead, I prefer to use *calling* to convey the idea that each of us has a divine and unique purpose in life. I hinted in the same chapter, however, that there is a problem with the idea of a calling, too. It is time now to explain why. Once again, I discovered this problem through life experience.

FATHERHOOD AS A CALLING

Lynda always wanted to have children. It was in her nature to be a mother. But we had difficulty conceiving a child. As time went on, she grew more discouraged. Strangely, her longing for children kept growing, in spite of the frustration. I felt as she did, or so I thought. I realize now, however, that I wanted children for her sake, not for mine. I operated under the mistaken notion that I had one calling, and that calling was my work. I was willing to care for children, of course. After all, if we had children, I would be their father. But the responsibility for the family would be Lynda's, not mine. I would follow her orders, respond to her cues, and function as a parent under her tutelage, like an enlisted soldier doing the bidding of an officer.

Lynda eventually gave birth to four children. She was overcome with joy. She embraced motherhood with flare and creativity. I did my part, too, but not with complete sincerity or commitment. While I could impress others with my fatherly skills, I could not deceive Lynda, who said to me on more than one occasion, "Jerry, you will miss out if you don't invest in these kids. Someday you will regret it. Don't let that happen."

Though I tried to listen to her words of warning, I could never quite make sense of them. I was too stuck on the idea that I had one basic calling—a calling to ministry, not to my wife and children. Not that I abused or neglected them. The problem was not schedule or effort. It was my heart.

Then the accident occurred. Suddenly I had no wife to shepherd me through parenthood. I had no maternal expert who could give me the proper cues and tell me what to do. There was no more division of labor. I was on my own. If my three kids were going to be raised, I had to do it myself. The world of home and family now sat firmly on my shoulders, and mine alone.

My journey as a father over these past eight years has been without question the most wonderful and difficult experience of my life. I was not a natural father at first; I am not sure I ever will be. I am too selfish and ambitious. But over time I have learned and matured. I am now so invested in my children and home that I find myself on the verge of tears whenever I talk about them. I no longer function as a father; I *am* a father. I no longer go home after work; I carry my home with me all the time. Fatherhood is central to my identity, as maleness is.

I chose in the aftermath of the accident to try to live a redemptive life. I had had enough of suffering and wanted no more. I realized that how I responded to the tragedy would set a trajectory for my children and how I functioned as a father would make all the difference in the world for them—and probably for me as well. I decided, therefore, to learn the art of fatherhood. I put my treasure into fatherhood, believing that my heart would follow. I experimented, failed, but kept at it. I prayed constantly. If I ever write a book on fatherhood, it will be entitled "How to Raise Children on Your Knees."

We have had our moments together. To this day my friends and I laugh over "Black Thursday," which marks a day in October of 1993 when I decided to stop using the accident as an excuse for the misbehavior of my kids and instead to begin to hold them accountable. On that day reality struck. My kids reentered the world of normalcy. I started to discipline them for behavior I had been tolerating until it became almost intolerable. Catherine and David spent the next two weeks in their rooms, or so it seemed at the time.

I can't say that the accident was the turning point of my life as a father. My conversion to fatherhood and home started before Lynda died, but the accident accelerated the process and made it a calling. Strangely, that calling also created a problem. I had assumed up to that point that I had one major calling in life—to study, teach, mentor, and prepare students for future leadership. The accident forced me to reconsider that assumption.

THE CONFLICT OF CALLINGS

I now know I have several callings. Each is important in its own way, though some are more important than others. It is the rare person who can concentrate his or her time and energy on just one major calling in life. Thomas Aquinas (1224–1274) could devote his entire life to study, writing, and teaching because he had time at his disposal. He belonged to the Dominican order, so he never married, never raised children, never managed a home, and never had the duties most ordinary people have. His productivity (e.g., the massive and erudite *Summa Theologica*) demonstrates his genius, to be sure; but it also reflects the simplicity of his life. He had few distractions—fewer than most of us anyway—though even Aquinas was required to serve as a religious statesman in medieval Europe, much to his irritation.

Most of us do not live like Aquinas. Our calling is plural, not singular. We may work as teachers, accountants, or social workers, and we may serve God well in any of those professions. But we are also students, husbands or wives, parents, church elders, committee members, neighbors, coaches, and volunteers. These various callings sometimes conflict. In my experience, in fact, they conflict often.

Part of the conflict comes because we have too much to do, as I described in chapter 3. Every one of us lives under enormous pressure. We are busy, and there is little margin of error in our lives. For example, I work without breaks when I am at the office, rarely stopping for lunch. I leave early from work two days a week to beat the kids home, and we eat snacks and chat about their day at school. I drive them to practices, lessons, and church activities. I get food on the table and clean up afterward. I make phone calls, help with homework, play games with them, and pray with them at bedtime. Later in the evening I grade papers, read, or write. Then I fall exhausted into bed.

I wish I could put all my responsibilities on a "to do" list and then choose when and how I will get everything done. But life never runs that smoothly and conveniently. Why does my job seem to demand the most from me on the weeks when my kids are busiest? Why do the kids always get sick when I have the least amount of flexibility in my schedule? Why is it that every babysitter I know always seems to schedule an activity on the very night I need one?

But conflict of activities is not the whole story. That is the *external* problem. I have a deeper problem as well—an *internal* problem, something that happens inside me. I think differently about life because my circumstances have forced me to take on a new identity. I used to wear several hats; now I realize I have several heads. I could take the hats off; it is not so easy to remove the heads.

My orientation has changed. At one time my professional roles of minister, then professor, determined how I thought, lived, and functioned in the world. But I am not just a minister or professor anymore; I am also a father, a home manager, a churchman, a writer, a friend, and a mentor. These roles also define who I am. Try as I might, I cannot confine them to separate spheres. They are all part of my essential identity. They are my calling.

Unfortunately, they do not always live in peaceful coexistence with each other. I am like a man divided against himself. The writer in me wishes the professor in me would go on sabbatical. The professor in me wishes the father in me would get a life. The father in me wishes that both the writer and the professor would take early retirement.

This problem is not going to go away. My calling is a plural, a permanent plural. So I must learn to be several heads at once. Efficiency does help. I believe that cordless phones, e-mail, bread machines, dishwashers, and crock-pots are God's gifts to busy adults. Still, efficiency is not the real solution. People who carry

around cell phones like appendages do not appear to be less busy
or more peaceful than anyone else.

The Bible doesn't seem to offer much help either. It does not
map out a schedule for us to follow each day, nor does it outline
a to-do list for us to check off. It does not tell us to rise at 5:30
A.M., spend two hours in personal devotions, serve as a social
worker in an economically deprived community, raise 2.4 children, and then lead evangelistic Bible studies once a week in our
neighborhood. The Bible allows us to exercise discretion. It gives
us the freedom to make decisions on our own.

How can we manage the conflicts that are bound to arise, considering our busy schedules and multiple identities? How can we
respond to the plural nature of our callings? How can we maintain sanity in a world that keeps demanding more from us?

I suggest that we follow three general principles: simplicity,
balance, and flexibility. These principles will help us fulfill our
multiple callings with some degree of grace and calm. No, they
do not guarantee that, should we follow them, all problems will
be solved. I think a certain amount of tension and conflict is
healthy because it unsettles us and reminds us of our need for
God. Some control over our lives is good; too much control is
not. It deludes us into thinking that we can manage our lives
without God's help.

SIMPLICITY

We will learn to manage our multiple callings better if we value
simplicity. Few things in life are truly important. Many of the
choices we make may appear to be weighty at the moment we
make them, but over time they often become less important. Such
choices—the career we pursue or the job we take—have an
appearance of ultimate significance when in fact they may not be
as significant as we think. I am not even sure God really cares all
that much whether we attend public school or private school,
become a carpenter or a teacher, marry Susan or remain single,
move to New York or stay in Boise. I think he is more interested
in the way we conduct our lives, no matter what we do and where
we live. We can do God's will nicely in any of those circumstances.

The apostle Paul kept emphasizing simplicity of life in his ministry. He wanted to make sure that new believers kept first things first and maintained one supreme concern in life—living for God. In his letter to the church at Philippi, he wrote:

> And this is my prayer, that your love may overflow more and more with knowledge and full insight to help you to determine what is best, so that in the day of Christ you may be pure and blameless, having produced the harvest of righteousness that comes through Jesus Christ for the glory and praise of God.[1]

According to Paul, the "best" he was referring to had to do with their relationship with God. The depth of that relationship would lead to purity of heart, righteousness of character, and fruitfulness of life.

Paul applied this principle to practical decision-making. The church in Corinth had questions about marriage. They wanted Paul to give them guidelines so they would know under what conditions marriage, divorce, and remarriage were acceptable. They were cautious about marriage in particular. Ironically, that caution had led them into immorality. Too many members of the church were single but not celibate. Paul allowed for marriage because he recognized that not everyone could be celibate and remain pure. But he had reservations about marriage too, because in his mind it made life more complicated.

Paul concluded, however, that the decision to marry or remarry was secondary. There was a more important issue at stake. Paul challenged the Corinthians to remain single-minded so that their lives would be free of entanglement, clutter, and worry. He wanted them to have one focus, one goal, one supreme concern in life, and thus to cultivate an "unhindered devotion to the Lord."[2] If believers in Corinth chose to live that kind of life, then the decision to marry or remarry would take care of itself.

Simplicity, therefore, concerns *how* we want to live our lives, considering life's complexity and demands. We may own many things, receive much recognition, and have more opportunities than we can possibly pursue. Still, we must maintain a single focus. Thomas à Kempis reminds us of the importance of such simplicity. In words that should haunt us, considering how preoccupied we are with wealth, health, status, and immediate happiness, he cautions us about overestimating what the world has to offer.

> It is vanity to seek material wealth that cannot last and to place your trust in it. It is also vanity to seek recognition and status. It is vanity to chase after what the world says you should want and to long for things you should not have, things that you will pay a high price for later on if you get them. It is vanity to wish for a long life and to care little about a good life. It is vanity to focus only on your present life and not to look ahead to your future life. It is vanity to live for the joys of the moment and not to seek eagerly the lasting joys that await you.[3]

I do not want to be simplistic, however, about simplicity. There is little hope that our world is going to get less complex and busy. There is little reason to believe that our schedules will ever become less demanding, our responsibilities fewer in number. The answer is not in returning to the bygone era of traditional societies, where people make their living with their hands, work at home, grow their own food, churn their own butter, and marry their neighbor. We cannot create a society in which there are no radios, MTV, Internet, malls, and cell phones. We can try, of course. But we will be lonely, for few people will want to join us. The simple life of traditional societies—which was not as simple as it would seem anyway—is past and gone.

Ignatius of Loyola has helped me to practice a realistic simplicity. Before Ignatius founded the Jesuit order in the sixteenth century, people joining religious orders lived the cloistered life. They followed a "Rule" that regulated their daily schedule, they wore a distinct style of clothing, and they lived in isolated communities. Ignatius, however, formed an order to serve the cause of missions and education, so he streamlined the traditional Benedictine Rule. Jesuits did not follow that older Rule, wear religious garb, or isolate themselves from others. They traveled to India, China, Japan, South America, and North America to win people to the Catholic faith, and they identified as much as they could with the host culture. This strategy made their life complex and messy because they involved themselves in society.

To help Jesuits remain faithful to God, Ignatius developed a series of spiritual exercises to be used in everyday life. Recently I started to use his "examen of consciousness" to help me keep my focus on God. This exercise is an excellent method of cultivating simplicity as the Bible defines it. Used at the end of the day, it requires adherents to review the day in light of God's presence and to reflect on God's will in the context of the ordinary circumstances of each day.

My spiritual director gave me a simple form to follow. There is a short version and a long version. The short version reads: "Jesus, you have been present with me in my life today. Be near, now. Let us look together at my day. Let me see through your loving eyes. When did I listen to your voice today? When did I resist listening to you today? Jesus, everything is a gift from you. I give you thanks and praise for the gifts of the day. I ask your healing for my life. I ask your forgiveness and mercy for my sins. Jesus, continue to be present with me in my life each day."

Ignatius believed that, however complex life is, we can still practice an internal simplicity. It is the simplicity that Jesus describes in the Sermon on the Mount, the simplicity that Paul refers to when he advises believers to pursue an "unhindered devotion to God." It is possible to embrace this kind of simplicity, no matter what our circumstances are. As Ignatius advised, we must keep asking simple questions. "How is God speaking to me? What is God doing in my life? How is God making his presence known when I am busy and distracted?"

BALANCE

Balance is another concept we must understand in relation to multiple callings. Balance means establishing proper priorities, choosing to do what is most important rather than what is most urgent, and organizing our lives around our central commitments.

It does not take a genius to discern what good order in life should look like. In his *Confessions* Augustine argued that nothing in the world is inherently evil. Evil is simply a distortion of the good, a disordering of life. Thus marriage is a good thing, but making marriage the goal of our lives is a bad thing. Success is a good thing, but not if it comes at the expense of family, friendship, and community. Evil puts last things first and first things last. It debases what is pure and exalts what is base. Evil thrives by distorting proper priorities.

Augustine argued that we should cherish and use God's gifts, but not put them above God himself.

> We may seek all these things, O Lord, but in seeking them we must not deviate from your law. The life we live here is open to temptation by reason of a certain measure and harmony between its own splendors and all these beautiful things of lower degree. . . . Sin gains entrance through these and similar good things when we turn to them with immoderate desire, since they are the lowest kind of goods and we thereby turn away from the better and higher: from you yourself, O Lord our God, and your truth and your law.[4]

For example, we would not find fault with a man who restores old cars as a hobby. If anything, we would probably watch him work his craft with great interest and awe. But if he neglected his wife and children to pursue his love of antique cars, we would conclude that his life is not ordered properly. Restoring old cars is not as important as caring for family. Likewise, we may applaud a scholar for her diligent study of classical philosophy, but if she ignored friends and family for the sake of writing still another book, we would say that her life lacks balance.

As a historian, I have studied the biographies of many great religious leaders, so I am well aware of the price they had to pay to fulfill their calling. I admire these leaders, although I do not always like what they sacrificed in order to succeed. John Wesley, for example, was unusually disciplined and dedicated. This eighteenth-century evangelist presided over a spiritual revolution that changed England forever. He traveled over a quarter million miles on horseback and preached over forty thousand sermons to reach people for Christ. He died penniless because he gave all his money away. He was largely responsible for starting the Great Awakening in England. Yet his marriage was not happy and his friendships suffered because he was so unbalanced.

Many Christian leaders whose names are household words have accomplished great things for God but have failed as husbands or wives, fathers or mothers, and friends. They took advantage of the loyalty of their spouses without giving much in return, neglected their children because they were too busy, and used—

or betrayed—their friends. I have watched several famous Christian leaders at a distance and observed with great sadness the contradiction between their public ministry and their private life.

Yet no one can deny the good they have done, the vision they have brought to the church, and the success of their ministries. Balance is a principle, but it is not a law. We should strive for balance but recognize that it is not always possible. For one thing, some people do not have it in them. They all too easily hurt others and themselves for the sake of their calling. But God is gracious enough to bless their work anyway. I am not convinced that the apostle Paul himself lived a balanced life, nor was he always pleasant to work with (as Mark, his young protégé, discovered during their first missionary journey).

Nevertheless, however often it is violated, the principle of balance is still applicable. We should maintain a balance in life that reflects the will of God. We may have too much to do and not enough time in which to do it, but if we strive for balance, we will create an order to our lives that reflects good priorities. Family will become more important than hobbies; friendship and service will hold careers in check; our concern for people will temper our passion for truth and vision for ministry. Good priorities will set a course for our lives and guide the choices we make along the way.

I have to admit that balance is a continual struggle for me. I can write about it more easily than I practice it. I am besieged by responsibilities and obligations, and I have difficulty sorting them out. I have my work, which demands as much as I am willing to give it. I have three children, whose personal needs and interests require me to spend time with them at home and on the road. Our home functions as a gathering place for their friends, too. I also have concerns about social causes, such as the poor in downtown Spokane. Moreover, I want to befriend three retired widows living a stone's throw from my house, and I want to participate in church activities.

I do try to strike a balance, yet I must also be realistic. I have endured periods when I had to work long hours for the college, but I have known during those periods that they would come to an end. I try to warn my kids when busy times are approaching. After they are over, we may celebrate by going out for dinner together. Likewise, I have coached my boys in weekend soccer tournaments, which means playing four or even five scheduled matches in two days. But then I cancel practice the next Monday to compensate and give some time off. What is most important is the overall pattern. Short-term imbalance is inevitable; long-term imbalance is destructive—to spiritual life, to family, to friendships, and to self.

FLEXIBILITY

Finally, we should try to be *flexible* because circumstances can often change suddenly and even irreversibly. There is nothing wrong with keeping a schedule and to-do list, nor with learning to manage our time as best we can, mastering the art of "multitasking," and becoming self-disciplined.

But we should beware, too. Control is a myth. It presupposes that the world is rational, predictable, and controllable. But the world is none of those things. A friend of mine was planning to play professional baseball and to marry his high school sweetheart. But a freak farm accident left him a quadriplegic. Steve suddenly lost control of his life. His baseball career ended, and his fiancée vanished. He has since developed a printing business, and he plans the schedules for dozens of sports teams on the south side of Chicago. He is as busy as ever serving God, although not in the way he wanted or expected.

The worst nightmare for a single working parent is a sick child. Yet all children get sick, including the children of single parents. Accidents happen at inconvenient times, and jobs put demands on us when we have the least amount of time to meet the new challenge. As Murphy's Law says, "If things can go wrong, they always will, and always at the worst possible time." I respond with cynicism when I hear self-help gurus dole out advice. One guru promises he can help people to reach "peak performance" if they will follow his program. I am more interested in learning how to maintain "peak survival." I think to myself, *I hope he has a lot of unruly kids.*

Life does not always run smoothly. A big crisis—even a little crisis—can change everything in a minute. We have dreams that appear to be from God, work hard to do his will, and live the best way we can. Then something happens—the stock market crashes, friends move, lovers betray us, health fails, tragedy strikes, our car breaks down, a nanny quits—and we find ourselves living in an unstable world, as if the ground underneath us has started to roll like waves on an ocean. In such a world as this, it is easy to get seasick. How can we do the will of God if God keeps upsetting our—and we assume his—plans? Why does God put obstacles in the way? Why would God play that kind of trick on us?

We can be certain of only one thing: Life will not turn out the way we had it planned. There will be surprises along the way, some little and inconvenient (like a computer crash or a child getting the flu), some big and catastrophic (an accident, war, or divorce). How we respond to unforeseen circumstances matters just as much as whether we can control them.

Several famous saints set out early in life toward a destination they never reached. Ignatius of Loyola, for example, planned to be a knight. He was wounded in battle and spent a year recovering. During that year he decided to become a soldier for Christ instead and spent months in prayer, meditation, and study. This period of intense reflection led him to develop a new way of practicing spiritual discipline, which he recorded in what is now known as *The Spiritual Exercises of St. Ignatius*. During that same year he outlined the foundational principles for the Jesuit order, which he founded in 1540. Ignatius never became the knight he aspired to be. But who would dispute the significance of his contribution to the church? Ignatius was flexible enough to adjust his expectations and move in another direction.

The apostle Paul wanted to preach the gospel in territories where no missionary had gone. But that clarity of calling did not always create a straight path for him. He rarely ended up where he set out to go. He spent only a few months in Thessalonica, barely getting the new church off the ground before enemies drove him out. He worked eighteen months in Corinth, yet the church there gave him the most trouble. He was beaten, shipwrecked, and hounded by opposition from the left and from the right. Jewish leaders persecuted him and Roman authorities kept throwing him into jail. Paul could have viewed much of his life as lost time, wasted time.

But Paul was flexible. He persisted in doing the will of God as it mysteriously unfolded before him, as if he were Alice making his way through the Wonderland of the Roman world. "For I have learned to be content with whatever I have. I know what it is to have little, and I know what it is to have plenty. In any and all circumstances I have learned the secret of being well-fed and of going hungry, of having plenty and of being in need. I can do all things through him who strengthens me."[5] Paul remained flexible, responding as creatively and faithfully as he could to circumstances beyond his control. He was also a man of prayer. We can only wonder if he had a good sense of humor as well, or at least an appreciation for irony.

If we want to do God's will, we must try to live life with a *light touch*. We should, of course, pursue our dreams, chart a course, make our plans, follow a schedule, and thus do what we think God wants us to do. But always, *always* with a light touch. We may discern at an early age what God wants us to accomplish and end up doing exactly that. We may dazzle the world with the perfect order of our lives and our incredible productivity. But we may also fail to get into medical school, break the record for consecutive losing seasons, or bury our only daughter before she has the chance to bury us. We may live most of our days in virtual chaos and have little to show for how busy we always seem to be. I remember many times coming home from work and asking Lynda, "What did you do today?" She would look around at a messy house and say, "I don't know what I did. But I was busy doing nothing all day long."

One of my favorite movies is *It's a Wonderful Life*. This film classic tells the story of George Bailey, a promising young man with a good heart who wants desperately to leave his hometown to find success in the world. He has dreams that are too big for little Bedford Falls. But circumstances keep getting in the way. The army rejects him because he has a hearing problem. His father's death forces him to take over management of the family's Building and Loan Association. A run on the bank soaks up his savings, preventing him from leaving Bedford Falls even for his honeymoon. Try as he might, he cannot escape. But he makes the best of it because he is a good man. He settles down, marries his high school sweetheart, and raises a family. But more, he serves the community by loaning money to poor people so they can buy a home and by showing generosity to everyone. He gives up his big dreams to live a little life well, though he never gets over feeling just a tinge of disappointment.

A crisis in the family business, however, caused by an inadvertently misplaced envelope, pushes him over the edge. He feels crushed by how his life has turned out, and he momentarily forgets what has made his life meaningful. He is about to end his life when an angel, Clarence, intervenes. Clarence gives George a precious gift. He lets George see what would have happened if he had never lived at all and what would have become of Bedford Falls without him. Clarence finally says to him, "You've been given a great gift, George, a chance to see what the world would be like without you.... Strange, isn't it? Each man's life touches so many other lives. When he isn't around he leaves an awful hole, doesn't he? ... You see, George, you really had a wonderful life. Don't you see what a mistake it would be to throw it away?" George's life was good because he chose to make it good, in spite of and perhaps because of the disappointments he faced along the way. He made the best of bad situations and was faithful to what he knew was right.

Faithfulness to God *is* God's will for our lives, even if we never end up doing exactly what we had planned. We should strive to stay true to God, however often life changes course. We may expect to follow one course, believing that God has willed it to be so, only to be forced to follow another. We will lose a spouse or a child, leave one career and take up another one, fail in a business venture, or end up in a wheelchair. We will get a flat tire on the way to an interview, break our grandmother's china, and come down with the flu the day before our wedding. We will lose control. But if we remain flexible, living life with a light touch, we will discover that God is with us still, calling us to do his will under circumstances that we did not expect or want. The Bedford Falls we wished to escape will become home to us.

➤

These three principles—simplicity, balance, and flexibility—do not promise that our days will be any less demanding, busy, or conflicted. We still have jobs to do, families and friends to care for, meetings to attend, projects to accomplish, meals to cook, laundry to fold, lawns to mow, teams to coach, and causes to uphold. We will face interruptions, disappointments, crises, and all the rest. Our many callings will vie for our attention like triplets crying for their mother, all at the same time. Simplicity, however, will remind us of the one thing that matters most: an unhindered devotion to God. Balance will enable us to order our lives according to good priorities. Flexibility will help us to adjust to the surprises we will face along the way. And God will remain absolutely devoted to us.

PART III

EMBRACING MYSTERY

8

LIVING WITH PARADOX

When I was nineteen years old, my best friend, Jerry Keizer, and I decided to take the "great American road trip." We left in early July from Grand Rapids, Michigan, to travel to a city outside Seattle for an August wedding. We knew both the place to which we were heading and the date we had to arrive. With destination and arrival date secure, we embarked on a great adventure, having six weeks to explore the West.

We decided to avoid freeways as much as we could. Once we hit Denver, which we reached in a dangerously short period of time, we decided to drive all the way to Seattle without using a main thoroughfare. We took back roads and slept in the car, in a tent, or in the lodgings of people we met along the way. We ate at local hangouts and met local people. At the beginning of each day we never knew where we would end up when the day was done.

Once we got hopelessly lost on logging roads in a vain attempt to take a shortcut to Mount Rainier. To make matters worse, we ran out of gas. After we were rescued, the foreman at a logging camp told us that the road we had intended to take no longer existed. It had been washed out ten years before, which said something about the accuracy of our map.

We took hikes that nearly killed us. On one unforgettable expedition to the bottom of the Grand Canyon of the Yellowstone, we took lots of food but forgot to pack water. We felt as if we would die of thirst before we made it out. Jerry Keizer chugged seven Cokes when we arrived back at the lodge.

But in all this adventure we never forgot our destination, which kept us on course and on schedule. Outside of that goal, we discovered that a whole lot of country lies between Grand

Rapids and Seattle. We drove on more roads than we could count, we saw more scenery than we could take in, and we met more people than we could ever hope to remember. We saw the wonder of America.

GOD'S REVEALED WILL

As I have argued in chapter 2, God has given us astonishing freedom in the Christian faith. If we seek first his kingdom and righteousness, which is his *revealed* will for our lives, then whatever choices we make concerning the future become God's will for us. There are many pathways we can follow, many options we can pursue. As long as we are headed in the right direction, all options can become his will for us. Yet only one option becomes the actual will of God—the one we choose. Only in retrospect can we see from God's point of view that there was only one way, the way we chose and the way God designed.

Basic direction in life is therefore supremely important. As my best friend and I discovered on our trip, we could travel highways or gravel roads, we could drive fast or take our time. We just had to keep *heading in the right direction*. Likewise, in our Christian journey we can face a variety of circumstances in life, whether planned and pleasant or unplanned and miserable, and still set a course for our lives that propels us toward God. That goal is the same for everyone.

I am *not* suggesting that all choices are relative, as if the choice of how to live matters about as much as the variety of candy we buy at a grocery store. The decision to seek first God's kingdom and righteousness forbids setting a direction for our lives that dishonors God. That one destination and direction preclude complacency, immorality, and relativism. Yet once we have decided to seek that kingdom first and become wholly God's, the world becomes full of possibilities. We can choose to marry or remain single, to live forever in a small town or move to Los Angeles, to become doctors or serve as teachers, to attend Harvard or to take up a trade. Listen to the apostle Paul: "For all things are yours, whether Paul or Apollos or Cephas or the world or life or death or the present or the future—all belong to you, and you belong to Christ, and Christ belongs to God."[1]

We know about God's will from the Bible, which contains the *revealed* will of God. The Bible tells us to love God with everything we have and above everything else. It commands us to love our neighbor as we love ourselves. It exhorts us to discipline ourselves in godliness, cultivate character, pursue wisdom, and live according to biblical truth. The Bible mandates that we offer ourselves as living sacrifices to God.

Even though the Bible may be clear on such matters, that clarity does not make our choices any easier. Knowing is one thing, deciding is quite another. Even with the Bible to guide us, it is still difficult to make decisions about the future with complete confidence and assurance. Should we accept the job offer, though it will require uprooting the family? Should we end an abusive marriage, though we know the Bible forbids divorce? Should we try to have a third child, though we are close to forty-two years old? The Bible does not tell us what to do in every situation. It establishes guidelines and principles, not a long list of rules. It sets the overall direction. But we must still make the practical decisions, trusting God to guide us and go with us.

GOD'S HIDDEN WILL

But there is a second way to understand the expression "the will of God." That will is not only revealed to us in Scripture, it is also *hidden* from us. It is mysterious and terrifying, like the unfathomable depths of the ocean, full of wonders and dangers. The hidden will of God consists of his sovereign control over the entire universe. *Everything that happens* is the will of God in this second sense because God rules by his providence over all of history. He has created time and the material world as the medium in which all creatures must live, but he himself transcends the limitations of time and the material world. Someday God will bring history as we know it to a glorious conclusion and utterly transform the material world. Then he will demonstrate just how complete his rule over the universe is and always has been.

God's will is hidden because at any given moment we cannot comprehend how he is working to fulfill his eternal purpose. God sees the end from the beginning and controls every aspect. Our vision, however, is limited because we are *inside* the story, experiencing it as it unfolds. In our perspective we see only a small part of the bigger picture. We can believe with confidence *that* God is in control, but we may not always know *how*. Thus, we are called to trust his sovereignty, believing that he will accomplish his glorious purpose.

Francis de Sales, along with many other Christian thinkers, has made this distinction between the *revealed* will of God and the *hidden* will of God, or what he called the "declared" will of God and "the will of God's good pleasure." Concerning the former, de Sales argues that God's will is clear. The Bible sets forth the truths he calls us to believe, the blessings we will receive, the punishments we can avoid if we live obediently, the priorities we should set, and the commands we must obey. We know these principles because God "has declared and revealed to us that he means and expects us to believe, hope, fear, love and perform it all."[2]

God's declared will expresses only his "desire," so that it is possible for people to obey it or oppose it. People, in other words, have the freedom to choose whether or not they will do his will. "That is why God, when he wants us to follow his declared will, entreats, encourages, impels, inspires, aids and abets us; when he allows us to oppose his will, however, he simply leaves us to our own devices, free to please ourselves."[3]

But de Sales believes that God's will is also mysterious and hidden. "Nothing happens but by God's will—by a positive or permissive will which no one can obstruct, which is known only by its results. These events, when they occur, show us that God has willed and planned them."[4] De Sales suggests that we often experience God's hidden will in suffering. A willingness to believe and love God through suffering expresses "charity's highest degree." Faith shows that we are willing to resign ourselves to the unfathomable will of God, even though we lack a clear understanding of why suffering occurs and what God intends to do through our suffering. De Sales counsels his followers to exercise "disinterested" love and faith as they make themselves open, available, and malleable before God.

> The heart of a disinterested person is like wax in God's hands, ready for every impression of the eternal will. Such a heart knows no personal preference, equally prepared for anything,

its one aim the fulfilling of God's will. It is not attracted by the things God wants, only by his will that wants them.[5]

GOD'S SOVEREIGNTY OR HUMAN FREEDOM?

The thought that God exercises sovereign control over history seems confusing and troubling. If we accept the idea of God's "hidden" will and affirm God's sovereignty over everything, we run the risk of becoming deterministic and passive. Yet if we reject the idea of God's hidden will and believe his power is limited, we run the risk of becoming insecure and fearful, especially when we face difficult circumstances. To resolve this apparent tension, each Christian community has tended to gravitate toward one of two extremes.

Some believers defend God's sovereignty as absolute, as if God controls history in the same way children play a game of army, deciding ahead of time which side is going to win. In this model, God follows no rules and gives no clues. His actions manifest no pattern. He operates almost according to whim as he exercises control over the affairs of humanity. Human beings seem powerless to alter his sovereign control. What God decides, God does; what human beings want or hope for doesn't matter. They are the objects of his control, not subjects who can influence him. Thus, if anyone is going to be saved, it is because God has decided to save him or her. If someone gets sick and dies, it is because God wills that death.

This view clearly upholds the idea of God's sovereignty, but it also makes God seem mean and manipulative. It likewise deprives Christians of the motivation to take responsibility for their actions. In fact, the notion of responsibility is meaningless because even a decision to take responsibility is a manifestation of God's sovereign control. If we do so, it is because God has willed it so ahead of time. Humans must do the divine bidding, like programmed robots.

Other Christians argue that God's sovereignty is limited by human freedom. God can only *influence* history because history itself is also subject to human influence. Human freedom, therefore, places limitations on God. In the beginning God chose to create human beings as free agents, and they are now free to make choices. These choices in turn affect God, who then responds to human choices with his own actions. Thus, God interacts with his creation, but he doesn't control it. According to this view, the future is unknown and unknowable. It contains an infinite number of possibilities. What eventually occurs depends not only on what God does but also on what human beings decide to do.

Both viewpoints present problems. The first one is unsettling because it suggests that God's sovereignty deprives us of our freedom and reduces us to mere pawns on a chessboard. God's will becomes synonymous with determinism. But the second perspective is also troubling because it implies God is weak and ignorant. He seems almost helpless, a force acting within history but not a transcendent power controlling history.

LIVING WITH PARADOX

Is it possible to believe both? I am comfortable living with paradox. Both my personality and my convictions make me so. Many people, however, are troubled by the apparent inconsistency of believing in two seemingly separate, disparate realities. I believe we can make a good argument for Christian paradox as long as we recognize the difference between a contradiction and a paradox.

A *contradiction* refers to two statements that conflict with each other. One can be true, or neither can be true, but both cannot be true. If I say, "It's raining cats and dogs outside," and my daughter says, "There's not a cloud in the sky," one of us, or both of us, are not telling the truth. Our statements contradict each other. The conflict between God's sovereignty and human freedom has often been viewed as a contradiction. Both cannot be true because they are mutually exclusive. They cancel each other out.

Or do they? Perhaps they are not a contradiction but a paradox. A *paradox* contains two statements that seem on the surface to be contradictory but are in fact, on a deeper level, simultaneously true. In science, Newton's view of the world does not allow for paradox. Everything operates according to physical laws that cannot contradict each other. But Einstein's view does allow for paradox. According to him, human beings can function on two levels of reality. On the level of human experience, time and mass seem absolute. On another level, time and mass are relative. It depends on point of view. What seems a contradiction is only a paradox.

God's sovereignty operates on two plains of reality. It does not contradict human freedom; rather, it envelops human freedom as a circle envelops a line drawn inside it. The best analogy I know to explain this paradox comes from C. S. Lewis. He used the example of writing a novel to make his point. The novelist stands outside the time and space dimensions of his novel. He knows the whole plot from beginning to end because, as the writer, he transcends it. If he wishes, he can write the last chapter first or the first chapter last. He can place characters anywhere he wants —in the mountains, on a deserted island, or in New York City—while he remains seated at his writing desk in Minneapolis. He can laugh when he is writing a tragic chapter or cry when is writing a happy chapter because he knows the novel's ultimate ending.

The characters, on the other hand, are confined to the time and space dimensions of the novel. Assuming that they are "real" characters who can act, think, and feel, they experience the story as it unfolds because they are part of the story. They are not the creator but the created. They respond to circumstances, make real choices, and thus contribute to the unfolding of the plot, but only as the author decides.

Up to this point it would seem that the novelist has all the power. His "sovereignty" and control are complete. He designs the plot, invents the characters, and writes it all down. He is the one who has the freedom, using it however he wishes. The characters may think they are free, but even this feeling of freedom has been given to them by the author. Their freedom results from the novelist's imagination. It is not real. Only the writer has true freedom.

But this view of the author's ultimate power doesn't square with reality. First, novelists themselves talk about creating characters that develop a life of their own. Novelists get to know them as people. They also talk about inevitabilities of plot, as if the characters themselves dictate what the novelist must write. The plot almost *has* to happen a certain way because of the personalities and choices of the characters. The characters become real, something separate from the mind of the author.

Moreover, what if a novelist decides to work himself into the story? He becomes, then, not only the author of the story, but a character within the story. This seems incongruous, but it is possible. Hypothetically, the novelist then experiences reality on two levels simultaneously. As the writer, he understands the novel as a whole and is in control. But as a character, he becomes a part of the plot and experiences the novel as an unfolding story.

THE PARADOX OF THE INCARNATION

Such is the mystery of God's involvement in history, especially through the Incarnation. God is the sovereign Lord of the universe. He stands outside space and time in the same way a novelist stands outside the story he is writing. The sequence of time the characters experience and the various locations where the action occurs are, from the novelist's point of view, only words on a piece of paper. Like a novelist, God is everywhere at once; he is "everywhen" at once. All places are "here" to God, all times are "now" to him (a subject to which we will return in the next section). God stands outside creation.

But God has acted in the time and space of history too. He invented time and space when he created the world. He has also revealed himself in time and space by intervening in history. He called Abraham to travel to Canaan and promised that he would be a blessing to the world. He commissioned Moses to lead the Hebrews out of slavery in Egypt. He sent Esther into the court of a Persian king, where she became queen. The Old Testament tells story after story of how God intervened in human history to guide, deliver, save, discipline, and protect his people.

Finally, God entered time and space personally when Jesus Christ, his Son, was born in a stable in Bethlehem. In that moment God became subject to all the limitations of time and space. Jesus Christ became a real human being. He had to learn how to walk, talk, and think. He fell down and cried. He ate and slept. He made choices without having the benefit of perfect knowledge. His was a real incarnation. He was not acting a part; he became the part.

How can God be both the author and character within his novel? How can he be both sovereign over time and space and yet subject to their limitations? It is a paradox. The Lord of history has written himself into the story because he saw where the plot was going and wanted to change its direction. He wanted it to end well. He entered the story as a character—he "condescended," as theologians call it—to win salvation for the world. Jesus Christ suffered and died as both God and man in order to open a way for human beings, the characters in the story, to be saved from a tragic ending. What Jesus has accomplished means that those who trust in him will continue to live after the story ends, entering into the larger world of the author himself.

THE POWER OF BIBLICAL STORIES

This paradox appears everywhere in the Bible, once we start to look for it. We meet real characters who use their freedom to make real choices. In many cases they see little of what is happening beyond their immediate experience. They cannot see that their lives are part of a much larger story that has significant implications for others and eternal consequences for themselves. They respond to a God they know as one who reveals his plan to them in part, but who at the same time remains hidden from them.

A good example is the story of Joseph.[6] Joseph suffered betrayal at the hands of his brothers, who sold him as a slave to a caravan of merchants traveling to Egypt. He found himself serving in the household of Potiphar, a member of Pharaoh's court. Joseph served Potiphar well and won his trust. But he was betrayed again, this time by Potiphar's wife, who tried to seduce the young Hebrew lad. When he rejected her advances, she falsely accused him of attacking her. Joseph was rewarded for his virtue by being thrown into prison. There, once again, his fortunes slowly rose. But he was disappointed yet again, this time when a servant in Pharaoh's court, cast into prison for a crime he did not commit, forgot to remember and reward Joseph for his help.

At this point Joseph could easily have lost faith and abandoned all hope. Three times he suffered betrayal; he received punishment for being righteous; and he spent more than ten years separated from all that was familiar to him. Amazingly, Joseph continued to believe in God, even in his darkest hour. Finally, after years of suffering, Joseph was released from prison. This time, however, he gained more than his freedom. Because he interpreted Pharaoh's dream accurately and advised him to establish a plan to avert the famine that the dream predicted, he was appointed second in command in Pharaoh's court. For seven years Joseph supervised a national project of storing grain. Then he supervised the distribution of the grain when the famine finally struck, all according to Pharaoh's dream.

Thus Joseph's story appears to end happily. He became a man of power, wealth, and influence. He married and had two sons. He was comfortable and secure in his new land. But the story did not end when his life became prosperous, as we would expect and hope for if we were playing Joseph's part. The famine forced his brothers to travel to Egypt to buy grain to keep their families alive in Canaan. Joseph recognized them as they approached the Egyptians for grain and, after testing them to see if they had learned their lesson, revealed himself to them, forgave them for their cruelty, and restored their broken relationship. Later, he moved the entire family circle from Canaan to Egypt, where they settled and prospered.

There are many such strange and wonderful stories in the Old Testament. We, as readers, understand them as the author does, standing outside the time sequence and space dimensions of the story itself. The power of these stories is lost to us because we are so familiar with them. We know how they end.

Thus, we often fail to sympathize with the characters, who have no idea what is happening to them. We forget to commiserate with their feelings of utter frustration, confusion, and doubt as they face circumstances that appear to violate God's goodness and faithfulness. Joseph, for example, had no idea how his story would be resolved. He is a character in the story, acting without benefit of the knowledge that we, the readers, have. He had to make choices with only limited information. He had to act in faith.

TWO PERSPECTIVES ON THE WILL OF GOD

The biblical stories provide two perspectives on the will of God. The author of the story provides the first perspective by informing readers of *God's role* in the story. We read that "the LORD was with Joseph," though Joseph had no proof of this. The author's perspective is informed by his knowledge of the *entire story*. He knows how it will end. So he can write with confidence that God was with Joseph. He knows too that God, sovereign as he is, is working out a plan that none of the biblical characters comprehends at the time. The author's perspective manifests God's hidden will, his sovereign control over time and history.

The second perspective comes from the characters themselves, whose choices demonstrate their importance in the plot and contribute to its development. Joseph obeyed God's revealed will in Egypt because he believed that God was with him, accomplishing some great purpose. Joseph had confidence that God's *hidden* purpose was being mysteriously accomplished, even though it is not until the end of the story that he received the evidence to prove it. Only then could he say to his brothers, "Do not be afraid! Am I in the place of God? Even though you intended to do harm to me, God intended it for good, in order to preserve a numerous people, as he is doing today."[7]

But because Joseph chose to do God's revealed will, he contributed something to the story long before it ended. He *believed* in the middle of the story that God was sovereign. He chose to trust God, even in the face of great agony and mystery. His obedience to the revealed will of God and his refusal to sin against God played a critical part in accomplishing God's hidden will.

What was the will of God for Joseph's life? On one level, it included all the events that make up the entire story. His will transcended Joseph's limited experience and perspective. It enveloped Joseph's life, however real and free his choices were. God simply accomplished his sovereign purpose. Joseph did not choose to do God's will at this point, though he did make choices. *God's will simply happened*, and the story ended well. As Joseph said to his brothers:

> God sent me before you to preserve life. For the famine has been in the land these two years; and there are five more years in which there will be neither plowing nor harvest. God sent me before you to preserve for you a remnant on earth, and to keep alive for you many survivors. So it was not you who sent me here, but God; he has made me a father to Pharaoh, and lord of all his house and ruler over all the land of Egypt.[8]

But on another level, God's will consisted of the wise choices Joseph made along the way, the course he set for himself while suffering, and the kind of life he purposed to live. At this point

Joseph did God's will. *He made it happen.* He could not always comprehend God's hidden will, especially in his suffering. But he did understand the revealed will of God. He knew he was called to trust God, show fidelity to others, work hard and responsibly, and maintain purity.

Joseph could have chosen disobedience at any number of points, and with good reason. He could have slacked off on his duties in Potiphar's house to undermine Potiphar's authority, seduced Potiphar's wife to satisfy his appetites, responded cynically to Potiphar's betrayal, exploited fellow prisoners to punish them for his misery, and lied to Pharaoh's baker and butler when they told him their dreams. Joseph could have justified such bad behavior by assuming God had abandoned him or perhaps did not even exist. But he remained faithful to God and his will.

The leaders of the early church likewise understood this tension between God's hidden and revealed will when they prayed. After suffering persecution at the hands of the Jewish authorities, they met together to ask for his help so they could continue in their missionary work. They recognized the gravity of the threats against them, but trusted God was still in control. They remembered what God had accomplished on the cross. In their prayer they described the dual roles that human choice and God's sovereignty played in Christ's death:

> For in this city, in fact, both Herod and Pontius Pilate, with the Gentiles and the peoples of Israel, gathered together against your holy servant Jesus, whom you anointed, to do whatever your hand and your plan had predestined to take place. And now, Lord, look at their threats, and grant to your servants to speak your word with all boldness.[9]

Paul states a formula that rings true to the entire Bible. He grasped this central paradox between God's hidden will, that is, his sovereign control over history, and God's revealed will, the role believers must play. "Therefore, my beloved, just as you have always obeyed me, not only in my presence, but much more now in my absence, work out your own salvation with fear and trembling; for it is God who is at work in you, enabling you both to will and to work for his good pleasure."[10]

GOD'S REDEMPTIVE PURPOSE

Joseph, Moses, Esther, Ruth, Paul, Peter, and a host of other biblical characters chose to do the *revealed* will of God. They trusted God, though at times there seemed to be no good reason for doing so. They demonstrated goodness, faithfulness, and compassion. They did not use their ignorance of the *hidden* will of God to excuse them from doing the *revealed* will of God. In the end, that hidden will enveloped their obedience—as well as their disobedience—creating a kind of glorious symphony out of the various instruments each played.

None of us will be able to comprehend the whole of God's symphony, at least not yet. All of us know enough, however, to do his will as it has been revealed. We know enough to believe God and obey his commands. We know enough to pray, though it does not always appear to do much good. We know enough to care for our family and friends, though they are wayward. We know enough to show compassion and kindness to sinful people, though we get nothing in return. This is the part of the score we must play, and must learn to play well.

The tension between God's hidden will and his revealed will finds ultimate resolution in his *redemptive purpose* (a subject to which we will return in the next chapter). God is doing something incomprehensibly wonderful—so wonderful, in fact, that it is too much for us to comprehend with our limited vision. His redemptive purpose is unfolding like a plot in a novel that would make Charles Dickens' complex novels read like a simple cartoon strip.

God's revealed will keeps us on course; his hidden will concerns the grand design of things. God's will is like a beautiful story that has heart. It calls us to life, not death; to active obedience, not passive resignation. As Rucker Blakeslee, an offbeat theologian if there ever was one, says to his grandson in Olive Ann Burns' delightful Southern novel *Cold Sassy Tree*:

> But I got one more thang to say. They's a heap more to God's will than death, disappointment, and like thet. Hit's God's will for us to be good and do good, love one another, be forgivin'.... Well anyhow, folks who think God's will jest has to do with sufferin' and dyin', they done missed the whole point.[11]

It is an act of utter audacity to believe that God's hidden will promises triumph and bliss when the story is complete. Who dares to believe that no matter how terrible life is—and it often is terrible—God intends to end the story gloriously. Peter Kreeft, a philosopher at Boston College, underscores the audacity of such faith when he argues that what happens on earth serves God's greater plan. Earth is therefore heaven's workshop, heaven's womb.

> Every atom in the quadrillion-mile universe and every "chance" event in its trillion-year history is deliberated and perfectly planned and controlled by God for the ultimate end of our good, our heavenly joy. Galaxies revolve and dinosaurs breed and rain falls and people fall in love and uncles smoke cheap cigars and people lose their jobs and we all die—all for our good, the finished product, God's work of art, the kingdom of Heaven.[12]

The difference between God's revealed will and God's hidden will is no mere intellectual abstraction, the stuff that philosophers and theologians debate. It has practical consequences for ordinary people. It has been significant to me for personal reasons. A drunk driver forced me to think about these questions, and my survival as a Christian depended on it. I *had* to think about them, for they assaulted me with the fury of a terrible storm. The tragedy of our car accident sent me on a religious search that continues to this day. I knew intuitively what I had to do to set my family on a course of healing. I suffered tremendously and wanted no more of it. I realized that how I responded to the accident would either help repair the damage done to me, my children, and many others, or push us further toward destruction. So my role was clear, right from the beginning.

God's role, however, was not clear. How, I wondered, could God allow such a tragedy to occur? Even after these many years I still do not understand why three precious members of my family lost their lives. It seems such a waste, a meaningless event, as if God were like a child who for no apparent reason squished three ants who happened to be crossing the sidewalk at the wrong moment. I still cannot find one convincing reason why it happened or had to happen.

I remember spending hour after hour pondering the tragedy in the months that followed, trying to make some sense out of it.

I looked at the event from within my own human experience. What I saw was horrible to me, very painful, very senseless. One man had used his freedom irresponsibly and had changed our lives forever. But was God in it, too? Did he play a role?

It eventually occurred to me that perhaps my vision was obscured by my own finitude. I could only see the event from my own limited perspective. I finally conceded that I could be wrong in the facile judgments I had made. So I decided, slowly and cautiously, to believe that God was still at work, however unfathomable and mysterious it appeared to me. The story of Joseph as well as many other biblical stories helped me to believe that my story could be part of a bigger story and that my perspective was like a blink of an eye in light of God's perspective. I started to believe that more was going on than met the eye.

So I concentrated on doing the obvious, not on figuring out the oblique. I figured that I had nothing to lose trusting in God, though I was aware that I had plenty to lose if I made the wrong choice. I lived in hope, invested in my children, and set a course for my life that would honor God and be redemptive for everyone concerned. I began to read the story of my own life through the redemptive story of the Bible, embracing the revealed will of God I already knew and trusting that God was working out his hidden will. That hidden will, I sensed, was not cold and hard, like an icy cliff, but vital and dynamic, like a rushing river. I learned to separate what I did know and could do from what I did not know and assumed God was doing. I learned to live with mystery. That decision saved my life.

SUFFERING RESPECTS
NO BOUNDARIES

No problem is more difficult to understand than suffering, especially undeserved suffering. If a drunken driver slams his automobile into a telephone pole and spends the rest of his life in a wheelchair, we rightly grieve over the tragedy, yet we also recognize that there are tragic consequences to bad decisions. We are rarely surprised when sexual promiscuity sends a friend to a clinic for treatment of some sexually transmitted disease. We support a judicial system that sends a thief to prison for five years. We recognize the risk involved when someone attempts to climb Mount Everest and dies on the way down. Risky ventures can result in tragedy. Foolish choices often lead to suffering. We mourn the tragedy but still admit that, in cases of wrongdoing and brinkmanship, people get what they deserve, sooner or later.

But undeserved suffering is an entirely different issue. Just this week I heard or read of several stories of suffering, and this week is not particularly unusual. A gunman rushed Capitol Hill and killed two police officers before he was stopped. A tidal wave crashed into the coast of New Guinea and killed thousands, including many children. A man in a pickup, distracted while reaching for his cell phone, drifted into another lane, struck a minivan, and killed two little girls. Cancer invaded a friend's body and consumed it. An avalanche killed two skiers who had accidentally wandered out of bounds at a ski resort.

Much of human history is a catalog of suffering, from the Ten Plagues in Egypt to the Black Death to the Holocaust. It comes in little doses or big doses, experiences that are soon forgotten and events that will remain in humanity's memory until history ends. Whenever I visit the graveyard where Lynda, Diana Jane, and my mother are buried, I always stroll past the new graves that have appeared since my last visit. I look at names and dates and wonder what happened to end their lives, especially if they died young. I also imagine how their loved ones must feel. I assume their experience of suffering is as wrenching as mine was, their feelings as raw as mine were. Suffering makes life so hard.

Thomas à Kempis dealt realistically with life's difficulties when he wrote:

> The days of this life are short and evil, full of sorrow and misery, where a person is stained with many sins, ensnared by many passions, bound by many fears, swollen by many cares, distracted by many curiosities, entangled by many vanities, surrounded by many mistakes, weakened by many efforts, weighed down by temptations, sopped by pleasures, tormented by wants. Oh, when will there be an end to all these things that have gone awry in God's plan?[1]

Where is God in all this suffering? Christians have pondered this question for centuries. It seems as if God has either power but no love, or love but no power. But if God has both power and love—muscle and heart, we could say—why do innocent people suffer? Where is God's muscle and heart when we need them? So I ask again, as I have done before: Does God will human suffering?

THE LOGIC AND ILLOGIC OF SUFFERING

Twice already I have touched on this critical question—in chapter 1, where I described my own experience of suffering, and in chapter 8, where I explored the relationship between God's hidden will and his revealed will. Now it is time to confront the question directly.

As I do so, I will appear once again to contradict myself. On the one hand, God does not will suffering because he does not create evil or pain. On the other hand, God does will suffering because he uses it to accomplish his redemptive plan. This apparent contradiction will not satisfy people who want an easy answer to the problem of suffering, largely because suffering of every kind raises perplexing questions about God's character and plan.

Suffering appears to run contrary to the will of God. God created the world a good place. Life as we live it now is not the way it's supposed to be, nor the way God designed it to be. Our abhorrence of suffering reflects a God-given impulse that runs deep within our nature. We recoil before suffering, not only because we dislike the pain, but also because we realize instinctively that we were not made for suffering. It is a violation of God's creation intent.

The book of Genesis tells the story of humanity's fall from grace and subsequent expulsion from the Garden of Eden.[2] Adam and Eve enjoyed bliss in the Garden before the Fall. Suffering entered the world as a terrible consequence of their rebellion against God. Mortality and pain resulted from their disobedience. God drove them from the Garden and appointed angels to guard the entrance so that the two of them could not reenter the Garden and eat of the Tree of Life, which would have sentenced them to live forever in a state of sin and misery. Instead, they were afflicted with pain and death.

The whole world—human as well as nature—now groans under bondage. God himself subjected the world to this bondage so that it could experience redemption and restoration. He sentenced the world to death to give it new life. Paul argues this very point when he writes:

> For the creation was subjected to futility, not of its own will but by the will of the one who subjected it, in hope that the creation itself will be set free from its bondage to decay and will obtain the freedom of the glory of the children of God. We know that the whole creation has been groaning in labor pains until now; and not only the creation, but we ourselves, who have the first fruits of the Spirit, groan inwardly while we wait for adoption, the redemption of our bodies.[3]

As Paul explains, God gives the Holy Spirit as a first fruits to ensure that the full harvest will come in due time. So, though we groan in our suffering because it is unpleasant and unrelenting, we also have hope that God will bring that suffering to an end. A taste of God's favor will give way to the final and complete banquet. God will envelop us with love as a mother cradles a sleeping baby in her arms. In the age to come, suffering will be eradicated, tears will be wiped away, and pain will be removed.[4] Believers will live in the full freedom and glory of being children of God, having received the promise of the kingdom.[5]

In the meantime, however, we suffer. Moreover, our experience of suffering does not follow strict standards of rationality or clear patterns of predictability. Suffering does not respect the boundaries of right and wrong, innocent and guilty, deserved and undeserved. More often than not, one person sins and another person suffers the consequences. A pregnant woman drinks too much alcohol and gives birth to a baby with fetal alcohol syndrome. Adolf Hitler caused the death of millions of innocent people. The Sullivan family, from a small town in Iowa, lost all five of their sons fighting because of Hitler's warmongering. Those sons fought in a war they did not start and did not want to fight.

Some people seem to be in the wrong place at the wrong time, and the suffering that visits them can have brutal consequences. I received a letter recently from a woman who told me her story and gave me permission to tell it to you. When Mary was five years old, her parents traveled to Europe for two weeks. She and her little brother, then only nine months old, were left under the care of her grandparents, who lived in the same small town as her parents. Her favorite aunt came to offer additional help. Before leaving, her mother said, in predictable fashion, "Be a good girl. Watch out for your little brother. We love you very much."

A few days later her grandmother and aunt took Mary and her baby brother shopping in a nearby city. On the way a speeding car failed to heed a stop sign and hit their car broadside. Everyone was killed but Mary. She remained trapped in that chamber of death for an hour before police could get her out. Her grandfather had a nervous breakdown when authorities told him about the accident, and he ended up in the hospital. It took two days for her parents to get home. By the time they arrived home, Mary had retreated into a cocoon of silence, refusing to communicate with anyone. She did not speak for two years.

She communicated again only after she buried the memory of the accident in her unconscious. Her life appeared to return to normalcy, and many years later she married and had a baby. But when her baby boy reached the age of nine months, she began to revisit the memory of the accident. The horror was so great that, for a time, she had to be institutionalized.

I have pondered Mary's story often. I have gazed on the face of that little five-year-old girl, trapped in that car for an hour with three loved ones, all dead. The scene fills me with terror. I want to reach back in time and reverse the sequence of events, sparing Mary from the horrible experience that marked her for life. She did nothing to deserve such suffering.

Sin ravages the human heart. Suffering is a consequence of sin. Yet how a person experiences suffering does not follow logically from the misdeeds that person has committed. Some people sin egregiously, yet live relatively happy lives, at least in this world. Others appear to live decent lives, yet encounter misery that makes the cruelest among us shudder. God did not will any of this; he does not want any of this. He condemns it and mourns it. He even suffered as a result of it. Jesus died on the cross because sin reigns in the world. God, therefore, does not will human suffering. It runs contrary to his original plan.

BUT IS SUFFERING GOD'S WILL?

Yet God allows our suffering. Though it often appears to contradict his revealed will, it fulfills his hidden will just the same. Ultimately God uses suffering, however horrible and undeserved, to accomplish his redemptive purposes. All events, both good and bad, fit into a larger plan that God is working out in history.

Suffering, then, is simultaneously both *inside* and *outside* the will of God. It runs contrary to what God intended for the world he created, yet also fits into his providential plan for history. The cross of Christ is the quintessential example of this paradox. It was history's darkest hour and greatest moment, an affront to the will of God ("You shall not kill") and the fulfillment of God's plan of redemption (Acts 4:23–31), a terrible injustice and the ultimate expression of God's perfect justice and mercy.

God's will is revealed to us in Scripture. He calls us to do what is right and good and condemns what is evil and unjust. But by his providence his will is also being worked out mysteriously in history so that even human behavior at its lowest and human suffering at its worst lead inexorably to a glorious ending.

How these two wills fit together is, once again, a paradox that works itself out in a redemptive story. Chaim Potok's *The Chosen* tells the story of two boys—Danny, a Hasidic Jew, and Reuven, a conservative Jew—as they become friends and grow up together in New York City. Danny's father, Rabbi Saunders, the leader of their Hasidic community, raises his son in silence, which utterly bewilders Danny. He cannot understand why his father is so distant and silent, why he afflicts him with such pain.

But there is a purpose to it all, as his father explains at the end of the novel. He says his own father raised him in silence too, in order to teach him about suffering. "My father himself never talked to me, except when we studied together. He taught me with silence. He taught me to look into myself, to find my own strength, to walk around inside myself in company with my soul." He discovered later that the suffering he experienced, bad in itself, had a good outcome.

> One learns of the pain of others by suffering one's own pain, he would say, by turning inside oneself, by finding one's own soul. And it is important to know of pain, he said. It destroys our self-pride, our arrogance, our indifference toward others. It makes us aware of how frail and tiny we are and of how much we must depend upon the Master of the Universe.

Rabbi Saunders experienced suffering on one level of his experience. But he learned to see it from a perspective outside his own experience when his father explained its purpose to him. His suffering was both painful and redemptive.[6]

Suffering was an idea I had pondered from a safe distance long before I experienced it so dramatically. I was a pastor and a professor, two lines of work that require one to think a great deal about these questions. But suffering suddenly crashed into my life like a meteor, devastating the landscape of my life. I knew immediately that the accident was a terrible injustice, as I still believe today. Even if I had found a way to blame myself for the terrible tragedy—I was, after all, far from blameless in the way I had lived my life to that point—I was never able to get to the point of believing that my children deserved such suffering. They were innocent in every way. Suffering was and always will be a terrible violation of what is right and just and true in the world. The accident was wrong, our suffering undeserved. As the book of Job reminds us, not everything that happens to us follows a clear pattern of punishment and reward.

I was, therefore, rightly outraged by the tragic event. I was angry at the driver, and I was dumbfounded before God. How, I asked myself, could God allow this injustice to occur? I could not fathom a God who would allow such a thing, who could see the horror of it coming and do nothing about it. The tragedy seemed to provide only more evidence of God's absence and the randomness of suffering. It made about as much sense to me as the actions of an abusive father.

Over the course of the next months I had conversations with many people who expressed similar sentiments about their own experiences of suffering. They had trusted in God, believing he would be good to them. But their trust in God had backfired, like friendly fire in a war. They had prayed for the safety of a loved one who was later killed, worked for the restoration of a marriage that ended in divorce, or hoped for the healing of a spouse, who instead withered away from cancer. Not that the problem of suffering was new to them. Every one of them had pondered it before. They knew that suffering did not start with them. Still, their experience of suffering had turned up the intensity of their emotion and raised the stakes in their quest for answers. Some told me their very sanity was at risk.

MAKING PEACE WITH THE SOVEREIGNTY OF GOD

About six months after the accident a good friend challenged my perspective. I was surprised by his boldness. Of all people who should have been spared admonition, I was surely one of them. Yet there I stood, mouth agape, as he said to me, "Eventually, Jerry, you will have to make peace with the sovereignty of God. Either God is in control, or God is not. You must decide which you believe is true."

That there is suffering in the world is so obvious that it hardly needs mentioning. M. Scott Peck was right when he wrote:

> Life is difficult. This is a great truth, one of the greatest truths. It
> is a great truth because once we truly see this truth, we transcend

it. Once we truly know that life is difficult—once we truly understand and accept it—then life is no longer difficult. Because once it is accepted, the fact that life is difficult no longer matters.

Surprisingly, we still respond with shock and anger when it happens to us, as if we are supposed to be the one exception to the rule. "Most do not fully see this truth that life is difficult. Instead they moan more or less incessantly, noisily or subtly, about the enormity of their problems, their burdens, and their difficulties as if life were generally easy, as if life should be easy."[7]

Life is difficult for everyone at times. We may be able to avoid some suffering, but not all suffering. We can eat healthy foods, exercise daily, fasten our seatbelts, drive the speed limit, build meaningful friendships, and think positively. Yet we must still face the reality that someday we may get cancer, die in a fatal car accident, face divorce, or fall into clinical depression.

What is God's role here? Why does he allow suffering? The answer we give will in large measure determine how we respond to the suffering that forced the question on us in the first place. Is God in control or not? If so, then we can trust him as he works out his redemptive purpose—that is, his hidden will—in our lives. If not, then we might as well abandon faith and find our own way through life without the help of God. The choice is that stark and simple, although the struggles and doubts we may have along the way are anything but simple.

John Calvin regarded suffering as one of the great tests of the Christian life. He acknowledged it was legitimate and even healthy to express human emotion in the face of suffering, for "adversity will always wound us with its stings." As Calvin put it so eloquently and compassionately:

> When we are afflicted with disease we shall, therefore, groan and complain and pray for recovery. When we are oppressed with poverty we shall feel lonely and sorry. When we shall be defamed, despised and offended, likewise we shall feel restless. When we have to attend the funeral of our friends, we shall shed tears.[8]

Yet Calvin believed that God is sovereign, working out a good purpose in suffering. Suffering makes us humble and hopeful, teaches us obedience, leads to discipline, and brings repentance.

Our suffering, then, fits into God's providential plan. It is right for us, therefore, to trust God, even in our suffering. "Whether we are afflicted with poverty, or exile, or imprisonment, or reproach, or disease, or loss of relatives, or any other similar calamity, we must remember that none of these things happen without the will and providence of God."[9]

THE STORY IS NOT OVER YET

That God works redemption through our suffering is foundational to Christian belief. Suffering never has the final word in a Christian's life. This past year I read Wallace Stegner's *Angle of Repose*, a brilliant novel about a bitter and disabled historian, Lyman Ward, who is writing a biography of his grandmother and grandfather, Susan and Oliver Ward. He chronicles the sad deterioration of their marriage. There is hope that the marriage can be restored. But in 1890, tragedy strikes, forever changing their lives. The novel ends just a few pages later. Though both his grandmother and grandfather lived together for another forty years, Lyman Ward says of their relationship, "It was all over in 1890." In his mind there was no longer a story worth telling, no possibility of redemption. He wistfully concludes:

> So they lived happily-unhappily ever after. Year after irrelevant year, half a century almost, through one world war and through the Jazz Age and through the Depression and the New Deal and all that; through Prohibition and Women's Rights, through the automobile and radio and television and into the second world war. Through all those changes, and not a change in them.[10]

But life does not have to end that way, no matter how terrible our suffering is. The story is never done, not until God is done telling it. And he will not be done until his redemptive purpose is accomplished. Sinfulness and tragedies and suffering and everything else never have the final word. God has the final word. The cross is irrefutable proof that God's hidden will, mysterious and unfathomable at times, is real and redemptive. God is sovereign. He is in control. He rules over time and history. Even our suffering serves his greater purpose, and that purpose has our ultimate benefit in mind.

SUFFERING OBSCURES SIGHT

Yet that benefit, however glorious, is still in the future. Words of assurance are easy to utter but hard to believe, especially when we are the ones suffering. Answers are helpful and necessary, but they can also sting. I get prickly when someone offers easy and untimely answers that show little sensitivity to people and their circumstances. God will bring resolution to human suffering— though not right away and sometimes not even in one's lifetime. Belief in God's redemptive plan does not always mitigate suffering or make it any less painful.

I backpack for a hobby. On many occasions I have trekked through forests so thick that I could see only a short distance behind me and ahead of me. I had no idea where I was except by consulting a map and using a compass. There were no landmarks, like lakes or rivers, no rises high enough to lift me above the forest floor, no open spaces to allow me to determine my location. Just forest, endless forest, and the trail I was following, which I was confident would lead me to my destination.

Suffering is like that forest. It encloses and overwhelms us so completely that we simply cannot see beyond the suffering itself. It is demanding, oppressive, and unrelenting. As a friend of mine once said, "I don't feel pain. I *am* pain. It is the only reality I know right now. It is the only thing I feel."

But I also remember occasions during a long backpacking trip when the trail led up a mountain pass where I gained enough elevation to get an unobstructed view of the vast landscape around me. From that pass I could see where I had come from. I could see lakes that sat only a hundred yards from the path I had followed, rivers and outcroppings of rock, and the spot where I had camped the night before. This pass gave me perspective.

Suffering, like the forest, obscures our vision. Thus, when we face it, it is all the more necessary to use two aids to keep us going. First, we should consult a map. A map can help us get bearings for the journey and locate our position so that we can see where we have come from and where we are going. Others, we discover, have gone before us. They have traveled over the same territory and charted their journey on a map.

The Bible is the map for Christians. It records the experiences of people who lived for God when there seemed to be no reason to do so. Yet they found God to be faithful. By reading the Bible we learn that suffering can serve a good purpose. We can therefore interpret our own suffering in light of that of biblical characters. We can believe that ours will end because theirs did and ours will be redemptive because theirs was. Like a map, the Bible allows us to locate our present position in life so that we never have to feel lost again. We gain confidence that there is more to life than meets the eye of immediate experience. We discover that suffering is not *the* story but *part of a bigger story* that turns out well.

Keep Trusting God!

Second, we should follow a trail—the trail of faith. If there is one consistent theme in Scripture, it is that God calls us to live by faith. According to the book of Hebrews, faith is "the assurance of things hoped for, the conviction of things not seen."[11] Faith helps us to see spiritual reality without physical sight. Moreover, "without faith it is impossible to please God, for whoever would approach him must believe that he exists and that he rewards those who seek him."[12] We must accept these promises *by faith* because our immediate circumstances may not provide evidence of God's existence and generosity. Suffering raises serious questions about God; faith enables us to endure. It closes the gap between objective knowledge of God, gleaned from the Bible, and subjective feelings about God, which may be colored by our suffering.

I had wondered for years why faith is so fundamental to the Christian life. My son David helped me to find an answer. When he was only eight years old, he asked me, "Why does God make it so hard?" Startled by his question, I asked him what he meant. He replied, "Why does God make it so hard for us to know him? We can't see God, hear God, or touch God. But we're still supposed to believe that he is really there?" His question got me thinking. Why is faith central? What keeps God from being more obvious? Why does he make it so hard to know him?

What would happen, I wondered, if God *were* obvious? I am not sure we would like the outcome. God's undeniable presence would make faith unnecessary. We would have no choice in the matter. We would *have* to believe. In fact, *believe* is hardly the right word. God's bright and blazing presence would overwhelm us. His ineffable glory would blind, crush, and annihilate us, sinful creatures that we are, which is hardly the goal God had in mind when he created us.

Could this requirement of faith, then, actually work to our advantage? I believe that God prefers to be subtle, choosing to woo and entice rather than to overwhelm and coerce. He gives us room to maneuver and the freedom to respond. He lets us choose for ourselves what we will do with him. He created us as individuals with hearts that feel, minds that think, and wills that decide. God does not absorb us into himself, as if he was a kind of giant black hole that cannot tolerate anything that has a separate and independent existence. Thus, we know enough about God to believe; we do not know so much that we *have* to believe. God invites us into a relationship with him, but he does not bully us.

In *The Screwtape Letters* C. S. Lewis used the clever device of correspondence between two devils to explore the nature of the Christian life. The "enemy," of course, is God because the entire book is written from the perspective of hell. Screwtape informs his nephew Wormwood that their "Father below" (Satan) wants to extinguish the individuality of every creature. He seeks to absorb, not love.

> The whole philosophy of Hell rests on recognition that ... my good is my good and your good is yours. What one gains another loses. Even an inanimate object is what it is by excluding all other objects from the space it occupies; if it expands, it does so by thrusting other objects aside or by absorbing them. A self does the same. With beasts the absorption takes the form of eating; for us, it means the sucking of will and freedom out of a weaker self into a stronger.[13]

Screwtape admits, however, that the "Enemy" (God) is different. While the Enemy insists on sacrifice of the self to him, in the end he purposes to give the self back again. Screwtape writes:

> Remember always, that He really likes the little vermin [humans], and sets an absurd value on the distinctness of every one of them. When He talks of their losing their selves, He only means abandoning the clamour of self-will; once they have done that, He really gives them back all their personality, and boasts (I am afraid, sincerely) that when they are wholly His they will be more themselves than ever.[14]

God respects our individuality. He does not want to obliterate us. So he lets us choose to believe or to disbelieve. He reveals himself, to be sure, and he invites us into a relationship with himself. But he does not coerce us.

So we know enough to believe there is a God who creates, loves, and saves. But we do not know so much that we are *forced* to come to such conclusions. We must therefore *choose* to believe. Such faith requires more than intellectual assent. It mandates active trust. We must live as if God really does exist, rewards those who seek him, makes us right with himself, and shows us the right way to live.

10

GETTING THROUGH SUFFERING

God invites us to trust him, even when nothing in our circumstances indicates he is trustworthy. Deprived of evidence, we choose nevertheless to believe that, even in our suffering, God is accomplishing some great purpose. Though our circumstances may cause nothing but pain, thus tempting us to doubt God, faith enables us to believe that God is working all things out for the good of those who love him. Again, as Rucker Blakeslee, one of my favorite theologians from fiction, says, "Well'm, faith ain't no magic wand or money-back gar'ntee, either one. Hit's jest a way a-livin'. Hit means you don't worry th'ew the days. Hit means you go'n be holdin' on to God in good or bad times, and you accept whatever happens. Hit means you respect life like it is—like God made it—even when it ain't what you'd order from the wholesale house."[1]

Faith means that although life does not appear to be turning out the way we had hoped, we believe that God's hidden will is being done on earth as it is in heaven. So we continue to endure, love, serve, and worship. We resist the temptation to turn bitter, seek revenge, view the world cynically, or whine about how hard life is, even though these temptations are as natural to us as hunger pains and fatigue. In short, we train our eyes to see signs of God's redemptive work. We wait patiently for God's will to be accomplished.

THE PRACTICAL SIDE OF FAITH

Such faith makes a practical difference. Take, for example, a woman who finds herself in a miserable job. She ponders whether or not to quit. But she needs the income desperately and has no prospects for another job. So she decides to stay because the future is unclear to her. She knows that today, just today, she should arrive at 8:00 A.M., do her job as best she can, and view it as an opportunity to serve God. She trusts that God is somehow working to redeem her life.

Or take a husband who feels trapped in an unhappy marriage. His wife is selfish and bossy. She ignores him and nags their children. He considers divorce but decides against it. In the meantime, he tries to love her as best he can, however unhappy he feels. He trusts that God is somehow working to redeem his life.

Or again, take a couple considering a move to another city to be closer to elderly parents. They feel a moral obligation to care for their parents. A move, however, would disrupt the lives of their children and would force both of them to take pay cuts at just the time when their living expenses are increasing. They have no idea what they should do. Still, they believe that whether they relocate or decide to stay, they are called to watch over their parents, provide help, and give advice when asked. They, too, trust that God is somehow working to redeem their lives.

Faith acknowledges need. Self-possessed people do not feel the need to live by faith because they are confident in themselves and their own human powers. In my mind such confidence is vain and foolish, for people are by nature dependent—on the natural world for food, air, water, and heat; on the social world for education, support, and love; and on the spiritual world for forgiveness, meaning, and purpose. Evelyn Underhill comments on this dependence: "I cannot by myself handle and purify the confusing energy of my half-evolved nature. I cannot really keep my resolutions, really govern my desires, set my life in order, cleanse my memory of all self-pity and all resentments, or kill self-love, self-interest, and self-will by myself. I acknowledge my need of help far beyond myself."[2]

Sometimes faith feels like hard work. Every Christian can recount experiences or describe circumstances that made it especially difficult to trust God. I know mine well. It is a scene I have rehearsed too many times. It goes something like this: I have a particularly busy week, so I stay up late at night to get my work done. I grow weary of the job, wondering if it is time for me to consider a move. Then, without warning, life at home starts to deteriorate. John becomes willful and negative; David uses sarcasm, driving all of us crazy; and Catherine procrastinates and gets defensive when I suggest she get her homework done. I lose patience and start to yell at everyone, which further poisons the atmosphere. Exhausted and discouraged, I crawl into bed at night thinking that the roof is caving in, our family is falling apart, and I am unfit to be a parent. I think God is playing a cruel cosmic joke on us. He snuffed out the life of Lynda, the one who was truly qualified to be a parent, and left me, a poor excuse for a parent, to fend for myself. I see myself trying to hold up a dam that is ready to burst, flooding us with still more heartache.

This is not an exaggeration. It is easy to lose perspective when you are a working single parent. But it is equally easy to lose perspective if you are terminally ill, chronically unemployed, unhappily married, displaced by war, or just sick of life. My area of vulnerability may be different from someone else's, my breaking point higher or lower, or my besetting sin in another area. Nevertheless, all of us have our limitations. All of us go through periods when we feel like a house of cards. I have heard it said that human beings are the most dogged and determined of all creatures. This may be true, but in my experience, human beings are also the most fragile.

Living by faith cannot always change difficult circumstances such as these. But it will give perspective to understand them, the soul to seek God in them, and the will to endure through them. Life is often hard and confusing. Bosses can be nasty, parents unreasonable, children disobedient, food and alcohol a temptation, loneliness unbearable, and daily tasks overwhelming. In such times, the life of faith will seem like all work and no play.

THE DELECTABLE MOUNTAINS

Still, there are wonderful respites along the way. God gives us those rare moments when we can clearly see the larger landscape of his redemptive plan, as if we have ascended to a high mountain pass and are looking down on the valley below. Such moments are rare but wonderful. In *The Pilgrim's Progress* John Bunyan tells an allegorical story of a pilgrim, Christian, who flees from the City of Destruction to follow the pathway of salvation to the Celestial City. At times the pathway leads him into hardship and suffering. It forces him to journey through the wicked city named Vanity Fair, up the Hill of Difficulty, into the Valley of the Shadow of Death, and across the River of Death. Surprisingly, Christian faces these challenges precisely because he stays on the pathway. In this way Bunyan demonstrates that the Christian faith does not ensure that life will be easy.

But Christian finds relief along the way too. At one point the pathway leads him to the Delectable Mountains, where he is given clarity of vision. He sees where he has come from and where he is going, to the Celestial City. He notices he still has a long way to go. There will be suffering and sacrifice ahead. But those few days spent in the Delectable Mountains allow him to view his journey from a transcendent perspective. Suddenly everything makes sense to him, everything becomes luminous, as if the fog has lifted and clear skies appear.[3]

Of course, Christian has to leave the Delectable Mountains and face the hard realities of life in a sinful world again. He has to live by faith, not by sight, and dare to believe in God when there is little evidence of God's involvement. As we learn from Christian's experience, it is difficult to believe that God is good when life is hard. "How can I believe in God," I hear someone ask nearly every week, "when my wife just left me?" Or "when my son just died of cancer?" Or "when I just lost my job?" Or "when my church humiliated me?"

There are no easy answers to these questions. Faith looks beyond immediate circumstances to the past, which tells the story of God's saving work in Jesus Christ, and to the future, which gives us hope that God will make all things right. Though our immediate circumstances can be overpowering, faith somehow helps us to transcend them and see the bigger picture of what God is doing.

GLIMPSES OF GOD'S PURE GOODNESS

How wonderful it is, then, when faith gives way to sight and we catch glimpses of God's wonderful plan. In this life such glimpses are never perfect and complete. Yet when they come, they make the spirit soar and give genuine hope that God will accomplish his final and perfect purpose in the world.

In *The Problem of Pain* C. S. Lewis wrote, "The Christian Doctrine of suffering explains, I believe, a very curious fact about the world we live in. The settled happiness and security which we all desire, God withholds from us by the very nature of the world: but joy, pleasure, and merriment He has scattered broadcast. We are never safe, but we have plenty of fun, and some ecstasy." Lewis did not have to look far for an explanation of this curious fact. If we start to feel secure, Lewis argued, we will try to make the world our permanent home. The world itself will then become an obstacle to our return to God. But, "a few moments of happy love, a landscape, a symphony, a merry meeting with our friends, a football match, have no such tendency. Our Father refreshes us on the journey with some pleasant inns, but will not encourage us to mistake them for home."[4]

I can testify to Lewis's point. There have been occasions when, in the oddest of times and places, I simply knew, in the depths of my soul, that God has been doing something so wonderful in my life that I cannot fathom it. I am in worship and suddenly know God is glorious beyond measure. I am listening to one of my kids practice piano and I start to smile, sensing in my heart that God is pleased with our home and my kids. I am lecturing to students and suddenly perceive that God is at work in their lives, preparing them for some great mission in life. I am reading the Bible and gain a sense of assurance that God's truth will triumph. I am listening to a beautiful piece of music and feel that heaven is closer than I realize. I am hiking in the mountains and see that God is making all things new.

For two years after the accident, I lived in darkness and chaos. My children were traumatized, and I felt exhausted most of the time. Night after night I cried out to God for help and relief, though none seemed to come. One night I took my three children to see *Les Miserables*. This musical tells the story of Jean Valjean, a bitter ex-con. He spends nineteen years in prison for stealing a loaf of bread before he is paroled. But he discovers that parole does not give him freedom. He is turned away from one village after another because of his prison record.

A Catholic bishop finally welcomes Valjean one night, giving him food and a comfortable bed. Valjean repays the bishop's kindness by stealing his silver. The police catch Valjean as he tries to escape. They drag him to the bishop's house for identification, but the bishop spares his life by insinuating to the police that he *gave* the silver to Valjean. After the incredulous police withdraw silently, the bishop says to a stunned Jean Valjean, "I have bought your soul for God." This experience of grace transforms his life.

From that moment on Valjean purposes to live for God. He escapes to another town, takes an assumed name, and becomes the owner of a prosperous factory and the mayor of the town. Later he pledges to a dying woman to take her child and raise her as his own. Though a merciless parole officer tries to put him back in jail for breaking parole, Valjean continues to live an exemplary life. He is wise and merciful. He shows unusual kindness to people, and he sacrifices his own life for the sake of others. On his deathbed he asks for forgiveness and entrusts his life to the good hand of God.

Something extraordinary happened to me while I watched the musical. I sensed that Jean Valjean's story was a metaphor for my own, a beacon of light showing me the way. It was so powerful that to this day I cannot talk about it without choking up. I sat in that seventh row of the Spokane Opera House, clinging to my children as if I was witnessing a miracle. I sensed that God was laying claim to my life, giving special grace to my family, and promising me that all would be well. The experience overwhelmed me. I knew from that moment on that God's favor rested on us. I felt relief, gratitude, and peace.

These occurrences are not as unusual as we think. I have heard many similar stories. Though brief and fleeting, such experiences give us glimpses of God's tangible goodness and place in us an intense longing to know God better. Most of us know many facts about God. We know God revealed himself in history, came in the person of Jesus Christ, and sent the Holy Spirit at Pentecost. He is working even now to accomplish his redemptive purposes. But on occasion we actually experience God, however briefly or dimly. We get glimpses of his glory. As Paul wrote so eloquently, "For now we see in a mirror, dimly, but then we will see face to face. Now I know only in part; then I will know fully, even as I have been fully known."[5]

Some people catch more than a mere glimpse of God's glory through mystical experience. They have a direct experience of him. The apostle Paul, for example, describes an experience of being taken up into the third heaven, where he "heard things that are not to be told, that no mortal is permitted to repeat." So ineffable was this translation into paradise that he did not even know whether he was "in the body or out of the body."[6]

This experience did not last, however. He spent the rest of his life suffering opposition, beatings, imprisonment, and deprivations of every kind. Moreover, God gave him a "thorn in the flesh" to keep him from becoming too elated and too dependent on his mystical experience. Whatever this affliction was, it forced Paul to live like the rest of us—"by faith, not by sight."[7] Paul recognized the fleeting nature of this glimpse of heaven when he concluded, "Therefore I am content with weaknesses, insults, hardships, persecutions, and calamities for the sake of Christ; for whenever I am weak, then I am strong."[8]

Saint Augustine, bishop of the church in Hippo, North Africa, from 395–430 offers one of the most famous accounts of a mystical experience. He lived a wanton life as a youth. He left his native North Africa to teach rhetoric in Rome and Milan. Through God's remarkable intervention he was won over to Christianity, but not until he was thirty years old. After his tumultuous conversion, Augustine decided to return to North Africa to start a Christian community with friends and family.

While waiting in Rome for a ship to take them home, Augustine and his dying mother, Monica, had a vision that manifested God's awesome glory to them. As Augustine describes it,

> Our colloquy led us to the point where the pleasures of the body's senses, however intense and in however brilliant a material light enjoyed, seemed unworthy not merely of comparison but even of remembrance beside the joy of that life, and we lifted ourselves in longing yet more ardent toward *That Which Is*, and step by step traversed all bodily creatures and heaven itself, whence sun and moon and stars shed their light upon the earth. Higher still we mounted by inward thought and wondering discourse on your works, and we arrived at the summit of our own minds; and this too we transcended, to touch the land of never-failing plenty.[9]

Augustine's vision is the exception rather than the rule. But it gives us another example of an occasion when the hard work of faith gives way to a brief moment of sight. In such moments we know beyond any shadow of a doubt that God is good to the core of his being and will make all things well. What makes Augustine's experience important is not what he saw but how it affected him. It awakened in him an even deeper longing for God. Not surprisingly, Augustine had many years of difficulty ahead of him. He became involved in virtually every controversy that the church faced in the fifth century, and he died while the Vandals, a barbarian tribe, were laying siege to Hippo. But he never stopped living by faith, even in his suffering. Augustine believed God for the glorious work he was doing. It was enough for him.

All will be well. Not because life will turn out that way naturally, as if there were some kind of universal law that ensures it. Life is not good because that is simply the way life is. If anything, life is often hard, mean, and brutal. But in the end life will turn out well because God is good and kind and gracious. He is working mysteriously to redeem us and restore the world to what he intended it to be. All will be well because God is God.

Saint Francis of Assisi had such a hope. He suffered more than most do, not only from physical infirmities that afflicted him but also from the burdens he bore for others. While praying one day, Francis received a word from God. "Rejoice, for your sickness is the earnest of my kingdom. Since you have been so patient, you can with certainty await this kingdom." To which Francis replied in prayer:

> *"I will rejoice*
> *at my tribulations and infirmities*
> *and be strong in the Lord,*
> *at all times giving thanks to God the Father*
> *and to his only Son*
> *our Lord Jesus Christ*
> *and to the Holy Spirit,*
> *for the great grace he has given me*
> *in deigning to assure me,*
> *his unworthy servant,*
> *while I am still alive,*
> *that his kingdom will be mine."*[10]

PART IV

GRASPING TIME

11

FACING WHAT WE
CANNOT CHANGE

The past has made us what we are, and we can't do anything to change it or its effects on us. The future holds the secret of what will someday be, and there is nothing we can do to control or know it, nor even to predict it. We live in the tension between the past and the future, like a paper clip pulled by two equally powerful magnets.

We have only the present moment in which to live. The unchangeable past lives in our memory; the unpredictable future lives in our imagination. We can be certain only of this one thing: We have only this present moment.

GOD'S TRANSCENDENCE

God is not bound by the present as we are. He transcends time. He dwells in eternity. All time is present to him. God is as alive a hundred years into the future as he is right now; he is as alive a hundred years into the past as he is right now. As the psalmist writes, "Before the mountains were brought forth, or ever you had formed the earth and the world, from everlasting to everlasting you are God. . . . For a thousand years in your sight are like yesterday when it is past, or like a watch in the night."[1]

In the film *Grand Canyon*, the Grand Canyon serves as a metaphor for transcendence. In comparison to the Grand Canyon, humans appear to be little specks of matter with life spans about as long as the tick of a clock. In the movie two strangers converse after they accidentally meet. Simon, a tow-truck driver, talks with Mack,

149

a lawyer, about a visit he once took to the Grand Canyon. He was overcome by its hugeness, and he felt small and insignificant.

> But the thing that got me was sitting on the edge of that big old thing. Those rocks and those cliffs are so old. It took so long for that thing to look like that.... When you sit on the edge of that thing you just realize what a joke we people are, what big heads we got thinking that what we do is going to matter all that much, thinking our time here means diddly to those rocks. Just a split second we been here, the whole lot of us. And one of us, that's a piece of time too small to get a name.... Those rocks are laughing at me. I can tell. Me and my worries, they're real humorous to that Grand Canyon.

THE POWER OF THE PAST

Unlike God, we cannot transcend time. We are bound by it. Take, for example, the past. We cannot change it, though it exercises great power over us. It affects us as a set of consequences from choices that were at one time made and cannot now be reversed. Many of those choices are our own. We chose to marry Elizabeth, to pursue a career in elementary school teaching, to smoke two packs of cigarettes a day for ten years, to collect firearms as a hobby, or to mug a stranger in Central Park.

Each of these choices has consequences that will affect us for the rest of our lives, though we can never be exactly sure how until we actually experience those consequences. We may enjoy sixty years of marital bliss. Then again, we may lose a spouse after only eight years of marriage. We may relish every day of a forty-five-year career as an elementary school teacher. Then again, we may start looking at the clock at 10:00 every morning. We may live to the age of ninety-five. Then again, we may die from lung cancer at age forty-two.

I think often about the course my life has taken and how weighty my choices have been. It is staggering to consider the cumulative effect of even one choice, which, once made, is impossible to reverse. For example, I chose to attend Hope College, almost on a whim. While at Hope College I met people who encouraged me to apply for a counselor position at a summer camp, where I was converted to Christ. After returning to Hope, I set a new direction for my life, which eventually led me into ministry. In my first job as pastor I met a high school student named Scot, who eventually became a Christian. Scot attended Northwestern College while I served as a chaplain there. At Northwestern he sensed a call to ministry, and he also met Patty, who became his wife. Now he is a pastor of a church in the Midwest, caring for a congregation of believers, and he and Patty are raising four children. Who knows what will happen to them?

The story continues, and it will continue to the end of history. Look at the staggering consequences of the single decision to attend Hope College—a calling to ministry, marriage to Lynda, the conversion of Scot, his marriage to Patty, and his calling to ministry. One choice sets off a chain reaction of events that keeps going and going.

Much of what happens in life can hinge on a single choice or event that seems, at the time, insignificant. As Richard, the main character in Robert Clark's novel *In the Deep Midwinter* says to his daughter after a period of bewildering events, "You choose one little thing, and everything that follows—maybe for the rest of your life—chooses you."[2] I wonder what would have happened had I chosen to attend another college. I will never know.

Our choices affect other people. Sometimes the effect is positive. I read recently about a woman who promised years ago to pay the college tuition for an entire class of elementary school children if they were willing to work hard enough to make it that far. Many of them did and have now graduated from college. Her benevolence has changed a whole group of people and set in motion a chain of events that none of us can predict. One of those students may become the president of Harvard University someday. Who knows where it will all end? The fact is, it never will end.

But bad choices have consequences, too. A husband gets involved with another woman, commits adultery, and divorces his wife. The wife is profoundly affected by her husband's choices. Colleagues and friends at an elementary school encourage a fellow teacher to apply for an open position in school administration, which she does. Eventually she becomes superintendent of schools and has to fire one of the teachers who encouraged her to apply. A woman smokes two packs of cigarettes a day and dies of lung cancer, which leads her grieving husband to file a lawsuit against the tobacco industry. An angry son of abusive parents steals a gun from his father's gun case and goes on a shooting spree, killing several classmates and a teacher.

I am not resorting to pure imagination. Such events really do happen, and they do have consequences. A man drinks too much, climbs into his car, and races down a lonely stretch of highway. Driving too fast as he approaches a curve, he swerves outside his lane and smashes into a minivan headed in the opposite direction. He does not know the people in that other vehicle. He did not have them in mind when he chose to drink too much and drive too fast. He was thinking only of himself—his own pleasure and his own problems. But his choice had catastrophic consequences for those other people. I know, of course, because I was driving that minivan. Just thinking about the power of his choice makes my soul shiver with fear, as if I were staring into a terrifying abyss.

The consequences of our choices are often permanent and irreversible. Lynda and I did not have to have children. No law required it. We chose to. Our decision was permanent. I cannot trade in my children for other children. They are *my* children, no matter what I do or what they do. I can choose to be a good father or a bad father, and they can choose to be good children or bad children. The choice I make about the kind of father I will be, just as the choice they make about the kind of children they will be, is secondary. We cannot change the fact that I will always be their father and they will always be my children.

So far I have mentioned only examples from the immediate and familiar past. But the distant past wields power over us too. We rarely think about how such events have shaped our lives— perhaps with good reason, for the very idea is staggering. Choices made long ago have created the conditions under which we now live. Emperor Constantine's conversion in A.D. 312 and the subsequent favor he bestowed on the church made Christianity the dominant religion of the West, which goes a long way to explaining why I am Christian and not a devotee of the cult of Osiris. Luther's decision to challenge the authority of the Roman Catholic Church contributed to the fragmentation of Christianity, giving rise to the many denominations we have today. The United States opened its doors to millions of immigrants in the late nineteenth and early twentieth centuries, making it possible for many Europeans to start a new life in America. That I am therefore a Christian, a Presbyterian, and a citizen of the United States is due to historical events that happened long ago. Had they been different, I could find myself living under very different circumstances. I could be a Muslim living in Libya and practicing Sufi mysticism.

INFLUENCE OR CONTROL?

But is the power the past wields absolute? During World War II Viktor Frankl, a Jewish psychiatrist and a concentration camp survivor, lost nearly everything dear to him, including his beloved wife. Suffering was imposed on him. He was clearly the victim of forces beyond his control. Millions of people from his background suffered the same fate.

Frankl observed that most prisoners in the camps allowed their circumstances to dominate their lives, which destroyed them in the end. Understandably, their lives became little more than an expression of the horrible circumstances under which they were forced to live. That was not true, however, for everyone. Amazingly, some chose, in the face of unspeakable affliction, to exercise the power of choice. They rose above their circumstances by choosing how they would respond to them. "Even though conditions such as lack of sleep, insufficient food and various mental stresses may suggest that the inmates were bound to react in certain ways, in the final analysis it becomes clear that the sort of person the prisoner became was the result of an inner decision, and not the result of camp influences alone." Frankl concluded, "Fundamentally, therefore, any man can, even under such circumstances, decide what shall become of him—mentally and spiritually. He may retain his human dignity even in a concentration camp."[3]

As Frankl observed, it was all too easy for prisoners to let their environment dominate them so that they became only what the camp conditions allowed. Many of us do the same with our past. We become only what our past allows, and we let it determine our fate. Of course, in ideal circumstances this may be an appealing option, if we come from stable, wealthy, happy backgrounds. But none of us comes from backgrounds so privileged and perfect that our past contains nothing we would want to change.

THE PRISON OF REGRET

There are at least two ways we let our past control us. The first is by living with *regrets*, the second is by living with *bitterness*. Let's begin with the former. No person lives a lifetime without ever making some bad choices—say, a youthful indiscretion, a bad business deal, poor academic performance during the first year of college, or a violation of marital vows. People make foolish decisions, which can lead to profound regret.

Anne Tyler's novel *Saint Maybe* tells the story of a young college student, Ian, whose older brother falls in love impulsively with a virtual stranger he meets at a post office. Ian does not trust this woman because her behavior is suspect. One day he mentions his reservations about the woman's fidelity to his brother. His brother is so shocked and upset that he jumps into his car, speeds off, crashes into a wall, and kills himself. Young Ian watches the whole scene unfold before him. "Ian went on staring into his own eyes. He couldn't seem to look away. He couldn't blink, couldn't move, because once he moved then time would start rolling forward again, and he already knew that nothing in his life would ever be the same."[4] And as the novel goes on to show, nothing ever was the same. Ian had to face the unspeakable truth that he had provoked his brother to commit suicide. Is it any wonder that he felt profound regret?

The Bible is full of stories of regret. One has special poignancy. One spring, when kings usually went out to war, King David of Israel decided to remain in Jerusalem and indulge his desire for leisure. One afternoon he woke from a nap and climbed to the roof of his palace, from where he could look out over the entire city. He spotted a woman bathing nearby. He saw she was beautiful, and he desired her. So he made inquiries about her and found out that her name was Bathsheba and that she was married to Uriah, one of his loyal soldiers. But he still sent for her and seduced her.

Bathsheba became pregnant, putting David in an awkward position. So he called her husband home from the front, hoping he would sleep with his wife while on his leave from war. But Uriah had too much integrity for that; he refused to enjoy the comforts of home and wife while his fellow soldiers were fighting in some far-off place. So David sent a secret message to the commander of his army, ordering him to make sure Uriah was killed in battle. When the deed was done, David brought Bathsheba into his harem. All was soon forgotten.

God was not pleased with David, however. He sent Nathan the prophet to confront him. David saw the error of his ways, repented of his sin, and accepted his punishment. The child conceived in the adulterous relationship died. But the tragic story did not end. Something insidious had wormed its way into David's soul, even after he repented of his sin, as if that one choice had disabled him spiritually. He became less decisive as a leader and less attentive as a father. When one of his sons, Amnon, raped a half-sister, Tamar, David did nothing. When another one of his sons, Absalom, murdered Amnon for his cruelty and then fled for his life, David again did nothing. When Absalom led a revolt against his own father to usurp his throne, David slipped away quietly, fearing a confrontation.

Finally the rebellion was squashed and Absalom was killed. David was overwhelmed with grief. He felt the pain of losing his son Absalom; he also felt regret because he knew why his son had died. His mind drifted back to that first decision to sleep with Bathsheba, and he saw the terrible consequences that had followed. In that moment David uttered one of the saddest laments found anywhere in literature: "O my son Absalom, my son, my son Absalom!" he cried. "Would I had died instead of you, O Absalom, my son, my son!"[5]

David's cry echoes down through history. It is the cry of regret. "O, my son Absalom!" We can easily substitute other names, other times, and other foolish choices. Such a cry may come from the lips of a father who has neglected a son, only to have that son commit suicide. It may come from a student who fails to study hard enough to fulfill his dream of becoming a lawyer. It may come from a coach who illegally takes money from boosters, causing a scandal that ruins his coaching career. It may come from a woman who has an affair that destroys her marriage.

I have my own regrets. I regret wasting my teenage years; I was lazy and never worked at much of anything until I started college. I regret working such long hours when I was a pastor. I regret the fights I had with Lynda. I regret the times I have been nasty, sarcastic, and explosive with my kids. I have said words I wish I could take back, and I have committed indiscretions I wish I could forget.

I became a Christian after my sophomore year in college. When I returned for my junior year, I was filled with enthusiasm. I wanted to tell everyone on campus about Jesus Christ. Though I had the necessary zeal for the task, I did not have the required humility. I hurt as many people as I helped, including some of my best friends, who soon enough became former friends. One said to me just before graduating, "If you are what it means to be a Christian, I never want to be one." True, his decision to follow or reject Christ does not depend solely on my influence, whether positive or negative. He is answerable directly to God. But to this day I regret my arrogance and judgmental attitude, which was disguised as Christian zeal.

Even little indiscretions can begin to gnaw at us, eventually leading to regret. A foolish comment we make about a friend's lack of coordination, which he hears from someone else, can create a strain in the relationship. A brief blowup at a meeting can alter the dynamics of a department. A missed opportunity for a conversation, badly needed by a troubled colleague, or a failure to show hospitality to a non-Christian neighbor can make people hostile to the Christian faith because of our callousness. Even little things can make us wish we could take something back or behave differently if we had the choice.

People with regret wish they could change the past, but they can never fulfill that wish. The past is beyond our reach, irreversible, like the loss of a precious family heirloom. We can merely rehearse a litany of "if onlys." "If only I had not taken that job," we say to a friend. "If only I had not drunk so much that night," we mutter to ourselves. "If only I had checked the tires before leaving on the trip." "If only I had spent more time with my daughter." "If only I had stopped smoking." "If only I had decided to stay in law and not run for political office." "If only I had waited longer before marrying."

THE POISON OF BITTERNESS

Regret is not the only way our past can control us. Bitterness can do the same thing. Regret usually involves choices we have made; bitterness usually results from choices other people make. It arises when we become acutely aware that we have been wronged.

Bitterness can turn the mind into a black hole of anger and revenge from which it is all but impossible to escape. The only thing a bitter person can think about is the hurt caused, the wrong done, the pain inflicted. A husband thinks constantly about what his wife did to spoil the tranquillity of their marriage. A woman spends every waking moment pondering what a business partner did to drive their business to bankruptcy. A quarterback replays the videotape showing a wide receiver dropping a pass that ruined the quarterback's only chance to get his team to a bowl game in his final season of eligibility. Bitterness poisons the soul.

Bitterness can poison everything else, too. A leader of the Warsaw ghetto uprising describes in the documentary film *Shoah* how he felt about Nazi brutality: "If you could lick my heart, it would poison you." Bitterness ruins health, destroys relationships, punishes friends and enemies alike, and wreaks havoc wherever it goes.

Shakespeare's *Othello, the Moor of Venice*, tells the story of a powerful nobleman, Othello, who falls in love with Desdemona, a woman of unusual beauty and goodness. They marry and experience great happiness together. Othello has an adviser, Iago, whom Othello passes over for promotion. Iago nurses his wound of bitterness caused by this snub and plots revenge. He feigns loyalty to Othello and manipulates his way into his confidence, all the while seeking his ruin. Slowly and insidiously he leads Othello to suspect Desdemona has been unfaithful. Othello becomes irrationally suspicious and makes wild accusations.

Meanwhile, Iago enjoys the power he wields and the evil he does. As he says in a soliloquy:

Divinity of hell!
When devils will the blackest sins put on,
They do suggest at first with heavenly shows,
As I do now.

Then, turning "virtue into pitch," he distorts the goodness of Othello and his wife, making a net to "enmesh them all." He succeeds all too well. Othello murders Desdemona and then, discovering his wife's innocence after her death, takes his own life.[6]

Bitter people have a certain logic on their side—the logic of victimization. Victims are quick to draw attention to the hurt done to them. It is true that one person's actions can have terrible consequences—a broken marriage, a disabled body, a lost job, a traumatized psyche. It is all so unfair. Victims are right. It *is* unfair; the pain *is* real; the loss *is* irreversible. Bitter people do have truth on their side. They are justified to feel rage. In fact, our entire society excels at the art of victimization, and it is not hard to see why. Everyone's experience is unique, after all. What right does anyone have to dismiss or mitigate the severity of someone else's pain?

But being right does not, by itself, make a person happy. Bitter people may be right, but they are also lonely. They may be able to make legitimate claims and accusations and win in a court of law, forcing everyone to concede that they are victims of wrongdoing. But is being right worth it? Is it worth the price paid in loneliness, isolation, and obsession? After bitter people win the trial and wring every concession imaginable from a jury, they are still left with their pain. They may be right, but their rightness has won them only a Pyrrhic victory. The years they have spent justifying their bitterness are wasted years, making the original loss pale in comparison.

I have never been given much to bitterness. I am more inclined toward regret because I tend to take responsibility for everything. Still, I have flirted on the edges of bitterness, largely as a result of the accident. Surprisingly, I have not felt bitterness toward the driver, whose own life had been a mess almost since the day he was born. Yet I have felt bitterness try to worm its way into my heart because of the circumstances I now face. I am busy most of the time, which makes me envy people who have more leisure time. I often feel isolated because I spend so much time at home.

Since Lynda died, I have discovered that intimacy requires so much effort and extra time that it hardly seems worth it. I attend social functions with other adults much less frequently than I used to. I feel cynical at times when I consider the loss and pain my kids have had to endure and will have to deal with in some way for the rest of their lives.

But I am deeply grateful that I have not become bitter. God's grace has delivered me from that peril. I think I have been kept from that vice by considering how bitterness would affect my own children. I want none of that poison in our home.

THE CHOICE TO GO ON

There is nothing we can do to change our past. It is as hard as granite, as immovable as a mountain. What is done is done. Regret, bitterness, revenge—none of these can alter what has already happened. No matter how many times we say "if only," regret cannot alter our past. No matter how bitterly we brood, blame, and accuse, the wrong done to us will remain as it is. No matter how often we rehearse a plot of revenge, we will never be able to reverse the course of events that created our pain in the first place. Regret, bitterness, and revenge will only ruin us. We will become prisoners in our own dark souls, suffocated by our own brooding thoughts.

Charles Frazier's novel, *Cold Mountain*, traces the Civil War journey of Inman, an injured deserter, who wants to return home to his beloved Cold Mountain and the woman who awaits him there. He endures profound suffering along the way, but realizes at the same time that obsessive grief and bitterness will leave him worse off than before. "You could grieve endlessly for the loss of time and for the damage done therein. For the dead, and for your own lost self. But what the wisdom of the ages says is that we do well not to grieve on and on. And those old ones knew a thing or two and had some truth to tell, Inman said, for you can grieve your heart out and in the end you are still where you were."

Inman knows that grief and bitterness can keep a person stuck in the past. He believes that, however severe the grief, "all your grief hasn't change a thing. What you have lost will not be returned to you. It will always be lost. You're left with only scars to mark the void. All you can choose to do is go on or not. But if you go on, it's knowing you carry your scars with you."[7]

Somehow, as Inman suggests, we must learn to move on, regardless of the severity of pain in the past. We cannot change what has happened. We do have one power within our grasp: We can trust God to *redeem the past*. To this topic I turn in the next chapter.

REDEEMING THE PAST

God can redeem our past if we let him. He redeems it by using the evil of what has happened to accomplish something good, thus transforming it so that it becomes like a vaccination. The poison ends up turning on itself, destroying the disease.

I have seen poor students become excellent teachers because their own failure as students showed them why students struggle and how they best learn. I have seen abused children become effective social workers because they understand how abuse starts and how it can be reversed. I have performed the weddings of young brides and grooms who have purposed to remain true to their vows, thus changing a direction set by their parents who, for whatever reason, could not make their marriages work.

Failures can give us clues to our calling. Charles Colson, hatchet man for President Nixon, was convicted of crimes associated with Watergate and spent seven months in prison. He turned his life over to Jesus Christ just before his incarceration. But his experience in prison did not leave him bitter or full of regret. Instead, it opened his eyes to the needs of prison inmates. He eventually started Prison Fellowship, a successful ministry to inmates and their families. Pope John Paul II grew up in Poland and witnessed firsthand the cruelties of communism. He has become one of the most zealous advocates of human rights in the world today. When still a teenager, Joni Eareckson Tada suffered a tragic accident that left her a quadriplegic. Her books, paintings, testimony, and ministry of hope now inspire millions of people.

It is easy to dismiss Chuck Colson, Pope John Paul II, and Joni Eareckson Tada as too extraordinary, like professional athletes or media celebrities, to serve as examples for ordinary people. But I

have observed the redemptive power of God at work in ordinary
people, too. One woman I know excels at encouraging others
even though she lost her husband recently in an automobile accident. I correspond with a teacher who invests time and energy in
troubled youth in spite of the fact that his father was brutally
murdered by just such a young person. I work with a colleague
who cares for more people on campus than anyone, though he
came from a loveless family. I have seen these people in action and
have benefited from their goodness. Each one of them is marked
by something from the past they cannot change. It is not in spite
of but because of past difficulties that they have become so kind
and influential.

EXPERIENCING REDEMPTION

God can redeem our past if we invite him into our lives and
ask him to give us grace. He will take what was once bad and turn
it into something good. He will make this work of grace happen
in our lives, but only if we are willing to do three things—receive
forgiveness, forgive others, and wait for God to work things out
for good.

First, we must be willing to receive forgiveness. I used to think
that if people had a problem with forgiveness, it was because they
refused to admit their need for forgiveness. They were quick to
accuse but slow to admit fault. They blamed more easily than they
accepted responsibility. Now I have come to realize many people
have a different problem with forgiveness. They cannot accept
God's forgiveness, and they cannot forgive themselves. They feel
so much regret that they are constantly reviewing their foolish
mistakes, playing the tape in their memory until their mistakes
dominate their lives. They hate themselves for what they have
done, and they cannot let the past go.

The problem is not with God. God sent Jesus Christ to deal
with the problem of sin once and for all. He promises to forgive
and to redeem. But we must be willing to admit our failures, take
responsibility for what we have done, and then accept forgiveness. We must be willing to let the past stand as it is, giving up all
rights to change it, deny it, or obsess about it.

Those who refuse to accept forgiveness pay a terrible price,
sometimes an ultimate price. I am no expert on the problem of

suicide, but I have had many conversations with people who have lost a loved one to suicide. In their stories one factor seems to prevail, especially among middle-aged Christian men.

These people appear to be good men, though perhaps given to perfectionism. Then something goes wrong—they are fired from their job, they embezzle money, or they have an affair. They inevitably face humiliation for their failure. Rather than admit doing wrong and accept forgiveness, which would mean loss of face, the only way out—at least in their minds—is to commit suicide. They cannot admit weakness and failure, a problem reinforced by living in a professional culture that shames people who feel fragile and powerless. Ironically, they often leave a note to the effect that they know they are doing wrong and are sorry for it. But they have decided to commit suicide because they did not want to cause any more hurt—as if their suicide would medicate the pain of their loved ones rather than exacerbate the pain.

It takes courage to accept forgiveness. Gordon MacDonald reached the pinnacle of success in evangelical Christianity when, in the late 1980s, he became the president of InterVarsity Christian Fellowship. Already a proven pastor and popular author, he stepped into that high-profile position with great expectations. But unknown to almost everyone, MacDonald had been having an affair. Shortly after assuming leadership of IVCF, the affair became public knowledge. MacDonald resigned in disgrace. Wisely, he sought help from friends, who advised him to withdraw from the public eye and submit to discipline. A group of men guided him through a long period of repentance and rehabilitation until he was ready once again to provide leadership for the church. MacDonald admitted his guilt, accepted forgiveness, and forgave himself as well. Gratefully, a capable but fallible leader was not permanently lost to the church.

Second, we must be willing to forgive. Bitterness can be just as ruinous to the soul as regret, if not more so. The one who suffers the most from bitterness is the one who is bitter. What infection does to the human body, bitterness does to the soul. It consumes. The antibiotic used to treat the disease of bitterness is forgiveness.

Forgiveness never happens in a moment; sometimes it takes a lifetime. Yet it begins with a decision. We must *want* to forgive and then *choose* to forgive, even if we do not feel like forgiving. Forgiveness, as Lewis Smedes argues in *Forgive and Forget*,[1] does not whitewash wrongdoing or justify evil. It assumes that the wrong done is truly wrong and deserves judgment and punishment. But forgiveness manifests a willingness to give up to God the right to judge and punish an offender, to see that person as a real human being, and to begin to wish him or her well. Forgiveness does not always restore the relationship, which requires movement from both sides. But it does let go of the hurt and move on. Forgiveness assumes that God is in control, that he will do justice at the proper time, and that he will make all things right in due time.

Thus, even when the relationship is *not* restored, because the offender doesn't care, or continues the offensive behavior, or disappears, or even dies, forgiveness works redemption into the heart of the person who does the forgiving. The act of forgiveness becomes a conduit for God's grace to work in that person, and God's grace can work wonders, whether or not the offender takes responsibility for the wrongdoing. Grace can heal the soul, cultivate character, create peace, and provide opportunities for ministry. It can transform a person so dramatically that he or she emits, as Paul testifies, a fragrance of life rather than an odor of death.[2]

It has only been in the last ten years that the mental health community has conducted research on forgiveness, and the results seem clear. Forgiveness mitigates depression and anxiety, increases self-esteem, and improves physical health and emotional well-being. It releases people from living in bondage and allows them to live in freedom. Forgiveness heals the soul.

An article on forgiveness in the January 2000 edition of *Christianity Today* tells the story of Sidna Masse, who became embittered after Diane, a friend and neighbor, was murdered. She learned later that Diane's husband was an accomplice. Sidna was enraged. "I had a dead friend and now lived behind three motherless kids," she said. "I felt I had every right to hate the murderer who caused this." But over time she began to notice that something was happening inside her own soul, something ugly and evil. The life sentence meted out to the murderer, Jennifer, did little to diminish her rage and hatred. "There was no relief in her sentencing. That's the thing with hatred and bitterness—it eats you alive. Every time I passed the house, I missed Diane and became angry all over again."

At first Sidna recoiled from the idea of forgiving Jennifer. But the teachings of Scripture persuaded her to reconsider. So she decided to write a letter to Jennifer to tell her that she had forgiven her. She described the impact of writing that letter: "A weight lifted. . . . That's when I learned that anger, bitterness, and unforgiveness keep you from experiencing the depths of joy." That letter was only the beginning. She began corresponding with Jennifer, and they have become friends.[3]

Forgiveness, of course, does not always come so quickly or end so happily. Forgiveness is a process, not an event. It is a decision of the will, not an emotion we feel. It sends us on a journey to which there is no obvious end. We may have to forgive a person many times over for a single offense as the consequences of his or her wrongdoing continue to plague us. I suspect that I will have to forgive the driver of the car when my children graduate from high school and college, when they marry and have children, because those events will awaken in me the feelings of loss that still live quietly in my soul.

Finally, we must be willing to wait for God to work things out for our good. As the prophet Isaiah wrote, speaking for the Lord God: "My thoughts are not your thoughts, nor are your ways my ways."[4] Neither does God's timing run on our timing. His timing can run both slower than ours and faster than ours. The Jews waited centuries for a Messiah to come. Obviously God took his time. But when he decided to act, he moved quickly and decisively, as the story of Jesus' life and ministry demonstrates.

Impatience cuts short the healing process. Real health comes slowly and often painfully. As anyone who has had major surgery will testify, the long-term benefits can be wonderful, though the short-term experience usually makes one think otherwise. In the case of redemption, the shortest distance between two points is not a straight line. Our human eyes see what we think God will do—or should do—to redeem the past. But our vision is severely limited. To accomplish his redemptive purposes, God sets in motion events that may follow a circuitous path to achieve the desired result.

So we must wait. But that is not all we can do. As we will see in chapter 14, we can also do the will of God in the present moment, however unpleasant that moment is. The past is over and done, but God is alive and well. Once we turn to him, we are immediately in the center of his will, regardless of the circumstances. God will begin at that very moment to work redemption into our lives, writing a story that will end in triumph, that will end "for [our] good."[5] God will somehow bring the consequences of the past on us in the form of a blessing. His grace will lead to a life of no regrets and free us from bitterness.[6] But we must be willing to wait for him to accomplish it.

REDEMPTION IN MY OWN PAST

I have seen God's redemptive power at work in my own family, although it took many years and engendered great pain. My sister, Diane, and I have lost both our parents. We lost our mother in the accident in 1991 and our father to cancer in 1999. We have spent many hours together reflecting on the past, searching, as if we were detectives, for clues to make sense of the past and find evidence of redemption. We have also sought to heal from a past that was not always happy or easy.

My mother grew up in a small town and came from a good, conservative Dutch family. She attended church and Christian school. But in her twenties she rebelled against her background. She dated men she should have avoided and eventually married one of them, my own father. She continued to live in rebellion until, several years later, her oldest brother exhorted her to return to God and the church. She heeded his advice, repented, and began to live for God again. Though her return to faith was genuine, she paid dearly for the decisions she had made during her rebellious years, including nearly thirty years of marital chaos.

My dad, one of the most likable and brilliant people I have ever known, came from a troubled background, which plagued him, like a stubborn parasite, his whole life. He was enormously successful in business early on, but fatal flaws in his character sabotaged his success and sent him on a downward spiral of humiliation and failure. He drank too much, cavorted too often, and tried too hard to succeed. He made many bad decisions and hurt many people, especially himself. He divorced my mother after three decades of marriage, and he remarried only a few months after the divorce. That marriage ended in divorce, too. He spent nearly thirty years enduring one crisis after another.

Obviously, he was not the only one affected. I still remember the whiskey glass that appeared to be glued to his hand, the nights he never came home, the shady characters he knew, the arguments that only ended after he stormed out of the house. He rarely attended my tennis matches and swimming meets, though I didn't care much at the time because his very presence embarrassed me. He was absorbed by his own neediness, driven by his own insecurity. If I could have viewed him more objectively, I would have felt compassion. But children are usually the last to feel or show compassion to parents because they are too close to the problem and too immature to feel anything but pain and outrage. During my teenage years I avoided or ignored him. When I became an adult, I started to challenge him, which led to years of conflict.

The story of my parents' lives could have ended badly, as badly as the plot foreshadowed. The relationship between my dad and me was strained for many years, though we never broke off communication. I wrote numerous letters to him. Much later, after his death, I reread some of the letters, which he had saved. My honesty and criticism startled me. I did not communicate much grace to him early on. I lambasted him for divorcing my mother and condemned him for remarrying. I disliked my dad during those years, and I saw little hope of redemption.

But life doesn't always play out the way we expect. God's presence changes everything, ultimately for the good, although it takes time. My mother's journey of faith started much sooner than my dad's. She became a woman of unusual faith and strength. Somehow she found the grace to rise above the pain of her marriage. She showed amazing restraint when my dad went into his tirades. She was kind and respectful without being a doormat. She never yelled or manipulated. She maintained poise and dignity in circumstances that would have pushed most over the edge.

She practiced hospitality, too. I have vivid memories of coming home from school and finding my mother providing comfort and counsel to the minister's wife in our church, who was weeping over the pain of living in a fishbowl and of trying to fulfill the expectations of a demanding congregation. I lived across the street from the high school. I went home for lunch almost every day, and I usually took ten to fifteen friends with me. Even when I had meetings during lunch, my friends went to my house for lunch anyway because they liked visiting with my mother.

Surprisingly, she had a wonderful sense of humor. In my younger years I had a tendency to exaggerate. When I was being disciplined, I would behave as if I was about to die a horrible death. I remember many occasions when my mother would have a hard laugh, then spank me or send me to my room. Somehow she learned to live in the tension of levity and seriousness. She had unusual goodness in her, a goodness forged in suffering.

After the divorce my mother moved back to Lynden, Washington, her hometown, and she went to work as director of nursing in a retirement home. She continued the trajectory of growth she had started many years before. She remained active in a church, provided hospitality to many, and showed gratitude and love to everyone she met. She excelled at being a homemaker, community leader, and friend.

She especially relished her role as a grandmother. She had a knack for giving special attention to the grandchild who was having the hardest time in life, whom she would invite over for a snack, call on the telephone, or give a special gift to. My kids called her the "outdoor grandma" because she played outside with them by the hour. She prayed faithfully for her grandchildren. She used to say that prayer for grandchildren is the primary calling of a grandparent.

When she died at age seventy-five, hundreds of people flocked to her funeral and lauded her as a modern-day good Samaritan. God turned her foolishness into something wonderful. The decision to repent and change invited grace into the home and set a course that resulted in profound healing.

My father's journey of redemption was harder. He endured years of financial hardship, which resulted in bankruptcy and led to the loss of a valuable piece of property on Lake Michigan that had been in the family for decades. He had to go to court more times than I can remember. He even spent time in jail. I felt shame that we shared the same last name, and I bristled whenever people said that I reminded them of my dad. I did not know then, as I do now, that resembling my dad is an honor, as long as I am reflecting what he could have become in his life had his redemptive journey started earlier.

When he hit bottom at the age of nearly eighty, he had only one way to look. He turned to God, and he found Christian friends who treated him with genuine kindness. He read Christian books and attended church faithfully. By then our relationship had been restored, which happened even before my mother died. We had both softened considerably. He had stopped trying to win my approval, and I had begun to care for him as the interesting, complex, broken man that he was. He became proud of me, largely because he saw me as the man he wanted to become, and I finally accepted the truth of who my dad was, not what I wanted him to be.

We talked on the phone every week or two, and he sent me newspaper clippings of stories about religion that appeared in papers and magazines he was reading. He was honest about his failures and regrets, too. He once told me, after watching me raise my kids during one of his visits, "Now I know what I missed. I was always too busy trying to make a buck. What a mistake I made." I think we had an unspoken agreement between us that I was somehow completing a story that he had begun, I was carrying on where he had left off. We never became as close as I am to my own sons, but we nevertheless shared a common bond and a sense of mutual appreciation.

In the fall of 1998 he discovered he had cancer. Typical for my dad, he was confident he could beat it. But in January he took a turn for the worse. The doctor summoned my sister, brother-in-law, and me to Michigan, where we had the rare privilege of spending three days with him before he died. We shared faith with him, prayed with him, sang to him, and spent many wonderful moments with his family and friends. We experienced a new level of intimacy and peace with him during those final days together. We were with him when he died. He told us he was ready to die, and he died believing.

Two days before he died I asked my dad what he wanted done at his funeral. He suggested a few hymns and biblical texts. Then he turned to me and said, "You must do it, son. You are the only one who can do it right." I will never forget that moment. His request was like a sign from God, who was assuring me that he was making all things good and right again.

I chose 2 Corinthians 5:16–17 as the text. At his funeral service, I talked about what it means to view someone like my dad
from a human point of view. What we saw in him was both glorious and deeply flawed. But that text does not end with a human
point of view; it ends with a divine point of view. "If anyone is in
Christ, there is a new creation: everything old has passed away;
see, everything has become new!"

My parents' journey was hard. There were many painful
moments along the way, for all of us. Even now I feel a great deal
of ambivalence—grateful for the way it ended, yet saddened by
the loss of my father as I think about all the wasted years. He
never really functioned as a father for me, at least not as I define
normal fatherhood. I am glad he died believing, though I wish he
had done better in the living. This longing will never go away.

The story did not end ignominiously or tragically, though it
seemed for many years that it would. I did not always believe that
God would or even could redeem what appeared on the surface
of things to be ugly, sordid, and evil. However real, the process of
redemption can be harsh and gritty, like stripping old paint off
furniture before it can be refinished. Even now I wish that my
dad's faith had taken firmer root and produced more fruit and that
I had been a better son to him. Yet I witnessed God's power at
work. God was telling a story that in the end turned out beautiful and holy. The pain was part of the story, but there was more
to the story than the pain. In the end our past was redeemed.

My story is only one. It is an example, imperfect and incomplete, of how God works redemptively. I know other sons whose
relationship with their fathers made more progress than mine did;
I also know sons whose fathers died before there was even a hint
of restoration. I have observed some marriages make it, against all
odds; others fail, though I thought there was still hope. The course
that redemption takes varies from person to person. It does not
always happen quickly; it does not always fix everything that was
broken. It does not always happen even within one's lifetime. But
that it does happen and will happen is sure because God is real and
good and true. However long, difficult, and perplexing, redemption will occur because God has pledged himself to it. Jesus Christ
is incontrovertible evidence of just how serious God is.

13

PREPARING FOR THE FUTURE

The world has just passed into a new millennium, crossing that magical barrier into the year 2000. Much to the surprise of doomsayers, the world did not end. Airplanes did not fall from the sky; gas, power, water, and other essential services were not shut off. During all the Y2K hype, I paused, as many people did, to dream about the future. I wondered what I would be doing in the year 2010. What would my children be doing? I tried on the idea of being a grandfather and felt comfortable in that role.

We like to dream about our future and imagine what we may be doing someday. But we should not be fooled. Our future constitutes a range of possibilities ahead of us, but we can never know for sure which ones will become reality until the future becomes the present. We cannot control the future. That we think we can is a foolish assumption.

Ignorance limits what we can know. Recently I heard a report on National Public Radio that surveyed predictions made by futurists at the turn of the last century. Like futurists today, they had predicted what would happen on the basis of what they already knew. Not one of them predicted the explosion of the technological revolution, the emergence of the Internet, the development of genetic research, or the rise and fall of Communism and Fascism.

Circumstances beyond our control will surprise us. A woman invests thousands of hours practicing the violin and becomes a virtuoso. A few weeks before her debut in Carnegie Hall, she loses a finger in a freak accident. A man proposes to his college sweetheart, and she accepts. They decide not to marry until she finishes a semester of studying in France. While she is there, she falls in love with a Frenchman and refuses to return to the United States. His heart is broken. No matter how confident we are of our plans, the future will always remain a range of possibilities, only one of which will become a reality. We can anticipate the future, but we cannot control it. We simply do not know what tomorrow will bring.

I have every reason to believe that I will be living in Spokane and teaching at Whitworth College ten years from now. But I could be surprised. This summer I am planning to take my children with me to Kenya, where I will be teaching at a university. Who knows what will happen as a result of that one experience? I may return to Kenya and teach at that university for the rest of my life. I could meet a missionary who invites me to move to Singapore. I could marry a widow with ten children. I could get sick and die. I have no idea what will happen. I can plan, I can predict, but I cannot know and control.

In Reformation times a woman named Katherine von Bora took vows to become a nun, which required her to confine herself in a cloister for the rest of her life. She wanted to pass her days living a simple, quiet life—doing chores, worshiping God, praying, and meditating on Scripture. But Katherine lived in a time and place swirling with change. She could no more ignore or avoid what was happening in Europe than could the pope, whose church was facing massive upheaval. Her convent was closed, her friends were married off to ex-priests, and she alone remained, without home and livelihood.

The man who took charge of finding husbands for her fellow nuns could not find a husband for her, so he married her himself! They had six children. Their home served as a center of hospitality for hundreds of people. It was full of music, conversation, and activity. Her husband faced constant controversy and opposition. He had a death sentence hanging over his head for all the years she knew him. They became two of the most famous people in Europe. Little did Katherine von Bora know, when she took her vows as a young woman to become a nun for life, that she would marry Martin Luther and be thrust into the whirlwind of the Reformation.

C. S. Lewis explained why utopian dreamers, who claim to know the future with such certainty, are usually wrong and often dangerous. The past and the present share one trait in common:

They are both real. The past happened; it is fact. The present is happening; it is also fact. But the future has not yet happened. It is not fact, only possibility.

Utopian dreamers try to convince others to accept their predictions for the future. The Aryan race will dominate history for a thousand years; the communist state will emerge forever as the perfect society; Jesus will return and establish his earthly millennial kingdom at such and such a time and place. These dreamers are as sure of the future as they are of the laws of nature. Ironically, some of them justify terrible crimes against humanity for the sake of that predicted future. They sacrifice everything for what they are positive will happen.[1]

But the future is not so predictable. No one can know with certainty what will happen next week or next year, to say nothing about next century. The future is slippery and elusive, and it will surprise us. We may experience tragedy just when we thought we had life by the tail; we may enjoy moments of pleasure just when we thought we would never pull out of a tailspin; we may find opportunity when we thought we were stuck forever in the same old routine. The world map will be configured in ways scholars and statesmen did not predict. An author may write a book that forever changes the way we think about the world. Other Edisons and Einsteins and Mother Teresas and Stravinskis and Martin Luther Kings and Joe DiMaggios will emerge and dazzle us with their brilliance, skill, and feats.

THE POWER OF FEAR

There are at least two unhealthy ways to respond to a lack of certainty about our future: fear and worry. Of these two, fear is more rooted in actual reality. We usually fear a specific object or situation—strangers, crowded rooms, snakes, rejection, or death, for example. We fear what we know. Fear has a clarity, sharpness, and immediacy to it. It is also strangely rational, at least to the person who feels the fear.

For example, I fear heights. When I am making my way to the top of a mountain on a chairlift, I feel genuine fear. I imagine the worst happening. I convince myself that, unlike every other person who has ever been on that chair before, I am in mortal danger.

I see the chair jumping the cable and hurling me to the ground. My fear may be irrational, at least in the minds of friends riding in the chairlift with me; but it is perfectly rational to me. I *know* something will go wrong. I feel it, then work it out logically. No one can persuade me to think otherwise.

Not that fear is always a bad thing. It can be a healthy reflex that serves us well. If the chair on which I am riding did jump the cable, I would probably be killed, or at least seriously injured. My fear is based on a genuine threat that, if realized, will do me real harm. When we fear, our body produces adrenaline, which makes the heart pump more blood, increases sensory awareness, sharpens our instincts, and infuses us with greater physical strength. Fear makes us ready to fight or flee.

In the film *Braveheart*, the main character, William Wallace (a historical figure who lived in the thirteenth century), leads Scotland in a revolt against English rule. He is captured and put in prison, where he awaits certain torture and death. He knows he will suffer unimaginable pain. Sitting alone in his cell, he whispers to God, "I am so afraid." He has good reason to be afraid, considering the cruelty of medieval torture. Yet fear concentrates his energy and turns his will into steel. He suffers and dies without crying for mercy or compromising his beliefs.

My youngest child, John, has typical childhood fears, which his older brother likes to dismiss in a supercilious tone—as if he never had such fears when he was younger. John is not unusual. Most children fear ghosts and monsters that hide during the day but come out at night. The fear is real enough. No, there are no monsters and ghosts hiding under his bed. But there are real beings populating the spiritual world that should awaken genuine fear in all of us.

When I was a college chaplain, I received a call one night from a student who asked me to visit him in his dorm room. I was not happy about being called at 2:00 A.M. But he said it was important, so I went to his room. When I arrived, I was surprised to find ten students who wanted to talk with me about *The Exorcist*, which they had just watched together. They were utterly terrified by the movie. We talked for two hours. I came away from the conversation feeling disappointed, not because the students were afraid but because they overcame their fear so easily. I wished that they had felt fear for a while longer. Certain powers at work in the world should make all of us shudder. It is to our peril that we think they are silly.

Adults have fears, too. Our fears are usually more practical and earthly. We fear a stock market crash, another world war, global warming, the loss of a job, or the death of a child. I think often about what would happen to me if I lost another of my children. I do not know how I would respond or what I would do. In my prayers I tell God that such a loss would be more than I could bear. This fear haunts me.

The Bible has a lot to say about human fear. The secret to overcoming fear is not to deny or dismiss it but to order it properly. In other words, we should fear the right things. A sense of proportion helps. We should fear the loss of a child more than failure in a job, sickness more than pain, hell more than death. And we should fear God most of all, because only he has ultimate and final authority over life and death. And if we do fear God most of all, our other fears will find their proper place. Jesus said, "I tell you, my friends, do not fear those who kill the body, and after that can do nothing more. But I will warn you whom to fear: fear him who, after he has killed, has authority to cast into hell. Yes, I tell you, fear him!"[2]

The Bible tells many stories of people who felt acute fear in the presence of God. Isaiah felt such dread that he wished he was dead. "Woe is me!" he said. "I am lost."[3] Moses hid his face from the brightness of God's glory, which threatened to consume him.[4] Thomas à Kempis warned: "Fear God's judgments. Dread the Almighty's anger. Do not presume to probe the works of the Most High, but look into your own failings, into how far you have fallen short, and into how many good things you have neglected to do."[5]

The New Testament, however, provides a useful counterpoint. It teaches that healthy fear of God—"awe" or "reverence" are perhaps better words—will actually mitigate our fears, even of God. The most common greeting angels imparted to people was "Fear not!" Jesus spoke with paradox when he commanded us to fear God, because he has absolute authority to cast us into hell, yet not to fear God, because he cares about us. "Are not five sparrows sold for two pennies? Yet not one of them is forgotten in

God's sight. But even the hairs of your head are all counted. Do not be afraid; you are of more value than many sparrows."[6]

As we fear God more, we will fear everything else less.[7] One big fear will mitigate all lesser ones. The famous seventeenth-century philosopher and mathematician Blaise Pascal wrote, "There is a virtuous fear which is the effect of faith, and a vicious fear which is the product of doubt and mistrust. The former leads to hope as relying on God, in whom we believe; the latter inclines to despair.... Persons of the one character fear to lose God; those of the other character fear to find him."[8]

THE PROBLEM OF WORRY

Worry is different from fear. If fear is like a raging fever, worry is like a low-grade temperature. It nags at us, simmers in our souls, or hovers in the back of our minds like a faint memory. We may fear certain realities, like death; we worry about vague possibilities. Worry distracts us more than paralyzes us. It is like a leaky faucet we never get around to fixing.

Not all worry is bad. Worry can make us wise, cautious, and conservative about serious matters. For example, I worry about my kids. Whenever Catherine gets in the driver's seat, I tell her to buckle up, observe the speed limit, and drive defensively. I warn my children about strangers, dangers, and evil in the world. I caution them about the insidious influence of TV, rock music, the Internet, and movies. I worry. Moreover, I am unapologetic about my worry.

My two teenagers think my worry betrays paranoia about the world and lack of confidence in them. They are forever telling me to "relax," "chill out," or "get a life." But I always respond the same way. "Worry is in the parental job description," I tell them. I remind them that the world is a dangerous place, and worry is an expression of parental vigilance.

Nevertheless, worry can cause problems, of which three come to mind. First, worry is rooted in unreality. When we worry about the future, we worry about something that does not yet exist. It *could* happen, but then again, it might not. What if we fail to get the promotion? What if we get fired from our job? What if we never get married? What if our kids get into trouble? What if the stock market crashes or our marriage crumbles? We worry about unforeseen and undesirable circumstances we *could* face.

Such worry is literally about *nothing*. We have no idea what will happen in our future. We can speculate and imagine, but we cannot know. Sales of this book could flop; then again, it could become a bestseller. I could lose my job next year; then again, I could win a major award for teaching. I could get cancer; then again, I could live to be a hundred. I could go bankrupt; then again, I could win the Lotto (okay, that's unlikely, because I never buy Lotto tickets) and retire to some Mediterranean villa. I do not know and cannot know what the future holds.

Worry makes the imagination run wild as we turn remote possibilities into raging realities. It erodes the spirit, distracts the mind, dulls our creativity, and wastes our energy. It prevents us from living fully in the present. The fact is, I have not even completed this book yet, so I have no idea how it is going to sell. I have not lost my job yet, and it is unlikely I ever will. I have not had health problems yet. What purpose is there in worrying?

Second, worry leads to indecision. That we have to make big decisions is unavoidable. We have to decide which college to attend (if we attend one), which major to study, which career to pursue after we graduate, and which job to take when we enter the workforce. We have to decide where to live, whom to marry (if we do), and what to do with our time and money.

It is easy to become frozen in indecision, like a deer blinded by the headlights of a car. We ponder which of the many options before us represents God's will, and we fret because we do not know which option is the correct one. What if there is no clear direction? What if all the options are good ones, though we can only choose one? What if we make a wrong choice?

So we weigh the options. We sigh because there seems to be no way of knowing which is the right or best choice, and we end up deciding nothing. François Fénelon, a mystic and spiritual writer living in France in the late seventeenth and early eighteenth centuries, thus advised: "Don't worry about the future—worry quenches the work of grace within you. The future belongs to God. He is in charge of all things. Never second-guess him."[9]

Indecision helps no one. We must realize one indisputable fact—we cannot control our future. It will continue to loom before us, forever out of reach. Whatever we decide—a trade school or community college? accountant or teacher? marriage or singleness? New York or Reno?—will always surprise us with strange twists and turns. Worrying about our future will not change it, nor will it help us make good choices.

Finally, worry causes distraction, which keeps us from giving our time and energy to what matters most—the present moment (the subject of the next chapter). As finite creatures, we have only so much time, energy, and ability. Worry divides us against ourselves. When we worry about what is beyond our control, we devote less of ourselves to what we can control. Ironically, worry keeps us from exercising the one power we do have over our future—the power to prepare for it by how we live in the present.

If students worry about final exams, they will be less likely to prepare for them. Anxiety about poor performance becomes a self-fulfilling prophecy. Likewise, if parents worry about raising teenagers, it will drain their energy to be attentive to them when they are young, thus contributing to the very problems they dread. Jesus said, "So do not worry about tomorrow, for tomorrow will bring worries of its own. Today's trouble is enough for today."[10] Paul advises us to make good use of our time as a way of combating evil, and he warns against worrying because it leads to lack of peace and fear.[11]

Overcoming Worry

There is no simple way to overcome worry. We come by it naturally, and there are too many good reasons why we should worry. But we can learn to control our worries. We can pray about them, prepare for the future, and learn to live in hope.

First, *prayer* mitigates worry. Paul wrote, "Do not worry about anything, but in everything by prayer and supplication with thanksgiving let your requests be made known to God. And the peace of God, which surpasses all understanding, will guard your hearts and your minds in Christ Jesus."[12] If we pray about our worries, we will find peace, gain greater confidence in God, and find relief from worry. When we pray, God changes us.

But prayer does something else, too. Spiritual writers have long argued that prayer changes God. He hears our prayers and acts. He alters the course of history as a response to our prayers.

Richard Foster makes exactly this point. When we pray, he writes, "we are working with God to determine the future! Certain things will happen in history if we pray rightly. We are to change the world by prayer."[13] History happened as it did because someone prayed. History will take a different course tomorrow because someone is praying now.

It is not as if God is like a genie in a bottle. Prayer requires humility, persistence, and patience. God will answer our prayers and change the future from what it otherwise would have been, but that future includes us. We will be actors in the very future we pray about. God will answer our prayers by *using us* to change the future. Moses was happy to hear that God planned to deliver the Hebrews from slavery, in response to their prayers. He was less happy when God said, "Come, I will send *you* to Pharaoh."[14] Moses did not initially consider *he* would be the answer to the Hebrews' prayer. When we pray, we should brace ourselves for what can happen. We may be the answer to our own prayer.

Every morning I pray that God will go ahead of me and prepare the way for what is going to happen that day. I pray him into the classroom and office and home. I ask him to protect me from temptation and keep my eyes peeled for signs of how he is working in my life. I visualize God clearing out a straight path for me to follow so that I can accomplish what is appropriate for each day. Isaiah's comforting words come to mind:

> In the wilderness prepare the way of the LORD,
>   make straight in the desert a highway for our God.
> Every valley shall be lifted up,
>   and every mountain and hill be made low;
> the uneven ground shall become level,
>   and the rough places a plain.
> Then the glory of the LORD shall be revealed,
>   and all people shall see it together,
>   for the mouth of the LORD has spoken.[15]

In addition to praying about the future, we can also *prepare* for it. One major way of doing this is to live well in the present. We can practice spiritual discipline, develop character, form lasting friendships, and become a person of faith. We can refine skills, like computing and speaking, and manage our resources responsibly. In doing so, we will be better equipped to do whatever the future requires of us.

What would such preparation mean for me? I can only imagine. If I pastor a church, proper preparation will help me preach good sermons and provide wise leadership. If I write a bestseller, I will be more likely to respond to my good fortune with humility and gratitude rather than conceit. If I adopt five children, I will be sturdy enough to handle the demands of being father to a large family. If, however, I lose my job, I will be ready to face the hardship with dignity and resourcefulness. If I write a book that flops, I will be glad for the impact it had on me as I wrote it and on the few people who do read it. If I lose another child—God forbid— I will be better prepared to endure it with the assurance that I loved that child as much as I could while he or she was still alive.

A good friend recently wrote me to express his own reflections on God's will. "In our instantly gratified world today," he wrote, "we have higher expectations of things coming to us on silver platters, including our vocational destiny." He referred to Abraham Lincoln as an example of someone who faced "failures, humiliations, and frustrations" before achieving his goals and accomplishing God's will. We should expect the same. My friend has personally endured much difficulty working for an inner-city community center—"at a measly $4.55 an hour to babysit screaming kids and deal with irresponsible parents who did nothing but criticize the staff and the program."

Yet that job inspired him to return to school to become a teacher. It helped him develop practical skills, creative lesson plans, and positive methods of communication, along with such character qualities as patience and endurance. Even the low wages worked to his advantage. "My service and experimental activities came as a donation under *my* control," he wrote, which relieved him of the pressure of high expectations. He concluded, "That whole year was an example of *preparation*. Isn't that in reality what most of life is? Every so often we celebrate the fruits of success, but let us *not* deceive ourselves into thinking that God's will means achieving a final product without preparation along the way."

Finally, we should live in *hope*. Christians have every reason to have earthly hope. Though we are mortal and life is fragile, we can take comfort in the fact that "the sun will come up tomorrow."

Having earthly hope means that we can attend school and earn degrees, get a job and make an income, set goals and plan schedules and take care of details, all the while assuming that life will continue here on earth for some time to come. There is a good kind of worldliness; there is much in this life worth living for.

God gave assurances of earthly hope to Noah after he survived the great flood. When dry land appeared and he released all the animals from the ark, Noah offered a sacrifice to God in gratitude for his deliverance. God then promised that he would never again destroy the earth in that way. The seasons would come and go, farmers would sow seed and harvest crops, and children would grow up and live on their own.[16] God's word to Noah ensures that tomorrow will be somewhat like today, that the natural world will function with some degree of regularity. Such earthly hope provides a good reason for us to live responsibly. As a mentor once told me, "Live today as if it were your last—but plan to live a lifetime."

That "last day," of course, will eventually arrive. The end will come—not just the end of our lives but the end of history. Thus, we should also never forget that we have a heavenly hope. The New Testament often refers to this hope, largely to encourage believers who are suffering persecution. It is grounded in Christ's second coming, who will bring about the world's final and complete redemption. Yet though a sure hope, it is also an unseen hope. "Now hope that is seen is not hope," Paul writes. "For who hopes for what is seen? But if we hope for what we do not see, we wait for it with patience."[17]

Paul looked forward to the resurrection of the dead. That was his final and greatest hope.

> Listen, I will tell you a mystery! We will not all die, but we will all be changed, in a moment, in the twinkling of an eye, at the last trumpet. For the trumpet will sound, and the dead will be raised imperishable, and we will be changed. For this perishable body must put on imperishability, and this mortal body must put on immortality.[18]

Earthly hope and heavenly hope exist in a creative tension. When health is good, relationships are strong, work is productive, and life is meaningful, it is entirely appropriate to live today with a view to tomorrow. But we must never forget our heavenly hope. This world is not all there is. Life on earth is important but not ultimate. It points beyond itself, toward heaven, which is our true home.

Though we were created to live in this world, we are redeemed to live in heaven. This world is wonderful, but it is also fallen, a gray and grim place where suffering often has the final word. Disappointment, insecurity, pain, and death remind us to turn our gaze toward heaven and to hope for final victory. Jesus will come again and establish his kingdom. Then all tears will be wiped away and all brokenness healed. In the end, nothing, not even the past or the future, will be able to separate us from the love of God in Jesus Christ our Lord.[19]

14

LIVING IN THE WONDER OF
THE PRESENT MOMENT

One of my favorite movies is *Groundhog Day*. If ever a redemptive movie was made, this is it. It tells the story of Phil Connors, an arrogant weatherman from Pittsburgh, who is dispatched to the town of Punxsutawney, Pennsylvania, to do his weather report live at their annual Groundhog Day Festival. Connors hates this assignment and likens it to purgatory. He does his weather report with obvious disdain and then urges the film crew to return to Pittsburgh as quickly as possible. But a winter storm turns them back. So Connors is forced to spend another night in Punxsutawney.

When he wakes up the next morning, however, he discovers that it is again February 2, Groundhog Day, which he is forced to live over again. The same thing happens the next day, too. And on it goes. Connors wakes up morning after morning, but it is always February 2. Every scene happens just as it did the day before; every character remains just as each one was the day before. He has entered a time warp.

At first, he is overjoyed by the experience. He can live as he pleases and not face any consequences. So he decides to experiment. He indulges his appetite for alcohol and sex. But soon he tires of pleasure and begins to despair, realizing that he cannot escape the day. He has entered into an eternity of Groundhog Days, and it is hell. He commits suicide dozens of times, only to wake up the next morning on February 2 with circumstances just as they were.

Connors finally makes a discovery. He realizes that although the day never changes, he can use the day to change himself. He can become a better person. At first he develops his talents. He takes piano lessons, masters ice sculpture, goes to school, memorizes poetry, learns a language, all by using just one day over and over again.

But then he discovers something else as well. He can help other people. He begins to roam around the town to learn what else has happened on Groundhog Day. He discovers that a man chokes on his food and dies, a couple breaks off their engagement, and a boy falls from a tree. Connors intervenes, altering the course of events. Every day he shows up at the same time and place to help people in crisis, saving all of them hundreds of times. He enjoys the role of serving others and becomes a hero—or better, a saint—in a town that stays forever stuck in one day. Connors only has that one day in which to live. His life is literally confined to the present moment, which goes on for what seems like an eternity. But he learns to live that one day well.

The story finally ends when Connors wakes up one morning and discovers it is February 3. But by then it is not just the date that has changed. Connors has changed, too. He has become a new man—musician, sculptor, poet, doctor, counselor, helper, friend to everyone—all in one day.

This is not such a fanciful story. As I have already suggested, God's experience of time and our experience of time are not the same. As an infinite being, God lives in all time as if it were the present. As finite creatures, we only have the present. What if, from God's point of view, every day is pretty much the same? What if dates and places, calendars and circumstances are irrelevant? What if the world is really like a Groundhog Day that God uses to change us so that we in turn can change the world? What if the passage of time (from past to present to future) is the least like eternity and the present moment is the most like eternity because it is the only moment we have to know the eternal God?

We can do nothing to change our past. Can regrets about yesterday change what has happened? Not at all! We can do nothing to control our future. Will worry about tomorrow give us any greater control over what lies ahead? Absolutely not! We can only live in the present. If we live for God, God promises to use the present moment to redeem the past, however unchangeable, and to prepare us for the future, however unpredictable, until all of life becomes a glorious testimony to his love and power.

GOD'S RADICAL GRACE

God promises to do this work of redemption and preparation because he is gracious. His grace is free, but it is not cheap. He abhors sin and evil, and he judges sin for what it is, an affront to his greatness and glory. But God is also good, kind, and gracious. He loves sinners and wants to show mercy. He sent Jesus to uphold his integrity and justice and to show his mercy. The cross of Christ is the crossroad where God's justice and mercy meet. It demonstrates how serious God is in dealing with sin, yet it also proves how earnest he is in giving mercy. The cross should sober us about the serious consequences of sin. It should also woo us back to God, who embraces us, prodigals though we are, as his children.

We need God's grace to do his will. Without that, we remain prisoners to our past and future, dominated by regret and bitterness or by fear and worry. Grace changes everything. It draws us back to God, placing us in the center of his will, no matter what we have done or how bad our circumstances. No one is so sinful as to be beyond God's grace. We can be rogues and misfits. We can be divorced ten times. We can be alcoholics, prostitutes, embezzlers, abusers, liars, or murderers. We can be Stalin or Hitler. What we have done matters little; what God has done matters a great deal. Once we turn to him in sincere repentance and faith, we become recipients of God's inexhaustible grace. From that moment on our life starts over, though the circumstances of our life may stay the same.

God's grace manifests God's character, and it is central to his plan for us. It is like a spring of living water, as Jesus said of himself. As God wills to give us grace, he also wills that we receive it and surrender to him. When we do, God will make this present moment alive with his power and do something wonderful in our lives. Thus our sinfulness, however despicable, cannot cut us off from God's grace.

Neither can our circumstances. We may be sick from a lifetime of smoking, be broke from bad investments, be on trial for past crimes, or be unemployed as a result of foolish choices or terrible injustice. It doesn't matter. The past is over, but God is alive and well. Once we turn to him, we are immediately in the center of his will. God will begin at that very moment to work redemption in our lives, writing a story that will end in triumph. He will bring the consequences of the past upon us in the form of a blessing. There is no place so distant from God that he is not present.[1] There is no deed so bad that God cannot or will not forgive.[2] What a comfort to know that we can be in the center of God's will once we turn to him! God's grace is that radical!

BEWARE OF PRESUMPTION!

But we must be wary of presumption. It is easy to take advantage of God's grace and put off doing his will. *If grace is always available to me*, we may think to ourselves, *then why not continue to sin?*[3] If we can always return to God and do his will, no matter what we have done, then why be in a hurry to do his will in the first place? Why not just enjoy the pleasures of sin and turn to God at a more convenient time? How do we find motivation to do God's will if the threat of forever missing that will is removed?

There are two reasons why we should avoid presumption. First, presumption is spiritually dangerous. True, choosing to pursue a course of action contrary to God's will does not change his mind about us. God will always love us, always forgive us, and always welcome us home again, no matter how wayward we have been. But disobedience can change our minds about God. Spurning grace and disobeying God hardens the heart. Every time we disobey God, calculating that at some later time we will return to him, we will find it increasingly difficult to return at all. We will begin to doubt our own sincerity, lose our capacity to discern right from wrong, and deteriorate to the point where we are no longer able to trust ourselves and the authenticity of our own repentance. We will become like a lover who takes advantage of the goodness of his beloved so often that he loses all capacity to know what real love is.

In *The Pilgrim's Progress* the main character, Christian, visits Interpreter's House on his way to the Celestial City. There he is taught a parable about hardness of heart. He sees a man in an iron cage. This man despairs because he has sinned against God and does not believe God will forgive him. But God has not locked him in that cage of despair. He has locked himself in. He does not really despair of God, although that is what he claims; he despairs of himself. He has presumed on the grace and goodness of God once too often. God will forgive him, but he can no longer repent. Presumption is dangerous because it turns us away from God.[4]

Second, presumption is foolish. As I tell my children, "I will always love you because you are my children. That is what parents do." But how I express that love depends on how they respond to my love. They can receive love the easy way, or they can receive it the hard way. If they choose to disobey me, they must face the consequences. They will have to go to their rooms, miss social activities with their friends, or do extra chores. My love for them will not change, but the way they experience it will. They will experience it as discipline, and they will miss out on enjoying their favorite activities, such as pizza and a movie on a Friday night.

We have freedom to choose whether or not we will do God's will. We do not, however, have the freedom to alter the consequences of the choices we make. If anything, our feeble attempt to weasel out of consequences only exacerbates the problem, sending us in a downward spiral of denial and deceit. Failure to do God's will, therefore, will inevitably make us wish we could reverse decisions made in the past. But that is impossible. Once we make a decision, it becomes a part of our unchangeable past, which in turn creates a new set of circumstances in which to do his will in the present.

WHY MAKE THE GAME SO HARD?

It is never too late to do the will of God because God's grace abounds for sinners. But it is always too late to change the consequences of our past decisions. Life is hard enough as it is, full of risk, pain, and confusion. Why make it harder by thrusting ourselves into circumstances we could have avoided if we had only done God's will in the first place? We can do his will while being married to a prostitute (as Hosea discovered), recovering from drug addiction, or serving time in prison, but why dig ourselves into a hole if we can avoid it?

The way our past decisions shape our present circumstances resembles a game of chess. We make a move with a selected piece. Once we lift our finger from that piece, that move becomes irreversible. It creates a new configuration on the chessboard for our opponent. Her move, in turn, reconfigures the chessboard for our move. Each move, in other words, creates the context for the next. We can make a series of bad moves and still remain in the game. But we will put ourselves at a disadvantage and find ourselves scrambling to survive. Why make a bad move if we have good ones available to us?

Robert Huntford's *The Last Place on Earth* tells the true story of the race to reach the South Pole between a Norwegian, Roald Amundsen, and the more famous Englishman, Robert Scott. Amundsen reached the pole ahead of Scott in 1912, then made it safely back to base camp. Scott died, along with his four companions, on their return journey. Huntford wrote his book to set the record straight, for it was assumed from the beginning that, although Amundsen won the race and Scott died, Scott was the real explorer, the heroic figure, and the true scientist. Scott was lionized after his tragic death, whereas Amundsen was shunned, especially in Britain.

Huntford sought to demonstrate that Scott was actually arrogant and stupid. It was not bad luck that led to his failure and eventual death; it was his ineptitude and lack of preparation. At every turn he made bad decisions; yet until the very end he could have salvaged the expedition and survived. One misstep after another kept setting his crew back, however, depriving them of food, time, and energy. He dug his men into a hole so deep that they could not get out.

Scott was too proud, however, to admit mistakes and listen to advice. For example, he refused to pack the quantity of food that advisers had suggested he would need in case of emergency. He got lost because he did not listen to the advice of his men. And he kept blaming bad weather and sickness for their problems rather than admit he had failed. He justified himself and his decisions to the very end, painting himself as a hero and insisting he was the victim of forces beyond his control. This self-justification was evident when, just before his death, he wrote in his diary:

We are showing that Englishmen can still die with a bold spirit, fighting it out to the end.... I think this makes an example for Englishmen of the future.... The causes of the disaster are not due to faulty organization but to misfortune in all risks which had to be undertaken.... I do not think human beings ever came through such a month as we have come through.

Huntford suggests otherwise. "Scott had brought disaster on himself by his own incompetence, and throwing away the lives of his companions. He had suffered retribution for his sins. But he was justifying himself, finding excuses, throwing the blame on his subordinates."[5]

Past decisions set the stage for present options. We can excel at stupidity, if we want to. We can sleep late, lose our job, commit adultery, gamble away our life savings, neglect our children, and deceive those closest to us. We can wait until the last moment before repenting of our sin. Amazingly, if we repent in sincerity, God will embrace us. But we cannot alter the consequences of our choices. So why put ourselves in a bad position if we can avoid it? Why make the game harder than it already is?

Take a college student. He frets about choosing a future vocation. His preoccupation distracts him, so he neglects his studies and gets poor grades. At the end of his sophomore year he finally decides to pursue a career in medicine. But his grades are too low for him to get into medical school, which only adds to his worries. When he does apply to several medical schools, they all reject him. Those rejection letters send him into a tailspin of depression. He thinks about enrolling in a graduate program in biology to position himself better to get into medical school the next year, but he wonders if it is worth the trouble and time. So he does nothing for a year. Once again, he applies to medical school and, once again, is rejected.

He finally concludes that the medical profession is not for him. He decides instead to enter a teacher education program to become a high school biology teacher. He postpones investigating options, however, because he cannot decide whether he wants to enter an undergraduate program or a master's program. So he misses the application deadline.

Or take the example of a husband who spends years driven by a desire for professional success. His wife and family pay the price. She complains, but he makes excuses, promising, "Next year, when things slow down, I'll spend more time at home." Finally, she files for separation. In her heart she wants to see the marriage restored, but she sees little evidence he is willing to change. The separation is her attempt to give him a wake-up call. But her husband assumes it is too late to restore his marriage and devotes even more time to his job. Years later, of course, he regrets the decisions he made as he realizes the treasure he lost in his wife and his children.

Again, take a young professional who rises quickly in the corporate ladder until she receives promotion to vice president of sales. She is likeable and sociable, and her savvy with people serves her well. But she doesn't like details and thus relies on loyal subordinates to handle them for her. As she is moving through the company, they warn her about her inattention to detail, but she simply smiles and says that she is grateful they make her look so good. The last promotion, however, puts her into a position where she has no one to cover her weaknesses. The president warns her about her failures, but she becomes defensive, accusing her fellow workers of jealousy and disloyalty. She eventually loses her job. But instead of learning from her mistakes, she hires a lawyer and files a lawsuit, claiming she is the victim of sexual discrimination.

As if playing a game of chess, these people made decisions that reconfigured the circumstances of their lives, each decision creating the context for subsequent decisions. Each bad choice put them into a more disadvantaged position, although never once were they completely devoid of good options. Their foolishness prevented them from seeing the options they did have. They failed, in other words, to take advantage of the options still available and continued to make bad choices. They never saw how they could do God's will that was staring them in the face.

MAKING THE MOST OF THE TIME

We could multiply these examples. God would be delighted to help people like this, not by delivering them from the consequences of their foolish decisions but by enabling them to endure and mature through them. Had they turned to God, they would have found themselves in the center of his will, and he would have given them grace to handle failure, divorce, loss of job, or the like. Although we at times see only failure, God views our circumstances from a larger frame of reference and wants to accomplish some greater purpose in them, in spite of our bad choices.

The will of God consists, in other words, of a life lived for God right where we are. It is not a set of ideal circumstances we may wish for ourselves. It is the godly course we set for our lives in the circumstances we face. We can start at any time. Once we turn to him, we receive grace and find ourselves in the center of his will, even if nothing in our current situation changes. He puts us on the course to the Celestial City and gives us the grace to do his will on the way to that destination.

The apostle Paul understood the urgency of discipleship when he told the church in Ephesus to make "the most of the time because the days are evil."[6] "Making the most of the time" does not imply that we should live a frenzied and frantic life. Piety does not require us to live in a state of panic, as if trying to escape a forest fire. Our view of time should be biblical, not modern. We should make the most of the time according to the biblical definition of time.

There are two words for time in the Greek language—*chronos* and *kairos*. *Chronos* has to do with clocks, calendars, schedules, agendas, and pressure. The clock ticks, the hours pass, and deadlines loom. *Chronos* requires us to get as much done as we possibly can. It demands efficiency, productivity, and punctuality. *Kairos*, by contrast, has to do with important events, the significance of daily experience, and the wonder of the present moment. It is transcendent reality invading earthly reality, eternity revealing itself in time, the extraordinary manifesting itself in the ordinary. We exist in *chronos*; we long for *kairos*. *Chronos* requires speed so life is not wasted; *kairos* requires patience so that life can be enjoyed. *Chronos* drives us forward to get things done; *kairos* allows us to relish the opportunity to do them. We perform in *chronos*, but we truly live in *kairos*.

We have all experienced *kairos*, though we are often unaware of it because such moments engender unselfconsciousness. We pause to watch snow falling late in the evening. We linger over the dinner table with close friends, lost in conversation. We gaze lovingly at a sleeping child. We read the newspaper over a cup of coffee on a lazy

Saturday morning. We take the extra time to reflect on a good book. We stroll lazily through the animal barns of a county fair. We finish a special project at work, knowing that we have done it well.

Vacations often create *kairos* moments. Last summer our family traveled for ten days down the West Coast. It took us two days to get used to being together. Once we adjusted to one another's company, we found great joy just being together. We camped on the beach, built sandcastles, took long walks in the late afternoon, and played Probe by the campfire. We caught an Ansel Adams photography exhibit in San Francisco. We took a twelve-mile hike through the largest stand of old-growth Redwoods in the world, which made us feel as if we were walking in procession through a cathedral six miles long. We ended our vacation at a Shakespeare festival in Ashland, Oregon, where we took in great theater and ate great food.

Music, books, hobbies, friendships, quiet moments of reflection, challenging projects at work—these create *kairos* moments for us. The way to find such moments varies from person to person and from one season of life to another. Right now music does it for me. After the accident I spent months listening to requiems. Then I entered a period of enjoying Celtic music. Now I cannot seem to get enough Mozart and Puccini operas. Writing this book has provided me with one long experience of *kairos*. Raising my kids has done the same thing for me.

Not that productivity is wrong. Sometimes we have to hurry. Contemporary culture forces us to do so with its schedules, tasks, and deadlines. But we must strive at the same time to enjoy our work and to "take pleasure in our toil," as Solomon wrote in the book of Ecclesiastes. In other words, we must enjoy doing what we do.

Thomas Kelly, Quaker mystic and philosopher, understood this sense of *kairos* well. He was concerned about the way time seems to control us, as if it were the master and we its slaves. A false view of time leads inevitably to strain, fatigue, and boredom. It deprives us of living by faith, of taking risks, of enjoying daily life with God. As he wrote sarcastically of life in his time: "No blind living, no marching boldly into the dark, no noble but ungrounded ventures of faith. We must be rational, sensible, intelligent, shrewd." Kelly believed we must orient our lives around a biblical understanding of time. He emphasized discovering the eternal in the present moment, or what he called the "Holy Now."

> The old life of one dimension, lived merely in the ribbon of time, was always a strained life. Had we calculated the past correctly? What unforeseen happenings in the future can arise and overthrow all our efforts? . . . And then comes the sense of Presence, the Eternal Now breaks through the time-nows and all is secure. A sense of absolute security and assurance of being linked with an overcoming Power replaces the old anxieties about the kingdom.[7]

The Amish also have much to teach us. Sue Bender was a busy, productive, professional writer who became increasingly unhappy with her life. One day she happened to see Amish quilts hanging in a store. The beauty and simplicity of the quilts told her she had something to learn from the Amish, so she decided to live with them for a while.

She never converted to their religion or joined their community. Yet she learned valuable lessons about how to live life in the present moment. "What I had been looking for was the calm and focus I felt when I was with the Amish doing the dishes. It was a state of mind I was after. My addiction to activity had diverted me from looking inside, fearing the emptiness I would find. Yet, beneath all the frenzy was the very thing, that inner calm I was seeking." Bender discovered the reason why the Amish knew how to live life to the fullest. It was the result of their view of life itself. "Their life is a celebration of the ordinary. . . . Through them I am learning not to rush through life in order to get the goodies. Their way of life delivers the goods, and that is quite different. How they live reflects what they believe. Their life is their art."[8]

MAKING LIFE AN ART

To make life itself an art—that is the goal of living in the present moment. We do not have to join an Amish community to live this way. Most of us are too entangled in the modern world to drop out anyway. We own homes in cities or suburbs, work in large institutions, and depend on technology for our survival. We live by the clock and keep long hours. The world is in us as much as we are in the world. Yet the ordinary tasks we do every day are alive with the presence and power of God, if we have the eyes to see it. They constitute the "sacrament of the present moment," as Jean-Pierre de Caussade wrote.

When I was twenty-nine, I came down with Rocky Mountain spotted fever, a disease that can be fatal to adults if not treated soon enough. The doctors were unable to diagnose my ailment at first, so I became critically ill. I ended up spending eight days in intensive care. I had severe double pneumonia and constant nausea, my temperature soared to over 105 degrees and stayed there for a week, my heart beat at 160 beats per minute, my kidneys and liver stopped functioning, and my heart stopped twice. As our family physician told Lynda, "Your husband was about as close to death as a sick person can get."

During my lengthy recovery, I saw the world through the eyes of someone who had almost left it. I remember relishing a stroll around our block in a Los Angeles suburb as if I was hiking through a national park, breathing the air as if I was inhaling pure oxygen, and gazing at flowers as if I was seeing color for the first time. I remember biting into a tomato and feeling the taste of it burst in my mouth like an explosive. The whole world was pulsating with life because I had the eyes to see it. I wish I could see the world now as I did then.

How can we make living ordinary life, as busy and crazy as it gets, an art? I am no expert in this matter. Sometimes I live more like a machine than a person. I get up in the morning and run all day long. I require little maintenance—just sleep and food. Put me to a task and I will get it done, efficiently and on time. I check off items on my to-do list with a sweep of my pen. I am the male version of Martha Stewart, only less famous, rich, and productive. I have turned life into a science, not an art.

Still, I am making progress. When I drive somewhere, I often turn off the radio so I can eliminate some of the noise in my life. I take time early every morning to listen to God, to pray, and to read Scripture. I meet with a spiritual director, and the two of us practice *Lectio Divina* (spiritual reading) together. I listen to music, read novels, and keep bees to slow me down. I also try to relish every moment at work as a gift from God, whether I am advising students, delivering a lecture, attending a meeting, or even correcting papers. What a privilege it is, I remind myself, to fulfill my calling at such an institution and among such people.

I am also learning from others how to live life well. I just learned that Ernest Hemingway quit writing at noon every day, even when he was in the middle of a sentence, in order to go fishing for the afternoon. C. S. Lewis took daily walks and answered every letter he received, though he could have easily excused himself from the responsibility. Suzannah Wesley, who raised nineteen children (including John and Charles, who became the leaders of the First Great Awakening in England), spent an hour a week with each child individually. Kathleen Norris, author of *Dakota* and *The Cloister Walk*, spends time every year in a Benedictine monastery, where she follows Benedict's Rule. Dale Bruner, a retired Whitworth professor, reads classic literature every evening. These disciplines refresh and restore, enabling those who practice them to return to their busy lives with renewed creativity, perspective, and gratitude.

It is especially difficult to turn our work into an art, using it as a means of living life for God in the present moment. Work requires efficiency and productivity. The pleasure we want to receive is subservient to the results we must achieve. How we perform is the means; what we accomplish is the end. Yet we can see our work as sacred, too. A recent graduate of Whitworth wrote to tell me how he has changed his attitude toward teaching high school history. "God has been showing me how I can serve and glorify him in all things, even when I am planning lessons and grading papers.... I feel like the division between what is 'spiritual' or 'ministry' and what is secular has disappeared. I feel like the sacred has expanded to cover all of life, and this doesn't dirty the meaning of sacred but broadens my understanding of it instead. I feel much more like I am about God's business in everything."

A. W. Tozer, a twentieth-century pastor, preacher, and spiritual writer, supports this view of work. He wrote that if one's motive is right, what a person does with his or her work can take on almost sacramental significance.

Let every man abide in the calling wherein he is called and his work will be as sacred as the work of the ministry. It is not what a man does that determines whether his work is sacred or secular, it is *why* he does it. The motive is everything. Let a man sanctify the Lord God in his heart and he can thereafter do no common act. All he does is good and acceptable to God through Jesus Christ. For such a man, living itself will be sacramental and the whole world a sanctuary.[9]

Martin E. Marty, the dean of American religious historians and my adviser in graduate school, has taught me more than anyone I know about how to take delight in living out one's calling. He has taught at the University of Chicago Divinity School for nearly forty years, sat on dozens of boards and committees, traveled around the world to speak, and written over fifty books. Yet he treats each assignment, project, book, or article as if it were his first. He relishes every moment he gets to work. He enjoys what he does, not because it is an idol to worship but because it is a calling from God. I used to think he was happy because he was so productive. Now I think he is productive because he is so happy doing his work. God made us for work, and he calls us to work six days out of seven. He has also created us with the capacity to enjoy our work, if we give ourselves to what we are doing and not simply work for what we can get, whether income, recognition, status, or power.

I admire people who take time to pursue hobbies, too. A dear friend of mine, Kathy, who teaches French at Wheaton College, is a master quilter. An old friend of mine has read virtually every one of Patrick O'Brian's seventy plus novels about ships and the sea. My next-door neighbor used to stay up half the night doing oil-painting in his garage. A friend who lives up the street races dragsters, just for the fun of it. A few of my colleagues at the college play basketball every Sunday afternoon without fail, even if they have to limp up and down the court. Every fall we bring our frames of honey to Wally, a local beekeeper, who extracts the honey for us. Wally's life is rich with hobbies. He plays oboe in an orchestra, raises fruit trees, keeps bees, and cultivates a magnificent garden. His home and property are more interesting than Disneyland.

Ordinary life gives us many opportunities to enjoy *kairos* moments. We must develop the eye of an artist to see and seize them. In pursuing our calling, we can take pleasure in everything we do because work itself has dignity. When spending time with colleagues or friends, we can lose ourselves in good conversation. When doing the dishes, we can reflect on the good things God provides. When tucking our children into bed, we can say a prayer over them, thanking God for the gifts they are to us. When waking up in the morning, we can rejoice that we have been given another day of life. We can train our spiritual senses, in other words, to embrace the "Holy Now" and to enjoy the wonder of the present moment.

PART V

MAKING DECISIONS

ATTENDING TO THE
LITTLE THINGS

Some time ago I heard a story that comes out of the Russian Orthodox Church. There was a rich and famous man who spent his life making lots of money and wielding power over others. His religious life suffered as a result. Though he espoused faith, he never had the time to practice it. Long after he had achieved success and fame, he decided to go on a religious pilgrimage to a city some distance away, where a famous holy man lived.

The rich man wanted to visit this man to learn what extraordinary act of service he could render to God and the church to demonstrate his devotion to God. When the day for his departure arrived, the train station was crowded with people who had come to send him off. They stood in awe of his achievements, and they marveled even more when he refused to ride in a private railcar, choosing instead to travel by coach so he could sit with the poor.

He took the only seat remaining, which happened to put him next to an old peasant who also appeared to be on pilgrimage. The rich man spent the entire day telling the old man about his life, achievements, and influence. He was surprised to discover how easy it was for him to talk with the lowly peasant. Finally he announced, "And now I am going on pilgrimage to visit our beloved holy man, who will tell me what great deed of service I must do for the church."

The train arrived at its destination. Once again, a throng of people was waiting outside. Assuming word had spread that he was on pilgrimage, the rich man remained in his seat, allowing other passengers to get off the train first. He heard the cheers of the people, which he expected was a mere warm-up to the mayhem that would follow when he appeared. He stood up, straightened his finely tailored coat, and slowly walked to the door of the train with his arms uplifted. What he saw shocked him. Not one person was waiting for him. The crowd had shuffled off, clamoring to see someone else. He felt humiliated.

Naturally, he wanted to know whom they were following, so he rushed to catch up with the crowd. "Who is it?" he asked. "It is the holy man," one of them panted with excitement. Pushing his way through the crowd, the rich man worked his way toward the center until he stood right behind the holy man. When the holy man turned around, he was horrified. It was the old man who had sat next to him on the train, the very man who had listened to him boast about his greatness. The rich man fell on his knees and asked, "What must I do?" The holy man replied, "Return to your home and serve the poor."

THE ORDINARY IS EXTRAORDINARY!

This rich man did not need to go on a pilgrimage to learn how to serve God. He traveled to the distant city because he wanted to do some extraordinary act of service, which would have only swollen his already bloated ego. If he had been humble in spirit and attentive to God, he would have understood he could serve God right where he was. God's will is done in the little things of life, daily and locally. God has shown us how to do his will in ordinary circumstances, which is the setting where most of life is lived. These circumstances are so mundane that it is easy—but in the long run fatal—to overlook them as unworthy of our attention and energy. To dismiss the ordinary as a lesser concern than the extraordinary is as foolish as an athlete who never practices except before the season's biggest game.

When they were younger, Catherine, David, and John used to ask me on special days, like Father's Day, "Daddy, what special thing would you like us to do for you today?" Of course, they wanted me to say something like, "Serve me breakfast in bed." I was always tempted to say (though I never said it because I thought it in bad taste), "Did you make your bed this morning? Did you empty the dishwasher? Did you sweep the driveway?

Did you fold the laundry?" To which they would have responded, "Yeah, yeah, we know. But what *special* thing would you like us to do for you today? What would really make you happy?" Again I would have said, "Make your bed. Empty the dishwasher. Sweep the driveway. Fold the laundry. Doing those chores would make me happy."

On Father's Day my children always wanted to do something extraordinary and heroic for me, which I would welcome and enjoy—and did, many times. But what really made me happiest then—and, for that matter, still does to this day—has less to do with extraordinary deeds on special occasions and more to do with their commitment to carry out daily, seemingly mundane tasks. I want my children to learn responsibility and obedience, not on those rare occasions when it seems important but every day, even when—especially when—it is not exciting.

Too often we behave like children. We want to know what extraordinary deed we can perform for God sometime in the future—the ephemeral "will of God" that we seek to discover. But it is not the big things we want to do with such bravura but the little things we must do every day that constitute his true will. God wants us to practice daily obedience. He calls us to serve the poor, love our children, befriend a neighbor, live with integrity in a world of dishonesty, and seek him above all. Daily obedience to God in the ordinary circumstances of life is his will for our lives.

Such obedience requires attentiveness to God in our present circumstances. How and why we got in those circumstances is worth exploring, of course. It does us good to consider why we are divorced or sick a lot or chronically unemployed or unable to make friends. It does us no good, however, to think about it too much. Regardless of the reasons, we are where we are. The will of God addresses what we are to do with and in our present situation. Circumstances themselves do not determine whether we are inside or outside the will of God. We decide that by *how we respond to God* in our circumstances.

Take, as one example, a man who has divorced his wife and married a younger woman. Though he had three children with his ex-wife, he was too busy making money and having fun to spend time with them. When his second marriage begins to crumble, however, he starts to search for answers. A friend from work invites him to a Promise Keepers rally. Over the weekend he gives his life to Christ. He acknowledges how foolish he has been and regrets the choices he made, choices he now thinks will forever keep him from God's perfect will for his life. But his friend encourages him to reconcile with his second wife, show kindness to his first, and care for his kids. He discovers it is possible to do God's will right where you are, even if you do not particularly like where you are.

LAYING A STURDY FOUNDATION

The most important decisions we make in life have to do with our way of life—habits, convictions, and direction. Too often we act like parents who agonize for weeks over whether the family should camp for a week in Yosemite or frolic for a few days in Disneyland. We forget that the most important decision—*to vacation as a family*—has already been made. The agony we experience to discover God's will can often be misplaced.

It is easy to miss the obvious. A couple may struggle for months over whether they should buy an existing beautiful home for $500,000 or build their dream-house for $750,000, never once asking whether they should spend so much in the first place. A man may wonder whether he should take a new job in Miami or stay in Kansas City, though the work he does in either place will make it difficult for him to be attentive to his family and active in a local church. Could our quest to discover God's will be sending us in the wrong direction?

We can always do the will of God as we know it in the present moment, however confused we are about the future. We can study hard, even though we may not have a particular profession we are pursuing. We can solve problems now that will equip us to solve bigger ones later on. We can meet needs that can turn us in a direction of service we presently know nothing about. We can care about people, learn to be good stewards, develop character and skills, and serve worthy causes. These simple commitments of everyday life lay a foundation for what is to come. The more diligent and faithful we are now, the greater our capacity to do the will of God later on.

Take marriage. Whether we choose to marry and whom we choose to marry matters less than what we do every day to build lasting friendships, long before we even consider marriage. Ultimately it is the choice to love that determines whether or not a marriage will succeed, for love creates the conditions for the success of marriage. Many marriages fail not because people choose to marry someone "outside the will of God," but because they did not learn how to love before marriage became a concern. The basic question to ask yourself is: "Am I capable of loving another human being until death us do part?"

Or take a calling. The calling we choose to pursue matters less than the little things we do every day that help prepare us. The world will always need hard workers, competent readers, careful writers, critical thinkers, good problem-solvers, cooperative colleagues, faithful subordinates, and fair-minded leaders. I teach at a Christian liberal arts college because I believe such a college lays a sturdy foundation for students. It provides them with a broad education that will be applicable no matter what they end up doing. Most students who graduate today will not stay in one profession for a lifetime. If colleges prepare them for one specific job, their education falls short. But if a college lays a sturdy foundation of knowledge, skills, habits, and convictions in the lives of its students, they are ready for almost anything.

THE SIGNIFICANCE OF THE ORDINARY

Ordinary life provides the proper setting for doing the will of God. A well-known speaker addressed a large crowd of students at Whitworth College several years ago. With intense drama he kept asking the students, "How many of you have really lived? I mean, *really* lived?" He was referring to living with adventure, taking risks to do big things for God, daring to live on the edge. He inspired everyone present. But when a colleague of mine told his wife about the message later that day, she quipped with a mischievous grin on her face, "Sounds just like a man!" She wondered if the speaker would say the same thing if he had to live like most ordinary people, who spend hours every day doing mundane tasks such as shopping for groceries or mowing the lawn. As Teresa of Avila, a sixteenth century mystic and leader of a religious order, once said, "God walks among the pots and pans."[1] Most people have to walk among the pots and pans, and it is among those pots and pans that we learn to "really live," doing God's will.

The New Testament addresses people who live ordinary lives. Jesus spent most of his time with regular people: women, children, fishermen, farmers, and so forth. He warned the rich about the dangers of money and assured the poor that God was watching over them. He promised that there would be a great reversal someday, when the last would be first and the first last.[2] So he urged people to live like servants.

> You know that among the Gentiles those whom they recognize as their rulers lord it over them, and their great ones are tyrants over them. But it is not so among you; but whoever wishes to become great among you must be your servant, and whoever wishes to be first among you must be slave of all.[3]

The apostle Paul made the Christian faith applicable to people in all walks of life. He demonstrated that believers could live for God right where they were.

- He exhorted slaves to take their discipleship seriously: "Whatever your task, put yourselves into it, as done for the Lord and not for your masters, since you know that from the Lord you will receive the inheritance as your reward; you serve the Lord Christ."[4]
- He charged Titus to teach the faithful in his church to live for Christ in the familiar setting of every day life: "Remind them to be subject to rulers and authorities, to be obedient, to be ready for every good work, to speak evil of no one, to avoid quarreling, to be gentle, and show every courtesy to everyone. . . . And let people learn to devote themselves to good works in order to meet urgent needs, so that they may not be unproductive."[5]
- He dignified common labor when he wrote: "Thieves must give up stealing; rather let them labor and work honestly with their own hands, so as to have something to share with the needy."[6]

The apostle used a simple formula to sum up his approach to the will of God: "So, whether you eat or drink, or whatever you do, do everything for the glory of God."[7]

We face our greatest challenges not when God requires us to live heroically and sacrificially but when he calls us to be faithful in our daily routines. Living with routine can easily lull us into complacency. Jean-Pierre de Caussade, an eighteenth-century Jesuit spiritual writer, advised that the secret of the spiritual life is surrendering to God in the ordinariness of the present moment. We must have eyes of faith and a heart of love to comprehend the significance of routine.

> The present moment holds infinite riches beyond your wildest dreams but you will only enjoy them to the extent of your faith and love. The more a soul loves, the more it longs, the more it hopes, the more it finds. The will of God is manifest in each moment, an immense ocean which the heart only fathoms in so far as it overflows with faith, trust and love.[8]

If we perceive the spiritual significance of the ordinary, we will recognize the incredible gift God wants to give us. This gift is his loving presence.

> When the will of God is revealed to souls and has made them feel that they, for their part, have given themselves to him, they are aware of a powerful ally on every hand, for then they taste the happiness of the presence of God which they can only enjoy when they have learnt, through surrendering themselves, where they stand each moment in relation to his ever-loving will.[9]

There is nothing more ordinary than routine work. God has created us to work—to plant soybeans, to transact business over the telephone, to teach math to fourth-graders, or to cook spaghetti. Daily labor has dignity and is good, if it is done to the glory of God and for the good of humanity. God gave us muscles and hands, creativity and brains so that we could write novels, play jazz, calculate a sum, and paint a house. We do the will of God when we work for his divine purpose in the world.

The Jewish expression *Tikkun Olam*—"Fix the World"—points out the divine purpose of work. God has made us his junior partners in helping to restore the world to what he intends it to be. We become coworkers with God not only when we win the lost to Jesus Christ, but also when we serve the common good, care for the needy, strive for justice, produce useful goods, provide helpful services, and create beautiful works of art. As Evelyn Underhill writes:

> Christianity is a religion that acknowledges that there is some-thing very wrong with the world and we are invited by God to cooperate with Him in putting it right. Christianity does not only offer redeeming love to each of us, but, as the earnest and token of our redemption, calls us to the high honor of cooperating in its ceaseless work. We, in so far as we are part of the Body of Christ, are each called to take *some* part with Him in the ceaseless work of saving the world, incarnating the Kingdom of God.[10]

Brother Lawrence believed it was possible to honor God even while doing common labor. He lived in a monastery in the seventeenth century. He spent much of his time in the kitchen, and he learned how to honor God while doing tedious work that appeared to have no spiritual significance. A fellow monk recorded their conversations, which has become a part of the spiritual classic *The Practice of the Presence of God*. According to Brother Lawrence, spiritual growth does not depend on changing what we do (the "works" God calls us to perform) so that we can do more "spiritual" duties; rather, it depends on changing our attitude about what we do. "Our sanctification [does] not depend upon *changing* our works, but in doing that for God's sake which we commonly do for our own."

Brother Lawrence believed that motive is critical. "The most excellent method ... of going to God [is] that of doing our common business without any view of pleasing men, and purely for the love of God." Thus this monk did not see prayer as more inherently spiritual than doing common labor, provided that one tries to serve God and commune with him while doing ordinary duties. "It [is] a great delusion to think that the times of prayer ought to differ from other times; that we are strictly obliged to adhere to God by action in the time of action as by prayer in the season of prayer."[11]

Routine tasks must have genuine significance to God because he requires us to spend much time doing them. A few years ago I read a feature in our local paper, the *Spokesman-Review*, about a retired man who devotes much of his time to chronicling his routine. He records his every action in a diary. He has written enough volumes to fill dozens of boxes with information about his mundane life. A sample entry into his diary goes something like this: "I brushed my teeth and gargled at precisely 8:05 A.M. I read the paper from 8:08 to 8:41 A.M. I went for a walk from 8:43 to 9:17 A.M. I weeded the garden from 9:20 to 10:13 A.M."

None of us would want to read his diaries, at least not for long. We would quickly tire of them. But he is on to something just the same. Most of us live as he does. We just don't bother to write it all down. Our lives are filled with the mundane, the forgettable, and the boring. We make beds, do dishes, shop for food, cook meals, run errands, write letters, take notes, sharpen pencils, answer e-mail, drive kids to practice and lessons, attend committee meetings, bring soup to a sick neighbor, sing in the church choir, weed a garden, make telephone calls, and balance the checkbook. We live an ordinary life, and we follow a regular routine.

I once tried to estimate just how much time we spend doing mundane tasks. According to my calculations, a person who survives to the age of eighty will live approximately 29,200 days or 700,800 hours. Of those hours, that person will spend roughly the following:

2,000 hours brushing his or her teeth (assuming four minutes of brushing a day)

204,400 hours sleeping (assuming seven hours a night)

43,800 hours eating (assuming ninety minutes a day)

58,400 hours doing chores (assuming two hours of chores a day, which includes meal preparation, shopping, house cleaning, bill paying, etc.)

14,600 hours traveling in a car (assuming just thirty minutes a day)

87,600 hours doing routine jobs at work, like filing folders, calculating grades, writing tedious reports, or cleaning paintbrushes (assuming three hours a day).

If anything, these estimates err on the conservative side. Most people spend more than thirty minutes a day in a car, bus, or train, and most adults spend more than two hours a day doing chores. Still, of the 700,800 hours we will enjoy on this earth by the time we reach our eightieth birthday, we will spend at least 410,000 hours—more than half of that time—doing routine tasks. Why did God create us that way? Why did he design life to be so ordinary? We fantasize about the glamour of being a Hollywood celebrity, a professional athlete, or a wealthy executive whose time appears to be spent doing really important things. Yet even famous people spend many hours each day doing a lot of nothing.

We can try to increase our efficiency by squeezing every minute of productivity out of each day. We can give our time to important matters instead of peripheral ones. But there is only so much we can do. We all have limitations. We have to sleep and eat and run errands. We need time off to take a walk and read a good book. We catch colds and get the flu. Eventually we will die. We must therefore learn to live life well—to live life for God—in the ordinariness of life.

DOING LIFE, NOT JUST GETTING IT DONE

I have dear friends who rallied to support me after the accident. Ron is a colleague of mine at the college, and Julie, his wife, works as a part-time nurse. They have three children. Julie felt a calling to be my son John's "surrogate mother" after Lynda died, so for four years she welcomed John into her home when I went to work in the morning. She treated him as if he were one of her own. John has been in school for many years now, so her role as surrogate mom has faded considerably, though she still cares about him a great deal. Still, Julie, Ron, and I continue to talk together about how our families are doing. We talk about problems, opportunities, and important decisions. Every so often Julie says to me, "What fun it is to be doing life together."

Many people pause for a few moments to celebrate when they reach milestones or accomplish important goals. Families throw birthday parties and couples go out for anniversary dinners to recognize the significance of having lived or having lived together for another year. Companies honor employees for years of service. Schools hold graduation ceremonies and hand out awards to acknowledge student achievement. My colleagues at Whitworth throw book-signing parties whenever one of our own publishes a new book.

A couple of years ago my family viewed a documentary at our local IMAX theater that told the story of a successful expedition to the top of Mount Everest, the tallest mountain in the world. The film begins by explaining the risk of spending more than one or two days in what is called "the death zone," which climbers enter when they reach 26,000 feet. The air is so thin at that elevation that the human body cannot tolerate climbing for very long. Even then, climbers spend weeks acclimatizing their bodies and carrying supplies to the many camps they must establish along the way. Yet however successfully they adjust and prepare, once they climb above 26,000 feet they have precious little time to reach the summit before they must turn around. The last pitch to the top requires so much from climbers that they must start the ascent as early as midnight in order to reach it before they run out of daylight, food, oxygen, and energy. It is considered a luxury for climbers to be able to spend an hour on the summit. In other words, climbers spend weeks of their time and thousands of dollars to reach a summit on which they will stand for an hour, if they are lucky! Many fail to get even that far.

The documentary made me think about the ambivalence of achievement. Is real pleasure gained in accomplishing some great feat, or is it found in the experience of trying? Do we find our greatest joy in getting done with something, or in simply doing it? Perhaps we are looking for pleasure in all the wrong places. Just living life, striving to accomplish a goal, and doing the will of God in ordinary life may hold the secret to finding real joy.

LITTLE THINGS MATTER A LOT

Newsweek carried a series of articles in late 1999 telling the story of the twentieth century from eyewitnesses. One issue was devoted to sports, telling stories of noteworthy athletes, amazing feats, unforgettable moments, and great sports dynasties. One of the greatest of all dynasties in college sports was UCLA's basketball program in the 1960s and 1970s. Its team won ten national titles, including seven in a row from 1967 to 1973. John Wooden was the coach of all these winning teams. A *Newsweek* reporter asked him to reflect on the secret to his success. Rather than picking successful offensive plays, recruitment strategies, or perimeter shooting, Wooden provided a different perspective: "I think it's the little things that really count." Those critical things could be very little indeed.

The first thing I would show our players at our first meeting was how to take a little extra time putting on their shoes and socks properly. The most important part of your equipment is your shoes and socks. . . . It took just a few minutes, but I did show my players how I wanted them [to put them on correctly].[12]

My son John, a fifth-grader, started playing on an Amateur Athletic Union basketball team this year. Our local AAU league is very competitive. The athletes are serious about the sport. John and his teammates imagine themselves as future NBA players. They try to imitate the fluid moves and brilliant shots of NBA stars. They are comical to watch because they are so inept. They pretend they are only one or two steps away from greatness, though most of them have trouble making layups. They have grandiose ideas, but their future success, as Wooden has recognized, depends on attention to the little things.

The apostle Paul took Timothy, his protégé, under his wing and trained him to be a pastor. He realized the success of Timothy's fledgling ministry depended on his attention to daily detail, so he wrote:

> Let no one despise your youth, but set the believers an example in speech and conduct, in love, in faith, in purity. Until I arrive, give attention to the public reading of scripture, to exhorting, to teaching. Do not neglect the gift that is in you, which was given to you through prophecy with the laying on of hands by the council of elders. Put these things into practice, devote yourself to them, so that all may see your progress.[13]

I used to envy people with extraordinary talent, quickness, and natural ability—people who could play competitive basketball without having to work hard, write excellent papers just hours before they were due, speak extemporaneously even though they never prepared ahead of time, or dazzle crowds with their magnetic personality. Not any longer. Mario Puzo once said that his idea of a hero is a man who simply knows what his duty is and does it.

The type of person who impresses me now is the plodder who enjoys the doing of life. Plodders keep the world going. I appreciate pastors who preach solid sermons week after week, students who turn in their assignments on time, having done the best they can, and managers who strive for the success of subordinates. I admire coaches who care as much about the players as they do about the record, custodians who take pride in their work, and colleagues who show up for meetings on time. It all comes down to our attention to the little things.

Many of us may have our fifteen minutes of Andy Warhol fame. We may win an award, receive a positive review for a performance, win a game in the last second, or see our photo in the paper. But for every fifteen minutes of fame we will spend hundreds of hours in routine. When I think about it, fifteen minutes of fame is not long. If we are living for those fifteen minutes, we are not living for very much. It is the time spent studying, practicing, working, serving, and sacrificing that counts the most. It is doing the little things every day that puts us on a trajectory of fulfilling the will of God.

16

Making Choices

Robert Frost wrote a poem about two roads diverging in a yellow wood. He chose the one less traveled, which made all the difference. Sooner or later all of us arrive at junctures where two roads diverge. We too must choose which one to follow. In some cases, however, both roads appear about the same. One is not less traveled; both are equally appealing. How do we choose between them? How do we make decisions about the future? How do we discern the will of God?

Take a high school senior. She receives literature from dozens of colleges. She narrows the field down to five schools, then visits the campus of each one and eliminates two more. The remaining three are equally attractive to her. Each has an excellent track program, a sport in which she hopes to compete; each has a strong biology department, the field of study she plans to pursue; and each has a rigorous general studies program, which satisfies her interest in the liberal arts. How will she choose?

Think about a young executive. He enjoys his job as a midlevel manager in a computer company. His wife has an enviable position as a reading specialist in an innovative elementary school, and his kids have excellent music teachers, good basketball coaches, and best friends in the neighborhood. The whole family loves their church. But a company on the other side of the country contacts him about changing jobs. The pay would be better, and the job itself is a perfect fit for his interests and abilities. The offer seems a once-in-a-lifetime opportunity, but his family does not want to move. How does he make a decision?

Or take two single people, both divorced with kids. They meet each other at a singles conference. There is immediate chemistry. So they begin to date and eventually fall in love. They are convinced that God has brought them together. They start discussing marriage, and both are excited about the idea. They have the energy and desire to start over. But their children are less enthused. There is tension whenever the families are together. Friends lend their support, but they, too, raise questions about whether the families can blend harmoniously. How do they discern God's will about their future life together?

Some choices, of course, are easy to make. If I have a choice at dinnertime between sweet corn and beets, I will choose sweet corn every time. If I have a choice between doing paperwork and reading a novel, I will read the novel. These choices concern personal preferences and little more. If all our choices were simply a matter of personal preference, most would be easy. But personal preference doesn't always help us decide which option is best.

Clear priorities don't always help either. It is easy for me to choose between spending time with my kids and fussing over my yard. My kids are more important to me than the yard. They are my priority. But too often my priorities conflict, like a classroom of rambunctious kindergartners vying for the attention of a teacher. It is not always obvious what my priorities should be in a given situation. I want to fulfill my contract and finish writing this book, for example, but not at the expense of my kids.

Moral convictions don't always clarify matters, either. If I had to choose between cheating on my income taxes and taking a summer job to make ends meet, I would choose the summer job because I know cheating is wrong. It is not God's will that anyone cheat. But moral convictions can collide and compete. Some issues are clear; others are ambiguous. My moral code tells me that serving the needy is right; it also tells me that paying attention to my children is right. But how much, in each case, is enough? Every hour spent serving the needy means one less hour at home with my kids. Is there an obvious right and wrong in such choices? I doubt it.

I wish there were. I hate to make choices. I am even stymied by a restaurant menu or the selection of clothes in a Lands End catalog. It all looks so good to me. When I have to ponder something as significant as a job change, I feel close to the edge. I want someone to decide for me. I write this chapter, then, as one who desperately needs to apply its advice to my own life.

GOD'S VOICE

Listening is an art as much as it is a skill. We may someday design computers that can carry on conversations with humans, but it will be difficult to build them with enough sophistication to decipher the complex nature of human communication. As we know from personal experience, people can use words to say one thing when, given gesture, tone, and timing, they really mean something different. Even the simple phrase "Thank you" can convey many different messages—sincere gratitude, profound indebtedness, acerbic sarcasm, polite indifference, patronizing irritation—depending on the tone in which the words are spoken and the context in which they are said.

If we want to make good choices, we must learn to listen to God. I don't believe listening to God is more difficult than listening to people. In some ways it may even be easier. Whether harder or easier, it is certainly different from human communication. God does not speak in an audible voice, nor does he use gesture and tone. Still, God does communicate, sometimes more clearly than we would like. He communicates with us to reveal his will and express his love. He does not communicate in "mixed messages," as we often do. He loves us and wants us to know him. So we must learn how to listen to one who communicates unlike anyone else. How do we listen?

The most obvious answer is that we should read Scripture, though that book should not be treated as a substitute for a living relationship with God. For example, we learn in Scripture that God speaks through fire, earthquake, and wind, but he also speaks in a still small voice.[1] He communicates directly to some,[2] but to most people he does so indirectly through nature and law.[3] He gives impressions and appeals to our intuition, which we often know as a feeling or sense of God's presence and will. He sends messages through prophets, seers, dreams, and visions. He reveals his will through the life stories of others who have gone before us. Finally, he came as a human being, Jesus of Nazareth, to show us in no uncertain terms who he is and how much he cares about us. There is no obvious pattern that emerges in these various forms of communication, except that it is clear God wants to communicate with us, however indirect his messages may appear to be.

We must be careful that we do not presume to know God better than we do. As I have already argued, we know God by faith, not by sight. This is how God has designed the universe. I am uncomfortable with anyone who claims to be on speaking terms with God, as if he or she belongs in the company of Moses and Elijah. There is too much of that in contemporary Christianity. It allows a few people to be demagogues and makes the rest of us suckers or cynics. We can know a great deal about God. We may even know God personally. But it is "in a mirror, dimly," as Paul wrote; it is not "face to face."[4] There will always be a degree of mystery and ambiguity in our relationship with God this side of eternity. We must learn to communicate with him in light of this limitation.

Still, God does communicate. Sometimes he does so through unusual circumstances. If something unexpected happens, we may suddenly find ourselves facing a new challenge and heading in a new direction. Corrie Ten Boom grew up in a normal Dutch family. For the first fifty years of her life she followed a simple routine. She lived at home and worked in her father's watch shop. She never married and never traveled. Then the Nazis overran the Netherlands and began to persecute the Jews. A leader of the underground, observing how devoted Corrie was to serving the less fortunate, asked her to join the movement. She did not hesitate one moment. The Ten Boom house was renovated to hold a secret chamber—a "hiding place"—for Jews trying to escape the Nazis. She spent years serving the cause. Eventually she was arrested and imprisoned. Corrie lost her father and her sister, but she survived.

After writing *The Hiding Place*, which tells the story of those traumatic years, Corrie Ten Boom traveled around the world, bringing encouragement and inspiration to millions. If someone had told her when she was forty that she would live such a life, she would have scoffed at the idea. "Who, me?" she would have exclaimed. "I am just a simple woman living a simple life. I am no hero. You must be talking about someone else." Then circumstances changed. God used them to speak to her, and the outcome was not what she or any other human being could have imagined.[5]

God speaks through dreams and visions, too. Just last week I had coffee with a member of our church who is the band director at a school in Bangkok, Thailand. He taught in public high schools in northwest United States for a while, but a devastating experience knocked him out of education for several years. He considered other options besides teaching, but he could never let a career in education go. Then he began to think about teaching abroad. One night he had a dream in which a close friend of his mentioned Bangkok. Just a few days later an opportunity arose to take a job in Bangkok. He believed God was speaking to him through that dream. He applied for a teaching position and has been serving there happily for two years.

A vision changed the direction of Paul's missionary work. On two separate occasions Paul attempted to travel to parts of Asia Minor to expand his missionary work there. He was turned back both times. Then he had a vision in which he saw a man from Macedonia beckoning him to come. Paul awoke the next morning, packed his bags, and sailed for Macedonia.[6] That vision launched him into a long and fruitful ministry of church-planting in what is now Europe. He started churches in such cities as Philippi, Thessalonica, and Corinth. He faced persecution in some of those cities, too, which reminds us that just because God speaks to us does not mean life will get easier. It may even get harder.

God also communicates through inspirational messages. I know a number of students who have attended one of the many Urbana Missionary Conferences held in Urbana, Illinois, every three years. Most return home the better for having attended the event. They reenter life where they left off and continue to pursue the interests and dreams they had before attending the conference. Urbana motivated them, though it did not redirect the course of their lives.

But a few students returned home knowing that God had called them to move in a new direction. They recounted a particular message they heard, seminar they attended, or conversation they had as a major turning point in their lives. From that point on they simply knew that God was calling them to work in an orphanage in India, to do youth ministry in El Salvador, or to become a medical missionary in Ethiopia. Why did that experience speak to them and not to others? Somehow they heard the voice of God, and they responded.

An entire church can speak with a prophetic voice. We have records in early church history of congregations of Christians who were certain God had called a particular person to assume a position of leadership, though none of these men sought or even wanted the position. They served in various capacities against their will because the church insisted that God had willed it. Ambrose became the bishop of Milan, Augustine the bishop of Hippo and a master theologian, Chrysostom the archbishop of Constantinople, and Gregory a great pope of the Roman church. These men wrote books still read today. They confronted emperors, marshaled the church's resources in times of crisis, contended against heretics, and faced tremendous opposition. They became giants of faith, not out of choice but out of necessity. They would not have voluntarily chosen the path their lives followed. But the body of Christ spoke with one voice, and God used that voice to call them into leadership.

These kinds of unusual occurrences don't happen often. We should not expect them to be daily events and become dependent on them. There is no need to sit by the telephone, waiting for God to call. For some reason we assume God has something to say about everything. I'm not sure this is the case. God may remain silent because he has nothing to say. His silence may mean little more than "Fine, you can be an accountant or a teacher, move to Orlando or stay in Chicago, marry Sam or remain single. It doesn't much matter to me. I'll bless you either way." Yet his silence may also mean he has something more important to say that we are not willing to hear. If we would bother to listen, we may hear God say something like "No, I don't mind whether you go to Harvard or to Spokane Community College, but I do mind that you are sleeping with your boyfriend. Stop it, please."

The extraordinary is just that—extraordinary, a departure from normality, an exception to the rule. It is not something we should demand or expect from God, though we should always be open to it and eager to respond. If God interrupts our lives, then so be it. We will never know ahead of time, but we should always be prepared. We can no more predict if or when God is going to speak in some extraordinary way than the Jews in Jesus' day could have predicted that God was about to become incarnated in the person of Jesus Christ. As Jean-Pierre de Caussade warned, "Faithful souls do not rely on miracles. Content in their unknowing, they leave them to be a light for others, and accept for themselves all that is most ordinary: God's order, God's way which tests their faith by concealing, not revealing himself."[7]

This first step—listening to God's voice—assumes God has something to say about our choices. If we want to listen to God, we must cultivate quietness of soul. Ignatius of Loyola prescribed the proper "occasions" when a good choice is made. Sometimes God simply moves the will to pursue a particular course of action. Ignatius believed such direct guidance, however, is the exception, not the rule. On other occasions God speaks through experiences of "consolations and desolations." Life experiences, in other words, help us to learn God's will. But most of the time God uses ordinary means to speak to us. We must learn to be tranquil so that we can listen and respond. Agitation and distraction prevent us from hearing God's voice.[8]

Some Christians practice fasting to quiet the soul. Fasting disciplines our appetites and increases spiritual sensitivity. In depriving the body of food, we end up feeding the soul. The body gets less, the soul more. The early church practiced fasting as a way of discerning God's will. Believers in Antioch prayed and fasted, for example, before laying hands on Paul and Barnabas and sending them off to do missionary work. Fasting and prayer made them better listeners.[9]

GOD'S GREATER PURPOSE

In addition to listening, we should also consider God's greater purpose and keep in mind the big picture of his redemptive plan. Ignatius advised:

> I must have as my aim the end for which I am created, which is the praise of God our Lord and the salvation of my soul. At the same time I must remain indifferent and free from any inordinate attachments so that I am not more inclined or disposed to take the thing proposed than to reject it, nor to relinquish it rather than to accept it.[10]

Francis de Sales believed that God's greater purpose is easy to understand. Its basic outline is obvious, if we want to know it. God is clear when and where he needs to be. When he is not clear, it is probably because there is no need for it. We can therefore enjoy freedom.

God's will is made known to us ... by what he disposes, what
he commands. This calls for no deliberation on our part; we
simply carry out God's orders. In everything else, however, we
are perfectly free to make our own choice of what seems
good—though it is not a question of doing everything that is
permissible, but only such things as are suitable.[11]

God's greater purpose is revealed in Scripture. Its main ideas
are clear. We should use reason to help us understand and interpret the Bible. It does not take a mystic, in other words, to discover what is truly important to God. He did not deceive us by
creating us with a brain, and he wants us to use it when we make
decisions. He may, of course, choose to intervene directly into our
lives. In the meantime, he wants us to learn to exercise good judgment. Though reason is not an infallible guide—the Fall, after all,
has tainted everything, including the mind—it is still a good one,
if the mind is yielded to God. Note what Ignatius has suggested:
"After having thus weighed the matter and carefully examined it
from every side, I will consider which alternative appears more
reasonable. Acting upon the stronger judgment of reason and not
on any inclination of the senses, I must come to a decision in the
matter that I am considering."[12]

God gives us a certain degree of freedom to make choices.
According to de Sales, once we consider his greater purpose, we
will discover a great deal of room to maneuver. God's will is like
several trails leading to the same goal. We can take any one of
them to arrive at our destination. It is a waste of time and energy
to try and make the "perfect decision" (assuming that there is such
a thing), if all the alternatives are good ones. Besides, our hesita-
tion to choose may keep us from making a good choice. "While
they busy or worry themselves trying to discover which is better,
they miss the opportunity of doing much that is good. Deeds give
God far more glory than any amount of time wasted in trying to
discriminate between good and better."[13]

KEEPING PERSPECTIVE

Finally, we should keep perspective. Lynda wrote her last letter just days before she died. The recipients of that letter, friends
living in the Midwest, mailed a photocopy of the letter back to

me. Her concluding line reflected her philosophy of life so well: "I am trying to live my whole life in the light of eternity." An eternal perspective will affect how we make choices. It stresses the important over the urgent, need over want, service over pleasure, people over things. A seminary professor told me just as I was beginning my first pastoral charge, "People and the Word of God are eternal. Most everything else is temporal. Make sure you invest in the eternal."

Ignatius suggested that when making a decision, we should imagine giving advice to another person and then simply follow our own advice. He concluded, "Then I will act in like manner myself, keeping the rule that I have proposed for another." He also counseled that before making decisions, we should try to picture ourselves standing on the threshold of death, peering in the abyss of eternity. Would we choose differently if we made our choices with the end of life in mind?[14] "I have never met a person," my friend Kathy once said to me, "who wished at the age of seventy-five that he had spent more time at the office when he was forty. If anything, I know too many people who regret not spending more time caring for their families or serving their communities." Perspective keeps the big picture in mind.

The people of God can provide perspective and thus help us make good decisions. Spiritual advisers and friends are in a good position to give advice because they care about us and see our strengths and weaknesses. The same is true with a support group. Since losing Lynda, I consult regularly with a group of friends. We talk about marriage, kids, jobs, and the like. We offer each other advice when an important decision has to be made.

The church, therefore, is a rich resource from which we can draw when we are making decisions. Yet I am cautious about the role of the church as well, for two reasons. First, a person is not necessarily wise just because he or she is a Christian. Even the most sincere believer has mixed motives and can give bad advice. Second, some Christian leaders excel at abusing authority. Particularly in more conservative Christian circles, pastors can make outrageous claims to authority and function as virtual dictators to their congregations. They assume they have the right to tell church members whom they should marry, what jobs they should take, how they should spend their money, or how they should use their time. The Christian church can become as cultist as any religious group, if not more so. Anyone who boasts that he or she speaks for God should be scrutinized carefully. As Jesus said, good leaders serve the flock; they do not dominate.

Sociologists have done research on why people join cults. The people most vulnerable to the influence of cults are genuine Christians who want security and an experience of authentic Christianity. They join groups that appear to embody what the New Testament promises—love, service, high standards, and serious commitment. Before long they become ensnared. By the time the real nature of the group surfaces, genuine harm has been done to them.

I met a woman at a funeral several years ago who told me, "All my close friends are dead." I was stunned by her comment. I asked her what had happened. She proceeded to tell me that while living in California she had found a community that was, as she said, "like heaven on earth." So she joined it. She left it just in time a few years later. The leader became more and more dominant and the group increasingly isolated until, feeling hounded by everyone, they bought property in South America and moved there. Several years later the entire community, some nine hundred people, committed mass suicide in Jonestown, Guyana. What appeared to be heaven on earth turned into a hell on earth.

Authoritarian churches do not have to go to that extreme to be dangerous. Anyone who assumes enough authority to think he or she can tell other people God's will for their decisions has gone too far. The church has one head, Jesus Christ. It is one thing to confront a person who is embezzling funds, committing adultery, or neglecting his children. It is quite another thing to presume to know that God intends someone to become a doctor rather than a teacher, or to marry Ed instead of Stan. I am not convinced God cares all that much about many of our earthly decisions, as long as we are seeking him.

There is another community of wise and seasoned people to whom we can look for perspective. I am referring to saints who lived long ago. I receive guidance from people whom I have never met, never spoken to, and never known personally. Though strangers to me, they have exercised profound influence over my life. I consult them when I have to make a decision by reading their writings and biographies. One of my favorite advisers is Augustine of Hippo (356–430), whose *Confessions*, an autobiography of his journey to salvation, has changed my life. I read the book many years ago but did not profit much from it, probably because I was not mature enough. I reread it in 1997. On page after page I found insights that have helped me to understand the nature of the Christian life and to make decisions about where I am headed in life.

CHOOSING AND BELIEVING

We should listen for God's voice, discern God's purpose, and keep perspective. Still, the time comes when we must make our decision. We must choose a college, a career, a job, a church, a house, and so forth. Can we ever know for sure that the choices we make are the will of God? If so, how? What criteria should we employ to judge the success of our choices?

Success itself is a dangerous term. If we judge the wisdom of our choices by how successful the outcome is, we will become confused and disillusioned in a very short time. Does success—whatever that means—verify that we have chosen God's will and failure indicate that we have missed it? Not necessarily. It depends on what we mean by success and failure.

William Carey believed it was God's will for him to become a pioneer missionary in India. He paid a huge price for it, for several of his family members died from disease while he was there. Should he have stayed in England instead? Samuel Zwemer spent his entire adult life as a missionary in the Arabian peninsula. He never saw one adult convert. Did he waste his time? I moved to Spokane to teach at Whitworth College. I felt strongly that God was in my decision. Two years later I lost three members of my family in the accident, including the very person, Lynda, who believed that it was "God's will" for us to move here. Did we make a mistake?

Benedict Groeschel, a Franciscan, cautions us about using success as the criterion for determining whether or not a decision is the will of God. Success is often misleading, and so is failure. Success can make us complacent and proud; failure can inspire us to work harder to accomplish our goals.

It is commonly thought that if we begin a project for the Lord, the pieces will fall into place. It doesn't work out that way.... Disasters befall projects of the good spirit, as well as those of the bad. Success has never been a sign of God's will. As Mother Teresa of Calcutta has observed, "God calls us to fidelity and not to success." It seems to me a sure sign that a certain project is the work of God if we have the grace to struggle on without bitterness in the face of difficulties and frustrations.[15]

Besides, what appears to be a failure one moment may turn into a success the next, though the opposite can happen too. We will never know, at least right away. My son David is considering transferring from a large public high school to a small private school. He wants to make a good choice. There are potential problems either way. If he chooses to stay, he will probably run varsity on a cross-country team that may very well win state. He would like that. But he could also get injured and have to sit out for a season, or he could fail to make varsity. If he transfers to the private school, he will probably play varsity basketball and soccer on teams that could go to state. But those teams could also play below their potential, forcing David to endure losing seasons. He will have to choose without knowing how things will turn out.

A decision made is final. We should not try to second-guess ourselves, wondering what would have happened if we had chosen differently. Of course, the results of our choices do matter. Every choice has consequences. I have chosen, for example, to remain single rather than to remarry after Lynda was killed in the accident. I have friends who would like to see me married again and have pushed me in that direction. They tell me it would be good for me—"You are the marrying kind," they say—and good for my kids—"Your kids need another mother," they add. But I have other friends who warn me about remarriage. They testify how difficult it is to blend families. As one colleague said recently, "Jerry, you're coaching a team in the fourth quarter. Keep your eyes on the game. Don't start looking in the grandstands!"

In one sense, their comments don't matter. For whatever reason, I have chosen to remain single and to raise my kids alone. Is it God's will for me to remarry? Who knows? I do know, however, that it is *not* God's will for me to obsess about it and thus neglect what I know *is* God's will, namely, to respond faithfully to him in the circumstances of my life as they are right now.

Choice implies risk, even when we choose wisely. I have made my fair share of "right" choices over the last twenty-five years. I seem to have chosen the "right" profession, taken the "right" jobs, married the "right" woman, made the "right" friends, and bought the "right" houses. But my choices have not always turned out well, even when I made them in good faith. I have suffered along the way, too. Sometimes I deserved it; sometimes I did not. But what I deserved or did not deserve is beside the point. What counts most is that I believe God is working in my life. He is writing a redemptive story. I can trust him and do his will where I am, whether or not I made the "right" choices, or whether or not those "right" choices had a good outcome.

Before it is all over, every one of us will make a few bad choices, and we will have to live with the consequences. But we will make a few good ones, too. Even then, not all choices, however good they are, will turn out well. We will take a job that seemed perfect for us, only to quit in frustration three years later. We will marry someone who exceeded our wildest dreams, only to wonder ten years later what went wrong. We will go to the mission field with high aspirations, only to get sick and have to return home. We will make choices in good conscience, but they will not always work out. We will be tempted in those moments to wonder if the choices we made were the will of God after all.

This natural tendency to doubt is why we must trust God and not look back. Life does not always work out as we expect it to. Even our best intentions and decisions can result in disappointment, failure, and suffering. But we must beware of coming to hasty conclusions about God's will. The story we are living is more wild and wonderful than we think. It is not over yet.

In the meantime, we have choices to make. After much reflection, we choose to become an accountant in a nonprofit organization, to live in Seattle, to remain single, and to attend a Free Methodist church. We could have chosen otherwise. As we look ahead, we see many good options for doing the will of God. All of them *could* be the will of God, but only one *becomes* the will of God—the one we choose. This choice is the one God will bless and redeem. We can be sure of this because God is good, and he has created us to be his. Thomas Merton wrote:

> Our vocation is not simply to be, but to work together with God in the creation of our own life, our own identity, our own destiny. We are free beings and sons of God. This means to say that we should not passively exist, but actively participate in His creative freedom, in our lives, and in the lives of others, by choosing the truth.[16]

As we make our choices, as we succeed or fail, as we experience bliss or suffer loss, we must never forget that we live in grace and can trust in God's sovereignty. Then, over time, we can look back and discern a pattern. We will see that God has been with us, accomplishing his unfathomable will for our lives. We will observe a redemptive story being written. God is using us to build his kingdom and working all things out for our good. In the end we will know that there was only one way, one will, one purpose. It is the one we chose and the path we took. It is also the plan God accomplished and the grand design he worked for his glory and our benefit.

ALL WILL BE WELL

Everything comes down to perspective. The view I have presented on the will of God does not spare us from the difficulty of having to make choices, nor does it save us from the agony of living with the consequences of our choices. Still, we can be certain that God will bless us. He will work redemption through the choices we make because he purposes to make all things right and good again through Christ.

If we seek first God and his kingdom, then whatever we choose becomes his will for our lives. In other words, we have the *freedom* to choose, the *confidence* of knowing that what we choose is God's will, and the *security* of having God's gracious presence in our lives, no matter where we go. We can follow the course set for our lives, knowing that God will go with us. He will never let us go; he will never leave us or forsake us. The good work that God has begun in our lives he will finish, regardless of the path we take.[1] God is that loyal to us.

The will of God involves how we live for him in the present moment, whatever the circumstances. Jean-Pierre de Caussade understood the simplicity of this perspective. Like so many spiritual writers, he stressed the significance of doing God's will in daily life. "To discover God in the smallest and most ordinary things, as well as in the greatest, is to possess a rare and sublime faith. To find contentment in the present moment is to relish and adore the divine will in the succession of all the things to be done and suffered which make up the duty to the present moment."[2] Intention and direction are everything. If we set our hearts to live for God, we can be confident that we will always be in the center of his will. We cannot lose with God. He works all things together for a good purpose.[3]

Thus, we can concentrate our energies on the journey itself and enjoy what happens along the way. The journey is sacred because it anticipates the destination. The *process* is central to the outcome. Every step we take has significance. As Oswald Chambers wrote in *God's Workmanship*:

> What men call the process, God calls the end. If you can stay in the midst of the turmoil unperplexed and calm because you see Jesus, that is God's purpose in your life; not that you may be able to say, "I have done this and that and now it's all right." God's purpose in you is that you depend upon Him and His power *now*.[4]

When the journey is over and, by God's grace, we reach our destination, we will see the utter greatness and grandeur of his eternal plan. We will discover in that glorious moment how everything fits together, perfectly and intricately. God's plan will seem like a vast landscape, gleaming in the morning sun. It will take our breath away.

The grandeur of this eternal plan overwhelmed Augustine. In *The City of God,* he set out to show the difference between God's eternal plan and humanity's temporal plans, between redemptive history and human history, or, as he put it, between "the City of God" and "the City of Man." The first refers to Christian history, to God's great plan to save and renew; the second refers to secular history, to humanity's futile attempt to bend history to its own selfish ends.

> We see then that the two cities were created by two kinds of love: the earthly city was created by self-love reaching the point of contempt for God, the Heavenly City by the love of God carried as far as contempt for self. In fact, the earthly city glories in itself, the Heavenly City glories in the Lord. The former looks for glory from men, the latter finds its highest glory in God, the witness of a good conscience.[5]

Augustine recognized that citizens of the Heavenly City—that is, the followers of Jesus—cannot be assured that life on earth will be easy. If anything, life will probably be hard *because* they are followers of Jesus. Still, they can be joyful and hopeful in the knowledge that their journey will end gloriously. "For all that, if anyone accepts the present life in such a spirit that he uses it with the end in view of that other life on which he has set his heart with all his ardour and for which he hopes with all his confidence, such a man may without absurdity be called happy even now, though rather by future hope than in present reality."[6]

Whether we choose wisely or foolishly, God will remain good because he is committed to us. He will go with us if we decide to move to Katmandu. He will prove himself faithful if we choose teaching over business. He will empower us to fulfill our vows if we decide to marry. He will show mercy and give comfort if one of our children dies of cancer. He will continue to rule by his providence if we go bankrupt trying to start a new business, fail in marriage, become a quadriplegic, or go to jail. He will smile on us as we go about the daily business of cleaning house, caring for a disabled neighbor, showing up every day for work, and raising our children. God will be there for us because he is God.

Here is the most wonderful truth of all: Ultimately, the will of God has less to do with the choices we make, however important, and more to do with the choice God has already made. He wills us to seek him because he has already willed to seek us. God is, as Thomas Kelly wrote, the great initiator.

> Religion is not *our* concern; it is God's concern. The sooner we stop thinking *we* are the energetic operators of religion and discover that God is at work, as the Aggressor, the Invader, the Initiator, so much the sooner do we discover that our task is to call men *to be still and know*, listen, hearken in quiet invitation to the subtle promptings of the Divine.[7]

The biblical story of the prodigal son underscores this truth. The younger of two sons claims his inheritance even before his father is dead, a callous violation of ancient Near Eastern norms. He then converts the property and livestock into cash so that he can go wherever he wishes. Jewish law did allow for such an action, though cultural custom disapproved of it. But if a son lost his inheritance to Gentiles, Jewish citizens from his community would disown him in a formal ceremony because he had dishonored his father and forsaken his heritage. The prodigal son knew that he could not return empty-handed. If he did, he would be sent away in disgrace.

He travels to a distant country, where he squanders his fortune until he becomes utterly destitute. He is so desperate that he hires himself out to hog farmers in order to get something to eat. He finally comes to his senses, realizing it would be far better for him to serve as a slave in his father's house than to work for Gentiles. He prepares a speech to give to his father, for he is certain his father will be distant and angry, reluctant even to give his son an audience. In his speech, he admits his mistake and proposes to pay off his debts by working as a slave in his father's house. So, with speech put to memory, he heads home.

Meanwhile, his father watches and waits, eager to have his son return. Far from being angry, he longs to see him again, in spite of the disgrace he has suffered. When he hears his son is coming home, he runs out to meet him, something a typical father in the ancient Near Eastern world would never do. He finds his son before he arrives home. The father doesn't even let him finish his speech. Instead, he embraces him with reckless love and welcomes him back into the family. He puts a ring on his finger, hangs a robe around his shoulders, and slips sandals on his feet to show that he is joining the family again as a son, not as a slave. Then the father throws a lavish banquet to celebrate the fact that "this son of mine . . . was lost and is found."

Thus, while the son has returned to pay off his debt and earn his father's approval, the father has already decided to forgive the debt and embrace him as a son. It is not the son who returns home; it is the father who brings him home. The father has "found" the son and makes all things well again.[8] Jesus is like that father, pursuing sinners. He invites us, though we are prodigals, into a relationship with him. The Pharisees were, therefore, accurate when they accused Jesus of being a friend of sinners: "This fellow welcomes sinners and eats with them."[9]

The story of the prodigal son reminds me of one of my favorite hymns. It, too, echoes the same glorious truth. God takes the initiative. God wills our redemption. God is good to the core of his being.

Come, Thou Fount of every blessing,
tune my heart to sing Thy grace;
Streams of mercy, never ceasing,
call for songs of loudest praise.

Teach me some melodious sonnet,
   sung by flaming tongues above;
Praise his name—I'm fixed upon it—
   name of God's redeeming love.

Hither to Thy love has blest me;
   Thou hast brought me to this place;
And I know Thy hand will bring me
   safely home by Thy good grace.
Jesus sought me when a stranger,
   wandering from the fold of God;
He, to rescue me from danger,
   bought me with His precious blood.

O, to grace how great a debtor daily
   I'm constrained to be!
Let Thy goodness, like a fetter,
   bind my wandering heart to Thee;
Prone to wander, Lord, I feel it,
   prone to leave the God I love;
Here's my heart, O, take and seal it;
   seal it for Thy courts above.

God chooses us, gives us grace, and redeems the story of our lives. That is ultimately his will for us. Only then does he call us to do his will in the ordinariness of life. The assurance we have that our choices are in fact God's will has nothing to do with the wisdom of our choices, though we ought to make wise choices— for our own sake and for God's glory. Rather, it has everything to do with the bounty of God's grace. He is the reason why we can march through life with bold confidence.

Jesus Christ is proof that God is faithful and will accomplish his plan. God will have the final word, and that word will be glorious.

> Who will separate us from the love of Christ? Will hardship, or distress, or persecution, or famine, or nakedness, or peril, or sword? . . . No, in all these things we are more than conquerors through him who loved us. For I am convinced that neither death, nor life, nor angels, nor rulers, nor things present, nor things to come, nor powers, nor height, nor depth, nor anything else in all creation, will be able to separate us from the love of God in Christ Jesus our Lord.[10]

Julian of Norwich, a fourteenth-century English mystic, grasped the radical implications of God's ultimate authority, which will be manifested so graciously at the end of time as it has already been throughout time.

> For as truly as we shall be in the bliss of God without end, praising and thanking him, so truly have we been in God's provision loved and known in his endless purpose without beginning.... And therefore when the judgment is given, and we are all brought up above, we shall then clearly see in God the mysteries which are now hidden from us. And then shall none of us be moved to say in any matter: Lord, if it had been so, it would have been well. But we shall all say with one voice: Lord, blessed may you be, because it is so, it is well; and now we see truly that everything is done as it was ordained by you before anything was made.[11]

I mentioned in the first chapter that if someone would have told me when I was twenty-five years old that I was going to be a widowed professor and an author, living in Spokane and raising three children on my own, I would have denied it or run away. I would not, in other words, have believed it or, if I had, I would not have received the news happily. But I did not know and could not have imagined the course my life has taken. I am as uncertain about the future now as I was back then about the future that is now the present.

Who knows what will happen? God knows because God is already there. I have this sense deep inside me that God is doing something wonderful. It is enough for me simply to abide in Christ, to choose as wisely as I can, and to catch my breath as the miracle of his will for my life continues to unfold. "All is well."

All *is* well because the will of God prevails, even if our will fails. God works things out for the good of those who belong to him. In the film *Apollo 13*, NASA is forced to abandon the mission to land Apollo 13 on the moon when part of the space capsule explodes on its way there. Both engineers in Houston and astronauts on board must figure out how to solve the problem so that the astronauts can return home safely. They have to make adjustments, but the problem seems insurmountable.

At one point a network news program broadcasts an interview between the captain of Apollo 13 and a reporter recorded several weeks before the space mission was launched into orbit. The captain reflects on his experience as a pilot during the Vietnam War. On one mission his jet fighter was hit by enemy fire. All the instruments in the cockpit went dead. Consequently, he had no way of determining his location or the location of the aircraft carrier. Fuel in his plane was running low. Worse still, it was the middle of the night and the sky was overcast, so he could see nothing. He felt as if he had little hope of survival.

While flying low over the water, however, he spotted a trail of something on the water colored a luminous green, as if a green highway was sitting atop the ocean. He suddenly realized that the luminous color was algae that had been stirred up by the wake of a large ship. So he followed the trail of color "all the way home" to the aircraft carrier, and he landed safely. As he said in the interview, "You never know how things will work out."

We never do know how things will work out, but we know that God will work them out. He will work them out for our redemption. We will fall in love, change jobs, bury loved ones, say good-bye to children, move to faraway cities, raise cats, lose a fortune on the stock market, go to war, and end up living in Singapore. Sometimes we will choose to put God first; sometimes we will choose not to. Still, somehow God will work things out for our good, both because that is his nature and because that is his will for our lives.

ENDNOTES

CHAPTER 1: WE NEVER KNOW HOW THINGS WILL TURN OUT

1. You can read more about what I learned through my grief after the accident in my earlier book, *A Grace Disguised: How the Soul Grows Through Loss* (Grand Rapids: Zondervan, 1996).

2. Barbara Holland, "You Can't Keep a Good Prophet Down," *Smithsonian* (April 1999), 69–80.

CHAPTER 2: OUR ASTONISHING FREEDOM

1. James 4:13–17.

2. Søren Kierkegaard, *Concluding Unscientific Postscript* (Princeton: Princeton Univ. Press, 1992), 88.

3. Matthew 6:34.

4. Matthew 6:33.

5. Luke 16:10–12.

6. Romans 12:1–2.

7. Ephesians 5:15–17.

8. See Romans 8:28–32.

9. 2 Corinthians 6:2.

10. 2 Corinthians 6:4–7.

11. Acts 13:1–2.

12. Acts 16:6–10.

13. Luke 22:39–46.

14. 1 Corinthians 9:16.

15. I Corinthians 3:21–23.

16. Thomas Merton, *New Seeds of Contemplation* (New York: New Directions, 1961), 14.

17. Ignatius of Loyola, *The Spiritual Exercises of St. Ignatius* (New York: Doubleday, 1964), 82–83.

18. Thomas à Kempis, *The Imitation of Christ* (Notre Dame, Ind.: Ave Maria, 1989), 30.

19. C. S. Lewis, *Mere Christianity* (New York: Macmillan, 1943), 168–69.

20. Joseph F. Powers, ed., *Francis de Sales: Finding God Wherever You Are: Selected Spiritual Writings* (Hyde Park, N.Y.: New City, 1993), 32.

21. Augustine, *The Confessions* (Hyde Park, N.Y.: New City, 1997), 39.

22. Matthew 11:30.

CHAPTER 3: OBSTACLES THAT GET IN THE WAY

1. C. Leslie Charles, *Why Is Everyone So Cranky?* (New York: Hyperion, 1999).

2. Power, *Francis de Sales: Finding God Wherever You Are*, 59.

3. Merton, *New Seeds of Contemplation*, 206.

4. Max Weber, *The Protestant Ethic and the Spirit of Capitalism* (New York: Charles Scribner's Sons, 1958), 181.

5. Matthew 16:25–26.

6. Anita Shreve, *The Pilot's Wife* (New York: Little, Brown and Company, 1998), 158.

7. Chuck Colson, "Killer ATMs: Urban Legends and the Net," *BreakPoint Commentary* (Oct. 19, 1999).

8. Anne Lamott, *Traveling Mercies* (New York: Pantheon, 1999), 100.

9. Ibid.

CHAPTER 4: SIMPLE OBEDIENCE AS A WAY OF LIFE

1. Scot Lehigh, "Spirit Search," Section E, *Spokesman-Review* (Jan. 15, 2000), 1, 3, 4.

2. Luke 9:23–25.

3. Dietrich Bonhoeffer, *The Cost of Discipleship* (New York: Macmillan, 1963), 62.

4. Evelyn Underhill, *The Ways of the Spirit* (New York: Crossroad, 1990), 217.

5. Alexis de Tocqueville, *Democracy in America* (Garden City, N.Y.: Doubleday, 1969), 294.

6. Exodus 3–33 gives all the details.

7. See 1 Corinthians 5 and 6 for the full story.

8. 1 Corinthians 6:12.

9. 1 Corinthians 6:19–20.

10. Luke 11:37–52.

11. Luke 11:39–41.

12. Dietrich Bonhoeffer, *The Cost of Discipleship*, 63.

13. Romans 1:5.

14. C. S. Lewis, *Mere Christianity* (New York: Macmillan, 1960), 172.

15. Matthew 7:13–14; Luke 13:24.

16. Matthew 5.

CHAPTER 5: DISTINGUISHING BETWEEN CALLING AND CAREER

1. Os Guinness, *The Call: Finding and Fulfilling the Central Purpose of Your Life* (Nashville: Word, 1998), 29.

2. Evelyn Underhill, *The Ways of the Spirit* (New York: Crossroad, 1990), 152.

3. Frederick Buechner, "The Calling of Voices," *The Hungering Dark* (New York: Seabury, 1981), 27.

4. John Calvin, *Golden Booklet of the True Christian Life* (Grand Rapids: Baker, 1952), 94–96.

5. See Isaiah 44:24–45:7.

6. Exodus 36:1.

7. Os Guinness, *The Call*, 46.

CHAPTER 6: DISCOVERING WHAT WE'RE SUPPOSED TO DO

1. Caroline Alexander, *The Endurance: Shackleton's Legendary Antarctic Expedition* (New York: Alfred A. Knopf, 1998), 165.

2. Anne Lamott, *Traveling Mercies* (New York: Pantheon, 1999), 84.

3. Elisabeth Elliot, *A Slow and Certain Light* (Nashville: Abingdon, 1973), 101.

4. Evelyn Underhill, *Practical Mysticism* (Columbus, Ohio: Ariel, 1914), 1.

5. Sally Magnusson, *The Flying Scotsman: A Biography* (New York: Quartet, 1981), 75.

6. 1 Corinthians 2:1–5; 2 Corinthians 10:10–11.

7. 1 Corinthians 15:10; 2 Corinthians 11.

8. Antony Storr, *Solitude: A Return to the Self* (New York: Free Press, 1988), 56–59.
9. Elisabeth Elliot, *A Slow and Certain Light*, 104.
10. Colossians 4:3–4.
11. Philippians 1:12–14.
12. Acts 11:19–26; 13:1–4.
13. T. H. L. Parker, "The Life and Times of John Calvin," *Christian History* 4 (No. 4, 1986): 11.
14. Parker Palmer, "On Minding Your Call—When No One Is Calling," *Weavings* 11 (May/June 1996): 20.
15. Elisabeth Elliot, *A Slow and Certain Light*, 108–9.
16. 1 Timothy 4:12–15.
17. Elisabeth Elliot, *A Slow and Certain Light*, 99.
18. Frederick Buechner, "The Calling of Voices," *The Hungering Dark* (New York: Seabury, 1981), 31.
19. Mother Teresa, *A Simple Path* (New York: Ballantine, 1995), 7.
20. Thomas R. Kelly, *A Testament of Devotion* (New York: Harper & Row, 1941), 29.
21. C. S. Lewis, *The Great Divorce* (New York: Macmillan, 1946), 107.

CHAPTER 7: MANAGING OUR MANY CALLINGS

1. Philippians 1:9–11.
2. 1 Corinthians 7:35.
3. Thomas à Kempis, *The Imitation of Christ* (Notre Dame, Ind,: Ave Maria, 1989), 30–31.
4. Augustine, *The Confessions* (Hyde Park, N.Y.: New City Press, 1997), 69.
5. Philippians 4:11–13.

CHAPTER 8: LIVING WITH PARADOX

1. 1 Corinthians 3:21–23.
2. Francis de Sales, *Finding God Wherever You Are*, 110.
3. Ibid., 110–11.
4. Ibid., 121.
5. Ibid., 126.
6. Genesis 37–50.
7. Genesis 50:19–20.
8. Genesis 45:5–8.
9. Acts 4:27–29.
10. Philippians 2:12–13.
11. Olive Ann Burns, *Cold Sassy Tree* (New York: Ticknor & Fields, 1984), 98–99.
12. Peter Kreeft, *Heaven: The Heart's Deepest Longing* (San Francisco: Harper & Row, 1980), 108–9.

CHAPTER 9: SUFFERING RESPECTS NO BOUNDARIES

1. Thomas à Kempis, *The Imitation of Christ*, 141.
2. Genesis 3.
3. Romans 8:20–23.
4. Revelation 21:1–4.

5. Romans 8:18–19.

6. Chaim Potok, *The Chosen* (New York: Ballantine, 1967), 265.

7. M. Scott Peck, *The Road Less Traveled* (New York: Simon and Schuster, 1978), 15.

8. John Calvin, *Golden Booklet of the True Christian Life* (Grand Rapids: Baker, 1952), 63.

9. Ibid., 65.

10. Wallace Stegner, *Angle of Repose* (New York: Penguin, 1971), 561.

11. Hebrews 11:1.

12. Hebrews 11:6.

13. C. S. Lewis, *The Screwtape Letters*, 89–90.

14. Ibid., 70.

CHAPTER 10: GETTING THROUGH SUFFERING

1. Olive Ann Burns, *Cold Sassy Tree*, 363.

2. Evelyn Underhill, *The Ways of the Spirit*, 206.

3. John Bunyan, *The Pilgrim's Progress* (New York: New American Library, 1964), 111–13.

4. C. S. Lewis, *The Problem of Pain* (New York: Macmillan, 1962), 115.

5. 1 Corinthians 13:12.

6. 2 Corinthians 12:1–7.

7. 2 Corinthians 5:7.

8. 2 Corinthians 12:10.

9. Augustine, *The Confessions*, 227.

10. *The Prayers of Saint Francis* (Hyde Park, N.Y.: New City, 1988), 39.

CHAPTER 11: FACING WHAT WE CANNOT CHANGE

1. Psalm 90:2, 4.

2. Robert Clark, *In the Deep Midwinter* (New York: Picador, 1997), 264.

3. Viktor Frankl, *Man's Search for Meaning* (New York: Simon & Schuster, 1984), 87.

4. Anne Tyler, *Saint Maybe* (New York: Alfred A. Knopf, 1991), 46.

5. 2 Samuel 18:33.

6. William Shakespeare, *Othello, the Moor of Venice*, in *The Complete Works of William Shakespeare* (Baltimore: Penguin, 1969), 1035.

7. Charles Frazier, *Cold Mountain* (New York: Atlantic Monthly Press, 1997), 334.

CHAPTER 12: REDEEMING THE PAST

1. Lewis B. Smedes, *Forgive and Forget: Healing the Hurts We Don't Deserve* (San Francisco: Harper & Row, 1984).

2. 2 Corinthians 2:15–16.

3. Gary Thomas, "The Forgiveness Factor," *Christianity Today* (Jan. 10, 2000), 38–45.

4. Isaiah 55:8.

5. Romans 8:28.

6. 2 Corinthians 7:5–12.

CHAPTER 13: PREPARING FOR THE FUTURE

1. C. S. Lewis, *The Screwtape Letters* (West Chicago: Lord and King Associates, 1976), 78.
2. Luke 12:4–5.
3. Isaiah 6:1–8.
4. Exodus 3.
5. Thomas à Kempis, *The Imitation of Christ*, 89.
6. Luke 12:6–7.
7. Romans 8:31–39.
8. Gordon Jackson, ed., *Quotes for the Journey: Wisdom for the Way* (Colorado Springs: NavPress, 2000), 56.
9. Ibid., 15.
10. Matthew 6:34.
11. Ephesians 5:15–16; Philippians 4:4–7.
12. Philippians 4:6–7.
13. Richard Foster, *Celebration of Discipline* (San Francisco: HarperCollins, 1988), 35.
14. See Exodus 3, especially 3:10.
15. Isaiah 40:3–5.
16. Genesis 8:21–22.
17. Romans 8:24–25.
18. 1 Corinthians 15:51–53.
19. Romans 8:31–39.

CHAPTER 14: LIVING IN THE WONDER OF THE PRESENT MOMENT

1. Psalm 139:7–12.
2. Psalm 103.
3. Romans 6:1–2.
4. John Bunyan, *The Pilgrim's Progress* (New York: New American Library, 1964), 39.
5. Robert Huntford, *The Last Place on Earth* (New York: Atheneum, 1979), 508–9.
6. Ephesians 5:15.
7. Thomas Kelly, *A Testament of Devotion* (New York: Harper & Row, 1941), 102–3.
8. Sue Bender, "Everyday Sacred: A Journey to the Amish," *Utne Reader*, 99.
9. A. W. Tozer, *The Pursuit of God* (Harrisburg, Pa.: Christian Publications, 1948), 127.

CHAPTER 15: ATTENDING TO THE LITTLE THINGS

1. Quoted in Evelyn Underhill, *The House of the Soul* (New York: E. P. Dutton, n.d.), 75.
2. Luke 13:30.
3. Mark 10:42–44.
4. Colossians 3:23–24.
5. Titus 3:1–2, 14.
6. Ephesians 4:28.
7. 1 Corinthians 10:31.

8. Jean-Pierre de Caussade, *The Sacrament of the Present Moment* (San Francisco: Harper, 1966), 62.

9. Ibid., 63.

10. Evelyn Underhill, *The Ways of the Spirit*, 188–89.

11. Brother Lawrence, *The Practice of the Presence of God* (New York: Barbour, 1993), 27–28.

12. *Newsweek* (Oct. 25, 1999), 64.

13. 1 Timothy 4:12–15.

CHAPTER 16: MAKING CHOICES

1. 1 Kings 19:11–12.

2. Exodus 3; Isaiah 6.

3. Psalm 19.

4. 1 Corinthians 13:12.

5. Corrie Ten Boom, *The Hiding Place* (New York: Bantam, 1971).

6. Acts 16:6–10.

7. Jean-Pierre Caussade, *The Sacrament of the Present Moment*, 69.

8. Ignatius of Loyola, *The Spiritual Exercises*, 84–85.

9. Acts 13:1–3.

10. Ignatius of Loyola, *The Spiritual Exercises*, 85.

11. Francis de Sales, *Finding God Wherever You Are*, 117.

12. Ignatius of Loyola, *The Spiritual Exercises*, 86.

13. Francis de Sales, *Finding God Wherever You Are*, 118.

14. Ignatius of Loyola, *The Spiritual Exercises*, 86.

15. Benedict J. Groeschel, *The Psychology of Spiritual Development* (New York: Crossroad, 1983), 156.

16. Thomas Merton, *New Seeds of Contemplation*, 32.

CHAPTER 17: ALL WILL BE WELL

1. Hebrews 13:5-6; Philippians 1:6.

2. Jean-Pierre de Caussade, *The Sacrament of the Present Moment*, 64.

3. Romans 8:28.

4. Oswald Chambers, *God's Workmanship* (Wheaton, Ill.: Van Kampen, 1953), 37.

5. Augustine, *The City of God* (New York: Penguin, 1984), 593.

6. Ibid., 881.

7. Thomas Kelly, *A Testament of Devotion*, 97.

8. The parable is found in Luke 15:11–32. For an analysis, see Kenneth E. Bailey, "The Pursuing Father," *Christianity Today* (Oct. 26, 1998), 34–40.

9. Luke 15:2.

10. Romans 8:35–39.

11. Julian of Norwich, *Showings* (New York: Paulist, 1978), 341.